Emotional Release for Children

Repairing the Past – Preparing the Future

Mark Pearson and Patricia Nolan

Jessica Kingsley Publishers
London and New York

All rights reserved. No part of this publication may be reproduced in any material form (including photocopying or storing it in any medium by electronic means and whether or not transiently or incidentally to some other use of this publication) without the written permission of the copyright owner except in accordance with the provisions of the Copyright, Designs and Patents Act 1988 or under the terms of a licence issued by the Copyright Licensing Agency Ltd, 90 Tottenham Court Road, London, England W1P 9HE. Applications for the copyright owner's written permission to reproduce any part of this publication should be addressed to the publisher.

Warning: The doing of an unauthorised act in relation to a copyright work may result in both a civil claim for damages and criminal prosecution.

The right of Mark Pearson and Patricia Nolan to be identified as authors of this work has been asserted by them in accordance with the Copyright, Designs and Patents Act 1988.

First published in Australia in 1995
by the Australian Council for Educational Research Ltd
19 Prospect Hill Road, Camberwell, Melbourne, Victoria 3124, Australia

First published in the United Kingdom in 2004
by Jessica Kingsley Publishers Ltd
116 Pentonville Road
London N1 9JB, England
and
29 West 35th Street, 10th fl.
New York, NY 10001-2299, USA

www.jkp.com

Copyright © Mark Pearson and Patricia Nolan 1995
This edition copyright © Mark Pearson and Patricia Nolan 2004

Library of Congress Cataloging in Publication Data

A CIP catalog record for this book is available from the Library of Congress

British Library Cataloguing in Publication Data

A CIP catalogue record for this book is available from the British Library

ISBN 1 84310 225 0

Printed and Bound in Great Britain by
Athenaeum Press, Gateshead, Tyne and Wear

The authors

Patricia Nolan and Mark Pearson are the authors of *Emotional First-Aid for Children*. Since the publication of this book late in 1991, and its heartening sales around Australia and overseas, they have received growing requests for training and support in the area of emotional release counselling (ERC) with children and with adults. Both are trainers in ERC.

Patricia Nolan has been working with children since her teaching career began in the early 1960s. She has always had a strong interest in those who have difficulties: 'the slow learner', 'the problem child'. At that time, before counselling was a widespread service provided within schools, she was drawn to informal counselling. Much aliveness came from relating with and drawing out from children the full potential she knew to be there. This commitment to the growth of human potential led her to community development work with Aboriginal people. It was through her informal, yet almost tangible, experience of the numinous with Aborigines that she was propelled into her own growth process.

Four full years of experiential and theoretical work became the seed bed out of which has emerged ERC for children. Patricia's training in Swedish massage and remedial massage adds significantly to her ERC skills.

Patricia and Mark worked together initially, running workshops and later, training in ERC. It was from this very rich and creative time that *Emotional First-Aid for Children* was born. Now they offer this second book. They are excited and inspired by the ripple effect as many more teachers, counsellors and parents train in and use these methods.

Patricia lives on the North Coast of NSW where she and her husband Steve continue to offer individuals and groups the opportunity to experience the fullness of their potential. Training courses in ERC are offered and details are available on application. (See page 202 for addresses.)

Mark Pearson began teaching primary school children, then founded a remedial reading clinic. He worked briefly with handicapped children at Cromehurst Special School. He has continued a special interest in the relationship between learning difficulties and emotional disturbances. As well as experience in private practice as a relaxation therapist and masseur, he has developed new methods of emotional release through Reichian-style bodywork.

He has co-authored a collection of children's stories published by Woman's Day. Several of his radio scripts for children have been performed on the ABC. He is the author of several cookbooks and a children's book, *Numbat – His Magic Quest*. He is the author of the first Australian book on transpersonal breathwork, *From Healing to Awakening*, and is currently completing a new book for adults, *Remember Who You Are! A Workbook for Self-Discovery*, and another for schools: *Teaching Self-awareness through Meditation*. He has two children.

Mark directs training courses in ERC at the Portiuncula Centre in Toowoomba, for the Victorian Emotional Release Counsellors, and for the NSW Emotional Release Counsellors Association.

Patricia and Mark began developing the ERC methods for children in 1987. As a result of lectures and seminars, groups of parents, educators and school counsellors around Australia and in New Zealand are now utilising the methods outlined in these books. Patricia and Mark are foundation members of the NSW Emotional Release Counsellors Association.

Acknowledgements

Our gratitude continues for our background of inner work with Ahrara Carisbrooke.

We appreciate all the feedback and contributions to this book from our colleagues and trainees.

We are heartened by the staff and children of St Joseph's Children's Homes, Grafton, who have continued to use ERC methods over a long period of time, and at such a day-to-day and moment-to-moment level.

Special thanks go to Elysha Neylan for so generously providing her observations of counselling sessions and developments of the exercises from *Emotional First-Aid for Children*, as well as the exercises on page 97 (My Fireworks Display), page 102 (My Real Face), page 103 (Am I a Puppet on Strings?), page 119 (What Does Your Heart Long For?) and page 121 (What Would You Really Like to Do?).

Special thanks go to Rosemary Pearson for her thoughtful editing and valuable suggestions for clarification of the manuscript.

Again, our gratitude to Sr Pat Quinn, Director of 'The Portiuncula' Centre for Spiritual Development, Toowoomba, Qld, for promoting courses and workshops through her centre.

We are glad of the support from the foundation members of the Victorian Emotional Release Counsellors and the NSW Emotional Release Counsellors Association for arranging courses and spreading information about this work.

All names used for children in this book have been changed
to protect their privacy.

This book has been greatly enriched by contributions from:
Elysha Neylan, Mary Peacock, Bernadette Wallis, Sonia Dayspring,
Maurine Boon, Irene Pecheniuk, Dorothy Bottrell, Lynn Bishop and
Margaret Thomson. Our thanks to all these enthusiastic explorers.

Preface

Our hope is that this book will contribute to enabling children everywhere to rediscover and remember who they really are.

Society is well geared towards helping children develop their skills in the outer world. The personality and the ego have an important place, but underneath these lies the essence, which has been covered by emotional pain and the rush to achieve externally. It is the essence, the core, that gives real 'life' to the person. What happens if this tender inner part is forgotten? The work presented here can be a way to help children return to the vitality and health at their core.

Our first book on this work was published in 1991 and sold out within its first year. The welcome this book received and the flow of requests, ideas and contributions from those now using it, encouraged us to put together the new material in this form and begin training programs.

> May you help children to take up the challenge
> of discovering who they really are.
> May you stand in awe before the mystery
> of their unfolding.

Patricia Nolan
Mark Pearson
Ellenborough

Other books

by Mark Pearson & Patricia Nolan
Emotional First-Aid for Children

by Mark Pearson
From Healing to Awakening

Contents

The authors	iii
Acknowledgements	iv
Preface	v
Introduction	ix
1 What is emotional release counselling?	**1**
Sources of ERC	2
Foundation principles	7
The child/adult concept	10
Behaviour modification and ERC	12
The basic tools of ERC	13
Signs that children need ERC	20
Signs of emotional growth	20
2 The effects of birth and childhood trauma	**22**
The role of birth in forming a child	23
The general influences of birth	24
The effects of different births	26
Childhood trauma	27
Raising an unarmoured child	31
Birthing games	32
3 Practical planning for ERC	**35**
Counselling sessions	36
Dealing with projection and transference	41
Affirmations and goal-setting	43
ERC and schools	44
Support groups	49
4 Encouraging children to talk about themselves	**53**
Beginning discussion	54
The hurt inner child within children	57
Body awareness	61
Journalling	72
Creative writing and storytelling	74
Drawing	79
Working with clay	84

5 Emotional release processes — 87
Introduction to processing — 88
Eye-to-eye processing — 91
Energy release work — 91
Reactions to parents — 100
Exercises for adolescents — 104
Work with anger — 112

6 The world of symbols — 122
Sandplay — 123
Gestalt work — 139
Dreamwork — 142

7 Moving forward on the inner journey — 147
Exploring the unconscious — 148
Visualisation work — 152
Relaxation and meditation — 159

8 Caring for the carers — 167
The hurt inner child in carers — 168
The child/adult concept in carers' personal development — 170
What is burn-out? — 171
Self-help methods for carers to use at home — 173

9 Stories from the counselling room — 175

Epilogue – New hope for children — 193

Appendixes — 195
Appendix 1: Milestones pro forma — 196
Appendix 2: The people in my life pro forma — 197
Appendix 3: Sandplay report pro forma — 198
Appendix 4: Choosing music — 200
Appendix 5: Contacts for workshops and training — 202

Glossary — 203

Recommended reading — 205

Index to exercises — 207

General index — 211

Introduction

There are two major strands, two continual themes, that support our work with children. Emotional release work is the first. It includes many practical processes that 'clear' trauma, release muscles, free repressed emotions and therefore energy, and allow a child to move into a happier state.

The second strand we call inner-life skills, the main skill being the ability to connect with and then articulate an inner world. It includes more subtle processes which enable a child to build on well-being, find their own form of inner growth: emotional, spiritual and intellectual.

The two strands support each other. Our work with children constantly crosses from one to the other and together they make up what we call Emotional Release Counselling (ERC). Work with normally well-adjusted children might focus on the second strand, but include the emotional release processes when needed. Work with abused, emotionally damaged children initially focuses very much on the first strand, but draws from the second processes that give hope and bring recognition of inner treasure.

Through our work around Australia we have seen a heartening trend in the number of childcare workers who have realised their own need for personal growth and healing and have courageously marched forward with this. Their transformation and release of the hidden negative parts of their emotional make-up will benefit all the children who have contact with them. And there is great hope in the fact that the more we have come in touch with our own needs and addressed these, the more we have in us to respond to children.

In many children today we see a depth of suffering that is held in the body and psyche, and may remain there for a lifetime. The pale face, the thin body, the dark eyes, the manic gestures, the sullen withdrawal all reveal the need for release. The widespread emotional wounding in children and adults is reflected in the current wounding of the planet. Just as many are now waking up to the environmental crisis, so many are now seeing, for the first time, what has been happening to the emotional life of the rising generation.

Those adults who have personally discovered the foundations of their own emotional formation in the connection back through time often feel a call to study child development and bring practical methods to healing children. This trend is obvious to us as we present workshops and training courses for teachers, counsellors and parents. It is heartening to note that *Emotional First-Aid for Children* was very well received. What was thought to be a highly specialised book with a small market swiftly proved to have very wide appeal and was soon being used in schools and counselling centres all around Australia and in New Zealand.

Our methods for bringing emotional release and healing for children have grown out of well-established methods used with adults. The most significant sources have been emotional release work; process-oriented psychology; the work of Carl Jung, Stan Grof, Arthur Janov, Fritz Perls, Wilhelm Reich; and especially transpersonal breathwork as it has been developed in Australia from Dr Grof's work in the USA.

However, transpersonal breathwork is not a process we use with children. It is perhaps the most effective part of current depth psychology for adult healing work. It uses breath to bring a connection to repressed emotions, to support the deep feeling of them, their expression and release. Restriction of breath is one of the main ways the psyche reduces the reception of feelings and reduces the general level of excitement in the body. The simple instructions to take deep breaths are what we use in therapeutic or counselling sessions with children. In observing children in the counselling environment and at home, it is clear that the breath is very often held when difficult feelings are approached.

Current emotional problems are linked with problems from the past. The work with adults dramatically shows that the imprints of childhood, infancy and the birth become visible in character. The imprints show up in the way adults relate, in the aggression, in the fearfulness, in the 'as if behind a screen or mask'. It is the same for children. There may be hurts or abuse from early childhood, or trauma from a difficult birth, which contain so much pain that the child must wait until adulthood to be ready to explore and release them. But the principles can be kept in mind when supporting children to feel deeply any current pain. This regular support to go into the ups and downs of their daily emotional life will ensure that new layers of repressed feelings are not added to the old.

An understanding of the link between strong emotional disturbances and past trauma or hurts will help parents be patient and find creative ways of assisting their children to share, or release, rather than hold in, their feelings. If they feel any guilt about past relationships with their children they could channel this feeling into some of the suggestions made in this book. This would help them deal with it, rather than have it impinge on the present relationship with their children.

The strength of the body–feeling–mind connection is observed clearly in adult breathwork sessions. Touch can bring up a memory. The memory will bring up a repressed feeling. Repressed feelings can often be detected under body aches and pains. Knowing the power of these connections will support parents in going beyond simple demands for external behaviour modification if they want the long-term good for their child.

The need for adults to release years of held-in sound, held-in screams of agony, yells of delight, is evident in almost every ERC session. If we can allow, even encourage, children to express themselves vocally and noisily – frequently – at appropriate times, we will reduce the loading on the unconscious. Of course children are noisy, but they rarely put the energy of the noise with the feelings that have generated its need.

With adults we use breath, sound, strong movement, touch and surrender in the counselling session. Working with children we use the same. As much as possible we use games and exercises that encourage the child to lie down, 'go floppy', relax their inner control of body and mind. We draw out their expression of fantasies, images and dreams, the representations of the unconscious. We use bioenergetics to loosen up body holding and prepare the way for emotions to flow again. We use strong physical exercise to address the excess energy – what some call nervous energy – that many disturbed children are burdened with.

The place for emotional release methods is in schools, as well as in the counsellor's private rooms. It would be a great service if we had all been taught how to safely express our rage, integrate our dreams, to give massage and guide ourselves into deep relaxation whenever necessary. What a boon to all relationships it would be if we had grown up knowing how to recognise and release the power of emotional hurts from the past. What a powerhouse of energy we would then have at our disposal.

The curriculum for life skills classes at high schools in Australia is beginning to move towards really useful areas. But usually there is no time for the inner life in school programs that are designed to inform the mind and provide employment skills.

We have enormous sympathy for those brave counsellors who may have hundreds, or even, in some cases, thousands, of children allotted to their care within the education systems. In many cases these counsellors have no supervision or back-up, and are so overbooked with clients that emergencies must eat into their own time. Many have shared with us their frustration, their sense that a deeper care, a deeper healing would be possible for their clients, if only there was time.

It is essential that we personally explore the exercises we present for children. Then we can be sure that we are growing – not living out our need to grow through the children. Then they can see, from our growth, what is possible. It is true that we all have layers of negativity which may scare us into constantly looking the other way – outward. But our systems, our psyches are yearning to release the old, and open to the new. This yearning is even stronger in children.

Parents can help children

As parents we may sometimes feel guilty taking time from our children and spending resources on our own personal growth work. Sometimes we can get the idea – which is often reinforced by those around us – that it is self-centred, selfish, egotistic to devote time to our own personal growth. It is often quite threatening to those around. The truth is that, before getting busy fixing up children, we must deeply know ourselves.

Any growth work we do for ourselves is the best possible gift we can give our children. Whether we intend it to benefit them or not, it will, because we will be different, more in touch with ourselves.

We are the models for our children. It does not matter what we say to them, it is what we *are* that they will learn from. So if our *being* grows, if our connection with ourselves deepens, if our negativity reduces – that is the model, that is the gift for the children. We are often afraid of our deep, so-called negative feelings: our grief, anger, rage, hate. To face these and begin to release them in our own private work enables us to deal with them confidently and safely in children.

Love is transmitted through the act of giving attention. When we are freed from some of the hungry inner voices that have been crying out for attention for so long, we are able to give it outwardly, paying attention to children. The fruits of listening to them, allowing their inner life to unfold and express, are healing and growth.

Emotions want to move. If they are stuck they become negative; mobilisation is essential. Paying attention to the inner life allows this vital mobilisation.

Through using ERC to open up parts of our vivid unconscious memories, we can grow to appreciate the importance of subtle and continuous watching of the inner life. We watch the flow or blockage of feelings, the fullness or stasis of bioenergy, the storehouse of negative patterns that often govern our 'adult' life. From this we begin to know, in a new way, what will support the unfolding of individuality in children.

The vital, first step in working with traumatised children, unhappy children, even normal children, is to notice our own energy levels and reactions. Then we need to access the traumas (the source of our problems) in ourselves. We need to recognise our own store of primal pains, our own held-down energy, and begin the work of clearing the issues that have patterned our adult response. Almost all of us need to open our bodies again, free our emotions and spirit.

If we are seeking children's growth we will be caught up energetically in our own. This will require *more* energy from us, more time, more effort, more standing aside from our own immediate comfort. If we are trying to modify their behaviour to make life more comfortable, a simple suppression of their potential will suffice!

Introduction

As parents begin to reclaim the depth of their own emotional life, and recall in vivid detail the feelings of their own childhood and relationship – or lack of it – with their own parents, they can quickly become better parents. To the degree that they are willing to face all the repressed feelings in themselves, they begin to support children in really feeling their lives day by day. For these fortunate children there are fewer repressions, less energy locked away, more immediate access to their lifeforce and the joy of being alive. These parents become more able to express their love directly, regularly, in words, touch, looks and exciting activities. An ideal way to begin this exploration is to form a support group (see page 49).

Most counsellors and therapists who work with children focus on the activities they *do*. Parents with problems with their children ask what they can *do*. It is a fact, however, that children learn most from what we *are*, not what we teach or say. It is of no use to teach them a behaviour, a meditation or an emotional release activity if we are not at the same time being true, living the things we try to teach them. The greatest need is to clear our own issues and come to a connection with ourselves. They will learn this from us, very directly.

Working towards all this, expressing ourselves, teaching from this state and knowledge will provide a direct model for children. They perceive at a deep feeling level how we are. That is what they really learn! No words can alter what they perceive as our true state. But above all they recognise, long for, need us to be centred and at home in ourselves. This centredness is the start of true relationship with children – and each other. So our growth work is really the biggest gift we can give our children.

CHAPTER ONE

What is emotional release counselling?

The structure of the one who is to render first aid
is very important. If he is emotionally blocked himself,
he will be prone to develop all kinds of cockeyed ideas
about what a child should be like or what to do
in the event of emotional blocking.
He will inevitably tend to run away from the issue at hand.
The greater his personal anxieties, the farther away his
judgment and practice will be from the requirements
of the situation.

Wilhelm Reich, *Children of the Future*, Farrar Straus Giroux, 1984.

Sources of ERC

ERC was born from the coming together of two interests in Mark and Patricia's lives. The first interest was our search for methods that would bring about emotional healing and evolution of consciousness – both for ourselves and our clients. The second was our background in teaching and our particular interest in children with learning difficulties.

Teaching personal growth methods and supporting individual clients in their healing journeys has always been a very creative activity for us. The groundwork for this creativity has been our personal use of ERC methods over many years. The fruits of this creativity are offered in our writing and teaching work.

Our methods have been refined through private counselling work, countless workshops and retreats with children and adults, and consulting work with various institutions around Australia.

Although we have gained much from the writings of Jung, Reich, Grof, Janov, Perls and other personal growth pioneers, our confidence, creativity and adaptability flow from the new energy released through self-discovery.

The formulation of our work with children has been greatly supported by our experience of the essential connectedness between the levels of the psyche – the unconscious, the normal waking state and the higher consciousness possibilities. These levels of consciousness within us are reflected in the range of exercises presented in this book.

Three levels of psychology

The marked progress in the effectiveness of psychological healing methods now used with adults and children owes much to the blending together of three approaches to psychology. ERC draws from all three. We categorise them as:
  level one: clinical and academic psychology
  level two: transpersonal psychology
  level three: sacred psychology

These categories do not relate exclusively to any one modality or belong to any one theorist, but cover a range of approaches, methods and knowledge. The inner-life skills outlined in this book draw inspiration from the methods of sacred psychology and from our own certainty of the value of the spiritual dimension for effective healing. The emotional release processes have evolved from current clinical and transpersonal psychology.

A discussion on how these levels of psychology contribute to work with children will necessarily include many generalisations, and for every statement there will be some exceptions. The three levels relate to different levels of the human psyche, to different levels of experience and consciousness. In essence, the three levels do not contradict each other, but offer a progressively wider view of the psyche and of the dynamics of healing methods. Most children have a natural ready access to these three levels.

Each level embodies more subtle ways of knowing. Whereas much of the knowledge of level one, for example, might be based on intellectual processes, for level two, knowledge comes from the emotional life, the body awareness as well as the intellect.

Many years ago Maslow began to bridge the levels in his formulation of the hierarchy of needs. He placed at the top of the pyramid the need for self-actualisation. In Jung's terminology this would be the need for individuation.

Level one

Level one is informed by what can be perceived by the senses in an ordinary state of consciousness. This 'ordinary' state of consciousness would seem extremely limited from the viewpoint of levels two and three.

Level one deals with the development of the psyche from birth to death. It honours clear thought and reason. It tends to doubt the idea of higher states or non-ordinary states of consciousness. When this resistance emerges in individuals it is usually a sign from the psyche that the person is ready to open to another level.

At this level the vastness and widespread impact of repressed memories and feelings tend to be ignored. Normally repressed people are regarded as normal, whereas at level two there is offered a new exciting view of what a healed life could be like.

The view of level one has tended to minimise the devastating effect of early trauma on children. Some schools of thought in level one aim effectively to change children's behaviour. This can be achieved but it does not address the need for emotional healing which opens the child to their full potential.

It is normal for adults working with level one healing modalities to be engaged in analysis for many years. Level one transformation and healing is a long, slow process. Children can sometimes spend most of their counselling time being tested, diagnosed and analysed. The need so often expressed by the counselling profession is for methods of healing that do bring change, that lead to resolution and happiness for the child. Those working with ERC see many and frequent examples of resolution of crises, transformation and a reclaiming of children's potential.

Functioning in a way that seems normal in society is an aim of level one methods. To achieve this these methods may support inner defences and bolster ego strength. They may modify a specific outer behaviour. ERC would use a behavioural problem as a gateway for healing work, which would then give the child the freedom to behave in accordance with their healed inner self. Level one may not recognise anything higher than the ego and its ability to mould behaviour in order to fit in, to get approval. ERC recognises the need for a child to develop a healthy ego, but knows there is much more.

Level two

Knowledge at level two is gathered by what is available to the five senses as well as what is perceived by other more subtle senses in a non-ordinary (to Western culture) or higher state of consciousness.

What is a higher level of consciousness? For many indigenous cultures the activation of the subtle senses and access to higher states of consciousness was/is part of everyday life. In simple terms, in our healing work, a higher level of consciousness, to begin with, means we have full access to our usual rational thoughts as well as the full awareness of emotions – where they are in the body, whether they flow or are blocked – and an awareness of the sensations of the body. The bringing together of these three functions activates a finer, clearer energy that is the gateway to level three.

Level two methods bring access and healing to the perinatal time, which is usually locked away in the unconscious. There is recognition of its dramatic potential for imprinting a child's character.

Transpersonal psychology has many definitions. Basically it is broader – 'trans' meaning across or beyond – than just biographical events. It integrates modern consciousness research with timeless methods and outlooks. From its perspective of higher, or non-ordinary, states of consciousness it can recognise the links between spiritual and psychological systems from the present and past. It tends to integrate rather than separate. It takes seriously experiences that come from a higher level or higher parts of the psyche, which might be dismissed at level one. It is open to the symbolic or mythological language that children and adults may use in articulating their own inner workings.

Level two methods awaken and utilise the full energy of the emotions. Researchers tend to be seekers themselves and so personally experience and, as well as their clients and colleagues, become their own subjects of study. Because of this personal experiencing, the fear of the human emotions is almost entirely reduced. Without this fear, more can be released and healed. Basic trust in the goodness and order of the psyche enables braver and bolder research. For example, the knowledge that under all anger and hate lies tenderness and love empowers a counsellor to lead a child into strong release of anger and hate. There is no fear that these are actually basic qualities which, if unearthed, will remain active and lead the child to become destructive or anti-social.

Without this fear of emotions, those working at level two can open to the full range of human experience and energy which leads to transpersonal or spiritual experiences. The importance of these energies in the healing process is recognised. First the body, feelings and mind have to be engaged in the healing process; then another energy is awakened that can re-order and heal. This other energy has many names in many cultures. It has been linked with nature and God. It does not depend on belief. Because of the opening to this natural healing force, transformation and healing are frequent in level two inner work. Moments of transformation often come quickly, and can often result in major changes.

Some of the main pioneers of level two are Dr Stanislav Grof and Christina Grof. The Grofs' research began at level one. They developed holotropic breathwork, and it seems their current work is leading more towards discoveries about level three. Christina has explored work with adolescents and their connection to the sacred.

It is from the methods pioneered by the Grofs that one basic premise of ERC has developed: that of the breath being a major tool in opening up our feelings. The influence of the perinatal time of development has been charted by Stan Grof, and this influence has been vital in bringing healing to many children. Where the Grofs' work has been most helpful is in re-establishing the link between healing and the spiritual energy of level three.

Dr Arthur Janov extended the understandings of level one with his work with primal therapy. His huge contribution to the understanding of the effects of traumas during birth and infancy has helped many. Janov's work has inspired other researchers, in particular Dr Frederick Leboyer. Our understanding of the mechanics of repression and how to deal with it owes much to Janov. Janov, however, denied the transpersonal or spiritual levels.

Dr C G Jung worked as a colleague of Freud. Based on his clinical observations and his own fearless self-enquiry, he tried to bridge level one and level three. Jung legitimised the role of imagination in linking into the unconscious. His active imagination and work with fantasies have been helpful in our work with children. His emphasis on dreams as an important road to the unconscious has helped us listen more carefully to children and respect their dream world. Jung encouraged the West to pay attention to myths and fairy tales, to see them as an important language of the psyche, a way of understanding beyond the limits of the rational.

Jung's colleague Dora Kalff extended his work with symbols by developing sandplay and promoted it as a valuable therapeutic tool. We have simplified the approach to sandplay and incorporated Gestalt processes.

Jung found that a large amount of inner suffering revolved around lack of meaning. He considered this lack of meaning to be the major disease of the twentieth century. Meaning, he found, came not from level one, but from experiences of level three.

The work of Dr Wilhelm Reich has a strong and growing influence. This is carried forward by many psychologists and personal growth explorers today. His colleagues Drs Lowen and Pierrakos developed bioenergetics, which has become such a valuable tool in our work with children.

Reich also began at level one. His work extended the boundaries of level one until he recognised level two. He brought the body and emotional release into the therapist's work. He too recognised the importance of the breath in allowing release of feelings and energy. He developed techniques similar to massage for helping the body let go of its holding, what he called its armouring. His descriptions of armouring in children have helped us develop gentle exercises that allow children to heal their body/mind split.

Through his more holistic approach Reich discovered the special energy that is available, and brings healing, when the whole body and psyche are very alive. His research extended to comprehend aspects of level three, but this part of his work was not taken seriously by most contemporaries.

Dr Fritz Perls, a leader of the Gestalt movement, outlined simple ways of learning from dreams, fantasies and symbols. Children readily learn these methods which help them reclaim their inner strength. His lifetime of work with clients, teaching and self-exploration led him to blend the best of psychotherapy with the teachings of Zen. He pointed the way to new links between the levels.

Supported by the inspiration from these and many other pioneers, we have spent ten years personally exploring our own inner world. We have been motivated by our search for and discovery of a better and fuller way of living. We have adapted methods and created many new ones, thus leading our clients through their emotional release to the experience of new inner-life skills.

Level three

The knowledge and methods of level three come from many sources. Mystics and saints of Christianity and Buddhism have explored and described meditation methods for bringing inner harmony and experiencing a different level of consciousness. In this century there has been a revival of interest in the practical application of the esoteric traditions of Sufism, Judaism and Zen, among others. These traditions reach us in the form of sacred texts, teaching stories, parables and in the new synthesis presented by G I Gurdjieff. These traditions have been linked by personal growth explorers such as Dr Fritz Perls, Ira Progoff and A H Almaas to the methods and frameworks of levels one and two.

Level three embraces all that is known in levels one and two, as well as the functions of full human development. The data has been collected over thousands of years by those following strict experimental procedures, and those firmly interested in the highest potential of the human psyche. The application of this collected knowledge leads to harmonious functioning of body, mind and feelings, and an opening to higher parts of the psyche – parts unknown to the other levels.

A person who has been fully engaged in growth work and persevered through personal emotional healing might find an inner 'homing device' which points them from level one to two, then on towards level three. Children have this homing device. When their basic needs are met, their curiosity turns naturally to inner aspects we would call 'spiritual'.

Sacred psychology is something that always was, always will be, but tends to remain in the background. There are many new attempts to encompass what it is, to understand its laws and methods. It is so vast that any one aspect or one method from level three can become the lifetime work of a seeker, psychological researcher or religious order. It is usually only known in fragments. Its full comprehension would require a level of consciousness broader and finer than any usual human level.

Its methods, interpretations and outer forms have changed with the times, but the core knowledge remains the same. It is often available through myths and teaching stories. Its influence is more obvious in the East and native indigenous cultures. The yearning for this level is reflected in the enthusiasm with which Western researchers are now studying the beliefs and methods of traditional healers.

Level three comes from a higher, evolved consciousness, so it includes knowledge of possible human evolution, what we could be when whole and complete. Its forms have been restated, reformulated for this century by G I Gurdjieff. His emphasis, which has been most helpful in healing work, is on the need to bring the three parts – the body, mind and emotions – together. From his work we also draw support for the need to have stillness and quiet at times for deep integration.

From Buddhist practice we have drawn ideas for relaxation and meditation. From Christianity we learn the importance of symbology, of stories or parables as a way of expression, and of the value of ego surrender to a higher level. Sacred psychology has been restated down through the ages by mystics and approached by scientists who have been able to transcend ego limits.

Many consciousness explorers are now working with the links between the levels. They are recognising that personal healing is so much more complete when conducted in the light of spiritual or transpersonal energy. This form of spirituality is not encumbered with dogmas, beliefs, superstitions or regulations. The spirituality of levels two and three comes from personal experience that is natural, intrinsic, inbuilt and available to all.

The intrinsic spiritual quality of children re-emerges as they go through their emotional release work. The more emotionally damaged they are, the more buried is this part of them. The more they release and heal, the more frequent and easy is their contact with this dimension within. The more they contact this dimension the more healthy and well-adjusted they become.

The boundaries of levels one and two are now being rapidly expanded. Understanding and interest in level three is also expanding. The world needs more of the influence of level three to help balance the apparent decline in society. This decline is evident in the destructive effect humans are having on nature, on the planet.

At the same time there is a growing power in the numbers of people beginning their personal development and moving towards interest in the higher levels. The welcome that ERC has received from childcare workers and the growing interest in helping children regain their wholeness is inspiring. It is our hope that this force will continue to be effective in the world and bring much good to the next generations.

What is emotional release counselling?

Foundation principles

ERC brings emotional healing. It can lead into therapy – a second level of aid – but usually children need to wait for deep-level healing until they are adults, or have a firmly developed ego. ERC stops the build-up of repressions and releases the day-to-day frustrations and hurts.

There is a clear difference between ERC and behaviour modification approaches. Generally, reward and punishment are used with behaviour modification to change a child's patterns of behaviour. There are firm guidelines for acceptable behaviour, which is very necessary, but this approach can often only deal with the outer child. ERC enables a child to feel some of the causes of their troublesome behaviour, release these and then naturally move into more positive expression.

ERC is based on the simple premise that to feel emotions and energy and to let them be expressed keeps us mentally healthy. We in Western society have learned to fear emotions, to hide them and lock away anything unpleasant. With ERC we simply find ways to release both current and old feelings in a safe and protected place. We recognise that the cause of many learning difficulties and behaviour problems lies in locked-away feelings in the unconscious.

ERC helps the psyche release trauma and emotional blocks that produce reactive behaviour. In ERC we use processing – structured emotional release – to heal problems based in the unconscious.

Negative feelings and memories in the unconscious are active and have an influence on how we make choices and live our lives. Bringing them to consciousness is the first step in disempowering them. Positive qualities, feelings and memories in the unconscious tend to be inactive, or overshadowed by the negative. Making them conscious empowers them to be part of our life – to be expressed and take their rightful place as background to our character.

Both children and adults have an inbuilt interest in self-discovery. Mostly this has been covered over by disappointment and trauma. ERC allows it to emerge again, forming the basis for further personal development.

The only way for adults to fully understand and effectively use the processing methods of ERC is to explore them in their own personal development work.

Understanding and freeing aspects of the psyche

Traumas are events so painful emotionally or physically that they have to be repressed from consciousness. They build up from womb to adulthood. These traumas that were too painful to feel are split from (as a safety mechanism), resulting in partial emotional shutdown. Shutdown, or repressed feelings, memories and thoughts, can have a powerful effect on how we think, feel and behave now – even though they are unconscious! In children, the repressed memories can lead to delinquent behaviour and, later, neurosis.

Processing is a structured, safe, supported method that allows an encounter with incomplete emotional expression and brings release. Anger, hurts, frustrations, grief, can be fully supported and fully expressed. The mobilisation of feelings that have been stuck will save a child having to act it out unconsciously throughout life. Children who use the processing methods will benefit from substantial support from the home environment.

The body, the mind and feelings work as a whole. What we don't let ourselves feel or express becomes stuck and causes muscular tension, or 'armouring' of the body, and destructive throughts in the mind.

Under muscular tension and pain are emotional holding and emotional pain. When the physical is focused on, and the breath increased for a moment, we can again feel – and ideally express – the underlying emotions. Then the body softens and we return to a state of relaxation and happiness.

Under anger and frustration are sadness and hurt. We try to reach under the layers to that hurt. Under the hurt is the original state of love and tenderness, which can then surface.

Attempts to be self-destructive or to take on blame must eventually be expressed outwardly towards another – where they really belong. This can be done through symbol work or through processing in counselling sessions.

Since healing takes place in the body, ERC works to help a child be deeply connected to the sensation within the body, to develop self-awareness. It is in early childhood that the mind/body split begins.

A child's body, in our culture, normally holds the energy of emotions, locks them in to some degree. The child is usually considered more 'grown-up' if unacceptable, embarrassing or negative feelings can be held out of sight completely. This holding takes place to a large degree through muscular tension. These tensions become chronic – they become permanent. Picture a child's feelings and energy as operating on three levels:

1 The core.
  Deep inside there is the strong flow of energy, life and emotions. This core energy is always healthy, alive, flowing and wanting to express. In a controlled, or armoured, child this flow from the centre of the core energy hits against the armouring and is stopped.

2 The armouring.
  This layer, as it were, just below the surface, just out of sight, stops the flow of lifeforce. Great tension is used to control and block expression. For example, great excitement could cause a child to jump about and annoy parents, so it is contained. We usually find that it is then experienced as anxiety. It is as if the positive has turned into the negative. In this intermediate layer all the positive and natural expression is blocked and seems to turn into destructiveness, spite, rage, anxiety, fear etc. Psychologically, this layer is where most of what Jung called 'the shadow' is held. Covering this layer is the persona.

3 The persona, or mask.
  The child has to pretend now, as the natural expression is blocked. The child may pretend to be nice, compliant, when adults are about. Often when alone with other children the negativities of the intermediate layer are expressed. Often the child comes to believe in this personality, or mask self, and is usually encouraged to strive hard to behave as if it were the true self.

ERC frees up the armouring, the intermediate level so that the core can again express in its natural positive way in the world. Real healing depends on the intermediate layer of energy and feelings being released.

Character changes can emerge only when this basic positive energy is free again. So-called healing modalities that try to rearrange the personality (although perhaps giving the child the

What is emotional release counselling?

experience of being accepted for good behaviour) do not bring healing. Negative feelings and expressions, and emotional pain, may be more successfully hidden for a time, but will have an effect on the persona at some later time.

Practical work with children

In counselling sessions, we work to reverse childhood shallow breathing patterns. Children reduce their breathing in order to reduce their feelings and to contain excitement. We help it to open again. We also work to free up restricted sounding and movement patterns.

The boundaries between what is done in the privacy of a counselling room and what is appropriate in real life need to be very clear. The aggressive expression acceptable in the processing room is not appropriate outside it.

Spend time developing trust before beginning confrontational work. Find the light before confronting the dark. Support children in finding some self-esteem, in feeling themselves as treasure, as something valuable, before asking them to deal with a past or present in which they may not feel valued.

It is often important to give an overview of some of the concepts before working with children and adolescents. For example:
- the conscious mind in relation to the unconscious
- trauma and repression
- idealised self vs. the shadow
- the wounded inner child

(See the notes beginning page 27 for introducing these concepts.)

Help them recognise defence mechanisms. For example, their ways of avoiding feelings, of hiding or covering what is felt, of getting a tough exterior.

Like us, children do not want to feel anything unpleasant. It is essential to spend time discussing some of the positive outcomes that ERC can bring. For example: happiness, academic improvement, self-confidence.

Group work is often better for older children and adolescents (groups of about six to eight are ideal). Groups create permission to feel, cry, express. In a group children learn that they are not alone in inner suffering, and the new friendships provide ongoing support after the official group times.

Working with your own children

ERC is difficult with your own children. Your children expect you to make them feel safe, loved, comfortable. In their eyes you are supposed to make things right, solve their problems, be there as a confidant when they need that, and remain (happily) excluded from their inner world if they happen to be in a closed-off mood. Even the most successful counsellor finds it easier to work with children other than their own.

Your own children expect you to have no needs of them. For example, all children resist chores around the house. The resistance will be greatly increased if they feel you have 'an investment' and emotional need – such as getting them to give back to you, to the household.

Similarly, children will close off if they feel your invitation to share their problems, talk about their inner world, comes from your own need for contact, your own need to feel needed. Often parents find they are struggling to give the attention that they lacked from their parents. In this case the timing will be determined by them, not by the child. Some parents have reported suddenly realising that they have been projecting their own needs of their parents on to their children. This has been the reason why their efforts to support have been ignored, met with cynicism or even strongly rejected.

Notes for teachers, counsellors and parents

It is vital that teachers, counsellors and parents are comfortable with the range and depth of another's emotions. Children need to sense that you are a safe environment for expression and release.

Be on guard against projecting your own needs or conflicts on to children. Patience is essential – your expectations can intrude on a process that has its own timing for each child.

Ideally, parents must open to growth and healing work too, since they are the models. This also prevents them inflicting their own inner suffering on to their children and gives them confidence in supporting the growth of their children.

Practise active listening: listen to the feelings carried in the voice, not just the meaning of the words.

Mirror back feelings, rather than always trying to solve problems for children. You can accept their feelings, acknowledge them, rather than trying immediately to do something about them.

Begin to recognise emotional triggers in children and in yourselves. These will become a guide to locating the unconscious problems that bring negative reactions, and opening the way for further growth.

Get to know your own wounded inner child, hear its needs, recognise what it reacts to, find how to let it heal.

Working with children will constantly bring up reactions in you and expose parts of your psyche that you may have tried to hide or totally forgotten. As a teacher, counsellor or parent, there will be some children towards whom you cannot warm, or who make you react over and over. You may have acknowledged the fact of these reactions and promised yourself: 'I won't react today!' Perhaps one of your own children becomes a problem and you feel you can't cope or you can't control your reactions.

The first step in resolving this dilemma is to acknowledge that while there may be an objective reality, namely a child with difficult behaviour, your reactions, your feelings about the situation are yours. It is these reactions that are your problem, not the child.

The child/adult concept

In ERC we distinguish between the happy, fulfilled, spontaneous aspects of childhood – which are fully integrated into us – and the hurt inner child. These positive parts – often called the playful, or magical child – are overshadowed by the hurt inner child. This part of us is like a separate identity, made up of unfelt, or blocked, feelings. The playful part is really us.

What is emotional release counselling?

At first the child does not use the mind to 'understand' hurts, it just feels the lacks, the disappointments, the longings, the traumas. Then it builds up a defence against these hurts – a survival mechanism. The child begins to blame itself for the lacks. It carries the load of the parents' shortcomings. This stops genuine self-esteem from developing. It leads to a few basic negative beliefs about self; these carry on into adulthood and sabotage life.

The child's guilt at not being good enough to be loved, seen, held etc., has strong undercurrents of resentment. Anger is the reaction to being hurt. These undercurrents have to be held down. An idealised self-image develops. The 'bad' is pushed down and forms the 'shadow'. A lifelong struggle develops between the ideal and the real (even though the real is often forgotten).

When the child's (or adult's) hurt is triggered by some incident in the present, all this unconscious resentment from the past comes up. This often happens in an 'over-the-top' way; the reactions are out of proportion.

In order to heal and release we must go back through layers of reaction:

1. false forgiveness
2. rationalisation, intellectual understanding
3. blaming others
4. feeling reactions: anger, resentment, hate etc. (the real feelings)
5. the hurt of not being loved, seen, held etc.
6. connection with our own resources – quiet, tender inner space

For integration, there needs to be recognition of:
- actions which might represent 'trying to win', 'trying to get it right' – this keeps children tied to the past
- the main survival or defence mechanisms the child has developed; for example isolation, self-blame, living only in head, disowning real self, etc.

For adults, after separation from the hurt inner child there is a change in *loving*: from expecting it to being able to give it.

Discoveries from several people working with ERC:
- To help a child to feel is to help the child to heal.
- Going beyond limits, facing emotional fears, allows changes to begin to happen in a child.
- Children are essentially good – our task is to discover the problems that make them appear bad.
- Breath, movement and sounding re-activate the emotions and open the energy and connect children to true self-knowledge.
- Healing work may begin with the healing of the personality, and it leads to deeper growth work that gives children an opportunity to experience their essence.
- We each have many opposites in our psyche, and we are more than these. We have opposite energies and if we experience one, the other must also exist. Helping a child to experience this frees them from being victim to any one energy.
- There is gift in everything. Every personal problem, when faced honestly, leads to more growth.
- The body knows and remembers everything that has happened to us – even from the time in the womb.
- The finer the inner focus, the better the connection to the inner world. The more inner attention is practised, the more feelings, memories, energies and authentic direction in life are revealed.
- Scattered energy, unfocused thoughts and revolving emotions, when released, give space inside for choice and intentional direction and stillness.

- It is every child's intrinsic right to unfold rather than be unfolded. Under ideal conditions they can discover who they are, what they are meant to do, rather than unconsciously follow old conditioning.
- To relate clearly, children have to be able to be separate, to distinguish self from other. This begins with the first separations from mother. When children are not separate, there is no real freedom to relate.

A story from a workshop

A mother of a preschool girl discovers her own projection

During a simple one-day workshop that was designed to introduce some of the ERC principles, a mother asked about the problem of helping children separate. She described a familiar scene: trying to leave a reluctant and crying daughter at preschool.

For three months she had been staying with her daughter for the three half-days that she attended preschool because the child would not allow her to leave. The child, she said, had a big problem.

Most parents will recognise the heart-tearing moment of abandoning their child at preschool or with a daycare mother – it is not an easy thing to do.

In this case it was the mother who could not leave the child. She stood up and agreed to try an experiment in the workshop setting. She 'became' her daughter. She stood like her daughter, pictured herself as the same size and with the same vulnerability. She began: 'Please mummy, don't go . . .' She felt some tears come to her eyes. Almost immediately she felt herself at the age of three, being left by her mother. Her mother had left her at the gate from day one of preschool. It was a terrible memory. She could feel some of the panic that she had felt thirty-two years before.

In briefly touching on this memory she could see how she had projected all her own childhood fears on to her daughter. This made it impossible to leave the child. Having recognised this, she realised that her own daughter was in fact much more secure, more loved, and it was really time to leave her to grow up. She recognised that this fear of her own was aroused every time she took her daughter to preschool, and that she may have to feel it herself, coming up inside from the past, instead of loading it on to her daughter.

Behaviour modification and ERC

Since *Emotional First-Aid for Children* has been published we have heard from many counsellors who have met resistance from colleagues when attempting to introduce ERC methods into a behaviour modification (BM) environment. It *seems* that there is a clash between the approaches.

Approaches that focus on control may seem to clash with approaches that encourage release and full expression. However, full expression is not the same as free expression. For emotional release work to be truly therapeutic there is an element of conscious awareness during the release. The child is guided to find the right time and place and method for releasing the destructive energies.

The BM idea of setting firm boundaries is integral in ERC. It is vital that children know clearly what is expected of them. ERC approaches have an advantage in that they can bring release of recurrent impulses that show as dysfunctional behaviour and negative expression. The child is then free to cooperate, conform and 'be part of'. The boundaries then become guidelines, models, not repressers of true feelings.

However, BM seems to work with the results of inner pain, the symptoms – the behavioural defences against feeling pain. ERC works with release of the pain. It is much more difficult, requires patience and great experience from counsellors, teachers and parents. It also requires emotional agreement from children.

Some people fear that teaching children to release violence might actually encourage them to express it inappropriately. This is a real concern. The use of ERC requires firm guidelines on what can release safely in the counselling room and what should be noted when outside for future inner work.

Held-in feelings or denied feelings will come out eventually, or make the child (or adult) sick in some way. The ideal for children whose inner pain has driven them to becoming behaviour problems would be regular, one-to-one healing sessions using ERC, combined with firm and consistent guidelines for outer behaviour.

The basic tools of ERC

These are some of the simple means and materials widely used in ERC work.

Breath

The most important and most powerful way to promote release is to encourage full breaths. Many references are made to this throughout this book. Most observers of child development have noted that children hold their breath when fearful, tearful, or excitable. Just a few hold their breath intentionally – sometimes as an attention-seeking device. However, shallow breathing or slowed breathing are the body's way of controlling emotions and excitement. In ERC sessions we simply reverse this habit. See more on page 91.

Sounding

We learn many ways of accommodating the world to gain approval or to get what we want. This means we suppress to some extent what we really want to do, who we really are. Many of us learned to be quiet. Free-flowing sounding in a safe place with a support person releases a lot of pent-up energy. Free sounding often leads to specific sounds or words and phrases, previously unconscious, being released. This can lead to emotional release, followed by a quiet state. See more on page 93.

Eyes

Many ERC exercises use the eyes – closing and opening – in order to assist focus within or on the outer world. When the eyes are closed there is usually more possibility of contacting feelings and sensations in the body, of watching the inner world.

In group work we may sometimes ask a child to use another's eyes as a focus point, to talk to. This allows a putting out of emotions towards an object or person. The eyes become the trigger and the reminder of reactions recent or past. Sometimes the eyes the child is looking at 'become' Mum's or Dad's, or all the teachers'. See more on page 91.

Cushions and mattresses

These are an essential tool in ERC. We use them firstly to mark out a safe, sacred space within which the child's inner work can flow out. We use cushions to make sure a child who might begin to express anger will not get hurt.

Lying down on the mattress can encourage letting go, surrender, becoming vulnerable. The conscious mind needs to relinquish control so that the unconscious can speak.

Surrender

Giving permission and encouraging letting go is something we use throughout ERC. We know that little real healing takes place while the ordinary mind is in charge. Surrender – lying down, closing eyes, relaxing muscles, dropping thoughts – is the state we aim for to allow the unconscious imprints, unconscious hurts to come to the surface. The state of surrender also encourages more subtle experiences that bring great positivity.

Working with coloured crayons

In exercises that use crayons to express inner images and states you will notice that we often say: 'What colour is it? What colour feels right for that?' This is a way of helping a child to look within more carefully. The intensity or faintness of the colour, the softness or hardness of it, the firmness or tentativeness of it are all subtle expressions of the true state of the child in that moment.

Drawings

When imagination presents something from the unconscious, or new contact is made with an unfamiliar feeling, it is good to record it. All too often the clarity of the experience can slip away. A drawing is a way to bring the new learnings to life. It can be used as a basis for further discussion and exploration. Drawings are very useful in drawing out inarticulate children. Drawing with the energy of anger, sadness, fear, love or joy enables that energy to be very alive in the child. Such energy can be released or celebrated as needed.

Mandalas

At the conclusion of an ERC session there is usually a need for an integrative exercise. We often use mandala drawings to achieve this end. These drawings are done when the child is still in touch with the energy and content of the session. A large circle is drawn on to the blank page to give a framework. The drawing can be in, over and around this frame. The drawing is allowed to flow out from a feeling state, rather than be planned and come from the intellect.

It is important to keep mandalas for a review at some future time. This review can highlight the journey aspect of the ERC work. Completing a mandala gives an internal feeling of completion. See more on page 79.

Sandplay

Sandplay is the choosing and arranging of symbols in a sandtray. The choosing is from many hundreds of symbols which are on shelves in the sandplay work space. The child can be attracted to or repelled by the symbols and arrange those which have strong energy for them in sandtrays. The child then plays with them in the sand until the picture feels right, or complete. Sandplay is described in detail on pages 123–139. Here we want to emphasise some of the benefits of this way of working.

When a child finds it difficult to focus, sandplay helps. There are definite boundaries in which the play of the unconscious can unfold. The movement it calls for in shaping the sand and in playing with the symbols can be invaluable for a child who is used to trying to resolve problems through discussion alone. They can be involved in a new way. The same is true for those who are very verbal. This process can be totally non-verbal.

One of the reasons for using this tool is the facility it develops within the child to feel congruence between the inner and outer worlds. A directive given to a child at the beginning of a sandplay is usually something like this: 'Work the sand until it feels right.' This calls for an outer action, that is, forming the sand, and an inner feeling that wants to have the outer just right.

Photographs can be taken of each sandplay and given to the child to keep in their special folder. This provides a record of progress.

Symbols

In sandplay, visualisation, mandala work and dreamwork we use symbols. Many children – and adults – can begin to face inner pain only in a symbolic form. They feel safe to acknowledge the symbol, and gradually become more directly aware of what is being symbolised. In some cases the unconscious will firstly present inner pain, traumas and terrifying memories in a symbolic form, gradually preparing the child to remember and feel directly.

As children use the Gestalt method (outlined on page 140) they return to a part of themselves from which they may have been disconnected. They can own this part and integrate it. The disconnected parts have presented as symbols in order to be re-owned. The symbols can be of positive aspects, such as talents, ability to care, etc., or of what are usually considered negative factors, such as unexpressed rage, an urge to seek revenge, etc.

Direct interpretive work with symbols is not useful for children, as they need to feel and understand the meanings in themselves. We have found that many positive or spiritual symbols are presented to children from their unconscious when there is a need to counter-balance heavier negative experiences from their outer lives.

Dreamwork

Dreams can give the counsellor an insight into what has been worrying a child and therefore provide an opening for more discussion and support. Through support using the Gestalt method, the child can release tensions, relieve worries and reclaim rejected parts of their personality. Working with dreams can reduce depression, increase self-esteem and reconnect a child with inner treasure – elements of which are revealed through the personal symbols of the dream.

Once we open to personal development work and begin to allow the unconscious to surface, to listen to it more, we find we begin to dream more, and remember the dreams more. It is as if the unconscious is excited to reveal more of itself. It is therefore essential in the overall work we offer, to include this tool. The simple Gestalt way of gaining meaning and new life from dreams is outlined on page 144.

To learn to work with our own dreams is a great gift and a significant way of continuing the day-to-day growth work at home without a facilitator. With the Gestalt method we can let go of the notion that only experts 'out there' can help us. We can find our own inner expert. Everyone who is willing can gain enormously from dreamwork.

Touch and massage

This is no doubt the most controversial area in work with children. Many government departments and counselling centres have had to set firm guidelines that preclude touching a client. Although this is understandable from the protection point of view, it denies the counsellors the use of one of the most natural and effective means of communication and healing. There are many ways of providing the experience of touch and massage that are completely acceptable; for example, working in small groups where children learn to give massage to each other.

Touch, with love, care and sometimes firmness, is appropriate at times. For example, a child may need to express a sound, but through habit the sound gets stuck in the throat. Careful upward stroking on the throat is a non-verbal encouragement to the body to release. A firm hand on the back can support a child who is trying to confront some inner terror.

Massage is a great help when children seem to be unaware of their bodies. This is probably most appropriate for parents to do. It is a very direct way to transmit love and care. Children love massage and are quick to grasp the techniques if taught clearly. Group work with older children giving and receiving massage has proved very effective for enhancing bonding in support groups.

Some children may be always hurting themselves or living in a fantasy (or mental) world. The massage helps them feel the boundaries of their body as well as what is taking place inside it. For hyperactive children a massage at night prepares the way for better sleep.

Bioenergetics and de-armouring games

These have been adapted from the work of Alexander Lowen and John Pierrakos. Sometimes a child's energy for life has been depressed. There is a lack of interest in daily activities, emotional depression, muscular aches and pains. Games that draw attention to this body energy and assist its release allow the feelings and energy to move again, to be expressed. This movement brings healing.

Some exercises intentionally bring stress to the body for a moment in order to make muscles let go. For example: 'See how long you can hold your arms up in the air.' Once the body relaxes and the energy moves again, emotions can flow and release will happen if it is needed.

Music

Music is a great aid to many of the processes. To make loud sounds in a silent room, or even make quiet ones, is often too much to ask of some children. To shout or scream or laugh or cry in the privacy of a room filled with strong music is much easier. Music can support both the release of a particular emotion and the release of energy generally.

Inward-turning processes can be aided by soft relaxing music which leads a child into a quiet space within, without the need to use too many words. Facilitators need to be ready to change music. For example, a quiet process may begin with silent inner focus, but this may transform into a need for strong expression. To encourage the completion of release, strong music is needed. After the release, either quieter music or celebratory dance music could be used.

We use a drum for rhythmic work, for bringing a group together, and as a signal to begin and end loud, noisy work.

Most of our exercises can be enhanced with background music. See the list of music on page 200.

Dance

In times of inner and outer freedom, when the body's energy is very alive, the natural impulse is to dance. Dance is a simple, creative expression that can bring a segment of work to a beautiful conclusion. Dance can be used as well, to help children connect with what is really happening in their energy. For example, they may begin energetically and then discover that their true state is the opposite. As they connect with their truth, emotions are often released and the emotional healing achieved.

Some children find that they are really themselves when they are dancing.

Meditation

We use this word to mean quiet times of inner focus when the child is guided to drop thoughts about external events and connect with the sensations of the body. Exercises are presented to assist children to move towards the possibility of being still and quiet for a time. This stillness, when not forced, can be very calming and healing. Sometimes the word 'centring' is used to describe this quiet tuning in.

Three-dimensional work

Sometimes it is important to give a child an opportunity to work in a three-dimensional way. Great benefit may come from making mother, father, teacher etc., out of clay. This is a more direct way of confronting real feelings about a person than using a ready-made symbol. This figure may be moved around, or even destroyed.

Moulding the sand in the sandplay tray is also three-dimensional work. It can be very healing to touch, to shape, to handle the sand. The physical involvement allows the emotional energy to be active also. Children usually feel comfortable in expressing themselves in this medium.

Journalling

We place a strong emphasis on the idea of ongoing growth work and sometimes refer to it as journeying. One method which assists a sense of individual journey is the keeping of a journal. For children we sometimes simply call it 'your special book'. We encourage them to write or draw a record of their work. It is a way for them to have a personal and private record of their emotional growth work. Some like to use it as a diary. The actual writing can be a process of growth and change. See page 72 for details.

Sharing

Group sharing times enhance the integration of ERC work. They have many purposes, and support the child in finding clarity and practising expression. They create a bonding with a group and allow the facilitator to assess the success of the program. Talking about inner work will usually ensure that the ordering and structuring functions of the mind come into play – this helps complete integration. See more on page 40.

Integration

The integration into ordinary living of the personal inner work that children accomplish occurs to varying degrees. It happens without effort or support when the child's process of dealing with a difficult feeling has been completed.

Sometimes, however, it will be helpful to a child if parents and/or the counsellor or teacher can assist in the integration. Irrespective of the depth of the growth process, one thing is clear and imperative: if there is no new life or empowerment of the child from the counselling situation which can be taken into daily living, then the ERC is non-productive. A lack of new life flowing from the processing work would indicate a blockage in the psyche of the child towards the unconscious material within, or to the process itself, or in the relationship with the facilitator. In such cases it can sometimes be important to stop the counselling work for a while if the blockage cannot be resolved.

Here are some examples of integration of the learnings from ERC work, and some ways of assisting integration.

- On page 138 there is a report from Patricia about Andrew ('Working with the Whole Child through Sandplay'). Patricia met Andrew's mother two months after the sandplay and asked: 'How is the frightened turtle in Andrew?' The mother's face lit up and she said, 'I haven't seen it since the sandplay.' This would indicate that Andrew's process was complete. He came through a block of fear, permanently. The effect on his ordinary life was apparent. The integration had happened.
- A very important aspect of the process of integration is letting the new energy exist and be fully felt and expressed in and through the body. Most exercises in this book are completed with an integrative action, such as:
  – writing
  – drawing
  – dancing
  – proclaiming, telling others
  – celebration

  This kind of integration at the time of the process is essential. It is another thing to live the new learnings each day. There is a leap to be made from the counselling room to the car, to the home, to the schoolyard, etc. When the child's process is partially complete, and this is something all counsellors will be familiar with, it would help if the counsellor worked out with the child what kind of help they would like from Mum and Dad. Together it could be decided that when Mum/Dad calls to pick up the child, the counsellor could help the child to share a bit about their process and ask for help in following up the new learnings.
- After a counsellor, teacher or parent has been working with a child a few times it is good to ask for feedback – simple questions such as: 'Do you think of the things you learn here in between times?' Such questions could help a child to begin to allow the connection between ERC work and daily life.
- Another simple method to support integration is the review of mandalas and completion drawings that have been collected together in the child's special book or folder. Reviewing these experiences and reading the summary words that accompany the drawings, or reports in their journal, can highlight the threads, the lines of growth and development. See page 73 for ideas on reviewing drawings.

What is emotional release counselling?

- On page 154 there is a visualisation exercise called 'Feeling My Roots'. The final question is aimed at helping a child make a bridge between this new time in their life and future times of fear. Perhaps a picture of a strong tree with thick roots could be displayed in the child's room to remind them of the true part of themselves they have found. Taking time to observe large real trees and feeling how they mirror the inner parts would be helpful.
- An 11-year-old boy found through sandplay a strength in himself that had been missing – due to his very low academic success. The finale of his period of inner work was a drawing of a wild strong stallion. Because of his limited drawing skills he felt unsatisfied with the drawing. It did not fully express the power he now acknowledged within. His carers helped him choose a large poster of a magnificent rearing stallion, which now fills the wall above his bed. This poster supports him in owning the good parts of himself. It reminds him of his strengths.
- A counsellor working with a 7-year-old boy uncovered his frustration with his father, who shouted at him. The child wanted to say – and did in his processing – 'Don't shout, just tell me!' The child's mother agreed to let the father know about this so that the child felt free and safe to say this directly, if Dad got angry with him again. The action that was needed for the child to integrate his process now had a place, an opening. This support made it possible for him to let his newly found sense of self live.

An integrative ritual

At St Joseph's Children's Homes in Grafton, personal work and healing emotional hurts are part of everyday living, and have been for many years. When a child is in a state of strong reaction ERC is available.

Patricia and her husband Steve go to the homes every two months for a three-day visit. The children make their own appointments for counselling work. They are able to use these times to give some continuity to their inner growth process.

At the end of the year the staff organise a special celebration that honours the efforts each child makes to become more fully who they are. Each child is consulted about how they see their growth. They make a statement that describes as well as they can how they have grown over the year; for example 'I don't have as many angry fits now.' This statement is written on a certificate. A room is decorated and the staff, carers, counsellors and children all gather together. The administrator speaks about the value of personal growth and commends the children on the efforts she has seen them making. She calls each child individually to proclaim how they have grown. Their certificates are presented and then later hung in their rooms to help them remember that they are becoming more whole, happy people.

The presentation is followed by a barbecue or party. This ritual and celebration definitely supports each child in their effort to grow.

Signs that children need ERC

There are a few indicators that children may be struggling to hold down deep emotional pains and could benefit from ERC counselling:
- continual lack of self-esteem
- lack of self-awareness; for example clumsiness etc.
- trying out of new roles, copying others
- inability to be alone for any length of time
- continual or periodic reading problems
- decrease in attention span
- chronically pale skin (not due to organic disorder)
- lingering illnesses without a clear cause
- a habit of lying, cheating and/or stealing
- chronic tiredness
- over-eating or not eating
- frequent stomach pains
- continuous sibling conflict – which may become more violent
- general destructiveness
- tantrums
- depression

Obviously there are a great number of causes for these, but quite often several will go together, and tell us that the inner stresses are getting too much to bear.

Signs of emotional growth

There are a few indicators that children's emotional health and general well-being are being achieved. Some children may show growth in one or two areas. Generally, depending on the time the counselling work has been conducted, five or six indicators can be observed. It is important to note that not all carers would really welcome these indicators. Growth for one person (child) in a close group dynamic calls for adjustments and growth in the others; and growth and change are often resisted. Signs of emotional growth in children are:
- deeper self-awareness
  - ready access to feelings
  - a knowledge of when release work needs to be done
  - a new ability to know what they want (and have more ability to express this and negotiate with 'authorities')

- recognition of positive changes in their responses to life situations
- expanded self-esteem
- more honesty in self-expression (this is not universally welcomed!)
- more alive energy – this might need some support into positive expression; those with hyperactive energy seem quieter, calmer, more 'at home' in themselves
- acting out after sessions (The issues and the emotions that have only been touched upon in the counselling session may be waiting to release fully after the session. For example, a boy who dealt with his hate of bullies and of being bullied, and worked with this in the sandtray, acted out some of this with siblings after the session. He was actually doing what had been done to him. He needed support in recognising the difference between 'expressing' in a counselling session and indiscriminate 'dumping'.)
- more willingness to reveal tenderness and vulnerability
- increased ability to cooperate and play with others
- more satisfaction in playing happily alone
- more spontaneity, more imagination, more creativity
- greater ability to share unpleasant feelings in order to let them go
- more peace and harmony at times *and* also, at times, more fully expressed anger and disappointment – children become more real and more able to release troubles
- increased ability to concentrate, extended attention span
- academic improvement, quite marked in some cases
- older children can find inner strength, as a resource

Some results of these indicators are:
- The child may receive disapproval from those around who are triggered by true, alive expression; for example 'We were never allowed to do that!'
- There may be a short transition time when hurt from the past comes up and creates a wider barrier between the child and the parent(s).
- The child's healing and freedom affect the family dynamics. Because they are able to be present in themselves, not defending against inner pain, they will not necessarily conform to the old behaviour patterns.
- If parent(s) are also working to heal themselves, a deeper, more direct, loving bond will form.
- If parents can work with the ERC methods, release is able to happen easily and naturally at home.

CHAPTER TWO

The effects of birth and childhood trauma

Blindly, madly, we assume that the newborn baby feels nothing.
In fact, he feels ... everything.
Everything, totally, completely, utterly,
and with a sensitivity we can't even begin to imagine.
Birth is a tempest, a tidal wave of sensations
and he doesn't know what to make of them.
Sensations are felt more acutely, more strongly by the child,
because they are all new and because his skin is
so fresh, so tender,
while our blunted, deadened senses have
become indifferent.

Frederick Leboyer, *Birth without Violence*, Alfred A Knopf, 1984.

The role of birth in forming a child

The effects of birth and the immediate postnatal time can stay in our system for a lifetime. They can positively or negatively influence character development and predispose a child to a particular attitude towards life. There are many positive effects of a good natural birth that stay with us and a memory in the unconscious of having accomplished a great deal. We focus here on some unfortunate effects from complications in the birth.

ERC includes an awareness of the effect of the perinatal time and embraces games, exercises and approaches to help a child release some of the dammed-up energy around birth. Deep healing of a highly traumatic birth may have to wait until the child has grown up and developed a mature ego capable of entering breathwork sessions that would allow the past to be fully released. However, games which help release the physical contraction, emotional closing and blocking of energy that are associated with birth trauma will always be helpful.

An overview

There is a memory in the unconscious of each of us, of the sensations and emotions of the time in the womb. There is a memory of the birth itself.

For many the birth is the first trauma. A trauma is an event or feeling that is too strong or painful to be integrated by the body, mind and feelings. The birth is the first separation. It can set a pattern for the way life is perceived and lived. Sadness at the 'expulsion from Paradise' and a lingering 'No!' to coming out into the world, can be a powerful initial imprint. For example, there can be imprints on the child's character that life is 'a long hard struggle', or 'all this work, then nothing!'

The way the child finally comes out into the world is a prototype of how it may face challenges. If it came out struggling it may tend to be in doing mode most of its life, to be driven into action all the time. If it came out having 'given up' it may tend to live life in a surrendered mode. If it came out only with help it may have a tendency to wait for help all through life.

The type of birth can contribute to personality patterns. For example, a child who experienced an obstructed labour may hate being stopped in anything. A forceps delivery may incline a child to believe 'I need help'. An elective Caesarean may leave a child with a lack of boundaries and body awareness.

The strong energies and emotions that surround the birth, as well as the baby's own strong emotions – such as fear, anger, outrage – can become locked up inside the baby. This perinatal energy may make the first contribution to muscular armouring and neurotic traits. This energy can be released somewhat through ERC methods, especially birthing games (see page 32).

Since the regular use of ultrasound began, it has been discovered that up to, and possibly more than, fifty per cent of singleton babies began as twins, one twin being reabsorbed by the mother during the first months of pregnancy! Both those who are born as a twin and those who experienced the vanishing twin have a sense of 'we' not 'I'. Those born as a twin often live as 'half of something'; they may exhibit the need for a fantasy friend or animal.

Negative emotional imprinting can result from a toxic womb experience or sense of not being wanted in the womb by mother or father.

A fearful temperament can be set from the fear experienced during birth. The physical crushing and pushing of the birth canal can set off a fear they may be held in for a lifetime. This fear is often projected out on to the world. It can come up in nightmares. The fears seem irrational unless the real cause is eventually recognised and released.

There is an inbuilt mechanism that constantly strives for all-round healing. This may mean that children access frightening aspects of their birth in dreams, or may project them on to people, animals, insects etc. These memories do not just lie quietly in the unconscious. The shocks of life, the challenges and the big emotional reactions continually trigger new areas of the unconscious to rise to the surface for release and healing.

The general influences of birth

We all carry imprints from our birth. These imprints are stored in our body and brain. Some have more impact on our future life than others. The experiences in the womb and in the birth process, the experiences immediately after the birth, relationships in childhood, adolescence and young adulthood, all compound and build on each other. These imprints are stored away together and determine many of our characteristic responses to life.

If these experiences were negative, painful or fearful, we repress the feelings and the memory of them. These memories – whether conscious or unconscious – determine the way we respond to the outside world. If we had a certain type of birth – say, one that was very long and difficult – there is a learning, not in thought, but through the body and directly from the feelings, that this lifetime is going to be tough and this world is a tough place. After birth we could be met with experiences that prove that this is true – being left alone, cold, surrounded by noise, and in the glare of hospital lights: all these experiences compound the learnings from the birth experience.

Of course if we are met with great love, great care and quiet warmth, in direct contact with mother, the rigours of the birth can be partly healed. The quality of the immediate postnatal environment and the state of our parents are vital in bringing healing to the struggle of the birth.

The power of these imprints can be gradually released. The trauma associated with them can be healed. But usually there is a build-up of stress in our psyche, based on these first imprints. 'Prototypical' trauma is Arthur Janov's term for the first imprint, to which the others seem to be added, and it is this collection of imprints, this conditioning, that determines how we deal with stress in our current life. The causes of our strong reactions to moments of stress can be traced back – through childhood, infancy, to the birth and the womb.

For most of us, our birth, whether complicated or not, would have been hard, with extreme discomfort. Before birth the baby is floating, totally supported, and then comes a contraction. For some the first powerful contraction is the first shock. There has been a change from the fun of the first gentle ripples to a dangerous expelling force.

Effects of birth and childhood trauma

For others it might be the sensation of the head engaged for a long time that becomes the start of a pattern. In deep-level therapy, some people re-experience and can clearly describe the severe claustrophobia of being ready to come out and the cervix not being ready to open.

The baby does not think like we do. It is well known that the thinking functions of the brain have not matured at the time of birth. However, the sensory receptors and emotional receptors are functioning. The baby is very open to the moods around it.

The baby's psyche disconnects from awareness of these moments – from the trauma, the pain, the fear of death – in order to survive. In order to go forward there is a cut-off from the pain. Unless there is immediate postnatal care, love and warmth of a high degree from parents, some part will then be locked away in the unconscious, possibly forever. And this forms the patterns of character.

The baby will receive and understand events from a point of view based on the very first lesson in life, the birth. As the child grows, its way of dealing with developmental crises, its way of receiving the world, relationships, all stress situations, is compounded – eventually affecting even the choice of career and close relationships.

Babies are born with a very sensitive physical and emotional awareness. This high level of consciousness means that we must exercise great care in handling them. Dr Frederick Leboyer advises us to make sure we do not create fear for the newborn; to make the transition from the womb to the world as gentle as possible by introducing the sensations of the outside world progressively; and that the parents and helpers should be there, be present, in a loving atmosphere.

In the ideal birth a baby will be born into a dim light, as the eyes are so sensitive. There should be no sounds at first, then gently the mother's voice is introduced and then the father's. The first touching must be careful, relaxed, so that the love can actually flow through the hands. Perhaps warm water is used to relax the newborn and allow a reconnection to the familiar and comforting skin sensation. Those in attendance need to be in a relaxed emotional state, as the baby perceives the state of those around. Every failure in these areas will add a strain to the baby, will bring an impulse to close down consciousness.

When we support children through ERC we might direct them to begin with a focus on whatever has been the trigger – what has set the current reactions or behaviours or symptoms in motion. In the counselling time they are often able to go back through time to the origins, to an early incident or even the first incident that caused a similar reaction of hurt.

This first prototypical hurt may have been in infancy or may be a stage of the birth. We support the child in focusing within and allowing feelings. This can allow them to feel the first hurt. When they feel the original hurt deeply, with its unexpressed pain and rage, there is an inner integration, a release of the energy that has been used to hold the pain from consciousness. There is freedom from that old emotional bind. This then shows in a new relaxed and positive attitude.

Ideally, birth could be an experience that sets positive imprints for dealing with the events and internal energies in our lives. It is only the negative aspects or moments when there was too much pain or fear that have to be released through deep-level counselling. The reward from reliving unfinished episodes is that the basic attitudes to life are able to change, to become very positive. Children can then meet life and its challenges more willingly and with creative energy.

The effects of different births

Our observations of the effects of birth trauma with many hundreds of adult and child clients are supported by the reports in the writings of Grof and Janov. Some typical patterns emerge. In considering these it is vital to stress that no judgement is being made on mothers or doctors. Intervention in deliveries is usually for positive, life-preserving reasons.

Firstborns

The journey of the firstborn out into the world usually takes longer, on average twice as long, as for the second born. For the firstborn there is more resistance in the birth canal, and the baby may spend more time with its head engaged in the cervix. Many firstborns have a vague sense of being more troubled than siblings, having to struggle more in life.

Nervous mother

If a mother is out of rhythm with herself and the labour process, the contractions will be uncoordinated, arrhythmic and the cervix dilation probably slower. The baby will be born out of rhythm with him/herself. This can sometimes be seen in jerky movements of the infant and a non-fluid way of walking. Some children have found a new sense of grace after a series of counselling sessions that released the energy that was most probably associated with an arrhythmic birth.

Anaesthetic

If the mother gives birth under the influence of general anaesthetic or pain-relief drugs she will not be fully connected to the force of the contractions. The chemicals also affect the newborn in some of these ways: shallow breath, poor temperature control, poor appetite, poor sucking and poor reflex activity. The chemical effects can last for months. Children born this way often have difficulty in completing projects, lose a sense of focus and have little sense of satisfaction from completed projects.

Manual help

A similar pattern to the one above can occur for those born with manual help, forceps: 'I can't do things myself, I need help.'

Induced labour

In the case of induced labour the child is pushed out into the world when the mother or doctor is ready or feels the time is right. The child born in this way can have a strong dislike of being pushed into projects before they are ready, can feel pushed even if this is not the case and can never be rushed.

Caesarean

Those born by caesarean section show some of the strongest character traits that can be traced back to the birth. Children born by non-labour, or elective, Caesarean have an easy access to spiritual dimensions, but often they lack stamina for effort in the world. The most pronounced influence is a lack of boundaries in the world. When working with those children it is necessary to frequently restate and define boundaries. Those born by emergency Caesarean usually after a long period of labour, experience greater trauma then those born by normal delivery.

Delayed birth and obstructed labour

Both delayed births and obstructed labours tend to produce children with a tendency to be out of rhythm, sometimes acquiescent and sometimes intolerant of waiting. Many of these are continually active as a defence against confinement. We suspect that the roots of many cases of hyperactivity (other than hyperactivity related to brain disorders) may lie here.

Breech

Breech births, where the feet or buttocks emerge first, bring the pressure of contractions on the head and face. Children born in this way often have mystery pains in the legs. They may have difficulty in standing up to things and a tendency to back away from challenges.

There are many variations in types of births and many external influences that enhance the trauma or alleviate it. No absolute statements can be made linking character and type of birth. The brief outlines above can increase our awareness of what initial traumas the child may have experienced and help us to choose processes to support them in their release work.

Childhood trauma

Children desire to be loved exclusively and without limit. They come out into the world expecting parents to live up to the womb experience: to be totally nurturing, present twenty-four hours a day, and not be shared with anyone. Some say they expected their parents to be the same as God. They would have been satisified with real mature love and warmth, but the capacity for giving this is rare.

In many children the pain of unfulfilment in their relationship with their parents has clouded over the strong original impulses of love that seem to be innate.

Children look towards their mother and father, their models, for encouragement, shelter and love. Many factors, such as the size of the family, whether both parents have to work, etc., as well as the emotional maturity of the parents, determine the parents' ability to give. Most children are still trying to get. If by some stroke of good luck parents are mature and do meet the child's needs, the child too grows to become emotionally mature, able to give.

Through ERC many children have grown beyond the hurt inner child, and that allows them the joyful experience of knowing their own innate wholeness. In this experience there is no hurt child, only freedom, peace and completeness.

Very few people truly leave childhood behind. Even though they may appear to mature and make their mark in the world, the motivation, the longing, remains the same: to get what was not forthcoming to the child. This explains why so few worldly achievements give lasting satisfaction for adults.

There are several main causes of childhood trauma and deep emotional pain. The main traumas come from direct abuse to the child. There is also the deep pain of parents separating, a pain that a growing number of children are experiencing these days. A teacher who does not like the child, or is unhappy and thus retaliatory with the class, can cause trauma. Some children find that their own academic limitations can cause them panic, embarrassment and continual turmoil. Frequently this disturbance is a secondary one, the primary one coming from the home life. Emotional pain is caused by prolonged neglect, not being seen, recognised or acknowledged. Over the time of growing up, even insufficient love becomes a trauma, something that cannot be integrated, something that leaves damage to self-esteem and self-image.

The trauma of abuse

In children who have been beaten, abused, emotionally or physically brutalised in some way, the tender, altruistic impulses are very deeply buried. They are locked away under the unfulfilment and hurts, and these in turn are beneath layers of rage and hate. Most children learn to suppress both the hurts and the anger at being hurt, needing to live in hope that if they are very good, they might finally get what they want.

No matter what the abuse has been – emotional or physical – it will be registered in the body. As for all ERC, the way into the memories is through work on something unsatisfactory in life now, something that has been created out of the old imprint or carries an 'over-the-top' reactive energy caused by the past.

Children may have great difficulty in speaking for themselves. They may appear to be unable to express feelings or thoughts and so be withdrawn, perhaps even failing academically. They may even stutter or develop a hunched body stance or a sunken chest. Energy and feelings are obviously held back.

In ERC a counsellor would notice these symptoms and would aim to help the child connect with the feeling in their body – the feeling of being withdrawn or of protecting or of keeping safe. This could lead to uncovering some decision made earlier (unconsciously, of course) such as 'I'll never say that again!' or 'I'll never speak my thoughts.' Such decisions are a way of surviving some form of abuse – perhaps that of being silenced repeatedly by an angry parent or teacher.

Children who have been punished physically for 'disruptive behaviour' (having high energy) will sometimes develop a very measured way of being in the world. Such control of lifeforce will one day want to burst out. Its first expression will be mostly anger or grief. Through ERC this abuse can be healed and the child (or adult) can reclaim their natural exuberance and decide for themselves when to express it and when to let it be quieter.

Sexual abuse

The deeper and closer to home the trauma, the longer the healing work will take. If the abuse was very close to home the child will be quite resistant to healing work. In cases where the abuse was by the father or stepfather, if the child knew that the mother was aware of what was happening and made no moves to protect, the scarring is very deep indeed. There is the trauma of the event(s) and the knowledge that the mother chose against the child – there is a sense that there is absolutely no safety anywhere.

Healing the shock usually begins with breaking the silence. Most abuse is kept secret in childhood. Sharing what happened and, more importantly, how it felt is the first step to releasing the trauma and shame. The speaking out is a healing process in itself and takes great courage and patience from the counsellor.

Shock from childhood remains in the body, closing down feelings and general flow of energy, unless it can be expelled through emotional release processes. Until counter-attack energy – the energy of rage – is activated, the victim state will remain. There is a need in processing to symbolically abuse the abuser, as well as those who did not protect.

Part of the victim state is the belief that the abused is too small or weak to counter-attack, or will be injured if the rage and hate come out (as may have actually occurred in the past). So all the fighting energy is held and can become a permanent state. An adult who suffers chronic depression or wishes to fight everyone and everything can emerge.

In cases of prolonged or repeated sexual encounter, the most difficult feeling to own will usually be the positive thing that the child got out of it: 'It was better than nothing, better than no love.' Some adults will say during therapy: 'In some way I allowed it, hoping that I would get some of the love I needed.'

To keep the hope alive of getting the right sort of love from the parent(s), the child will usually transfer the 'badness' of the abuser on to themselves. It is an unconscious attempt to keep the image of the parent intact. This is a very powerful force in all children. If the parent is seen in all their imperfections and with their immaturity, there is no chance of getting the love and care that is needed. 'If I am bad, that is why this is happening to me. If I am the cause, then I might be able to change things. If they are the cause, it's hopeless!'

The result is very low self-esteem. Children who have low self-esteem need much work to access the good in themselves, the treasure, the strengths. When they come to puberty, or if the abuse took place after they reached puberty, the badness is very often transferred on to their own sexuality. This is sometimes reinforced through strict religious teachings that deny the body and sexuality, resulting in an imprint that, at core, they and their sexuality are evil. What happened to them is then seen almost as just punishment. Great support is needed in placing the blame where it belongs. This will bring up many feelings that go beyond the abuse experience, that relate to feeling unsafe in the world, and the general lack of love in their environment.

In all cases, the dealing with memories and suppressed feelings – whether recent or from years before – will put the child into a very unsettled state. Some adults even use this as proof that too much delving into the past is not good. This stage will throw into turmoil school work and relationships. There will be forces within the child that strongly resist the healing/remembering process. So patience will be needed to accompany them through the 'yes/no' of facing the pain.

For their growth into balanced adults, it is vital that all measures are taken to ensure that these children do not take on an identity that comes from what happened to them. If they live under a label of 'abused' or 'survivor', if this becomes a means of feeling special, of standing out from others – and we have seen this often – there is much more resistance to growth and healing work.

Children of separated parents

The place of a stable family life in the healthy development of a child has been well-researched and seems obvious to most of us who work with children. The norm in our society is that separation between parents is bad. The fact remains that there are growing numbers of single-parent families and ERC counsellors are called on more and more to help children make the adjustments to this.

Prior to parents deciding to separate, or revealing the decision to their children, the children actually know that something is not right, that something is 'going wrong'. Clear communication will help children cope with what is happening between parents. Feeling one truth and being told another will not only confuse children, it will teach them to doubt their own intuition. Children's intuition is usually active and accurate.

Children will often consciously and unconsciously make efforts to get the family structure working again. To them, the outer family structure is like a mirror to their inner wholeness. When parents split it is like a tearing of two halves inside. The same inbuilt movement towards wholeness that we all have contributes to the long-term longing of the child for the parents to re-unite. It is as if the masculine and feminine inner parts are being torn apart as the outer models separate.

Parents are often surprised to find that their children wish for the family to be back together again even after many years, and even though they may rationally understand that it cannot work. It is very helpful to bring this desire to 'fix things' to consciousness. This brings relief and freedom.

Some children come to counselling because they are continually blaming themselves for the parents' separation. This blaming of themselves may have resulted from an overheard and misunderstood comment made by one of the parents. It may endure because the child desperately longs for the image of the parent(s) to stay intact – along with their hope of resolution of problems. This self-blaming is one of the major contributions to low self-esteem. It can affect school work, health, morale, and even result in the child becoming self-destructive. ERC methods can help the child become free of this blame.

There is a great need for the children of separating parents to release their feelings of anger and hurt and fear. The conflicts and highly charged emotional atmosphere that usually surround a separation will negatively affect a child's academic, eating and sleeping habits.

When children visit the non-custodial parent it takes them time to reconnect, to open again emotionally. One effect of the coming and going between parents' homes is that children have to open and close emotionally. Parents who have been looking forward to a visit from their children are often dismayed when children seem cold, distant and uncommunicative. Children have to be given time to adjust, as well as time to express how they feel. Many children will try to hide feelings of awkwardness and this will actually compound them.

Where children have been told by one parent not to talk to the other parent about life at home, the secretiveness will add another strain that reinforces the barrier to easy relating.

Adolescent boys who live with their mother will usually blame the mother for the separation. This may be open and expressed (and painful for the mother), or it may be quite unconscious. Again, the need to keep the image of the father intact, the model of masculinity, may override any facts. This blaming of the mother often shows through the rebellious behaviour and the constant tests of authority.

The way that the parents relate to each other after the separation will often become a model of relating for the children. Where it is not plainly aggressive, this relating will usually be cold and distant, a mere exchange of information. Children absorb this. The lack of physical contact and warmth in relating can be assimilated by the children. Parents should ensure that the relationship with children does give freedom for warmth, affection and touch to be experienced.

When parents enter new relationships or remarry there may be a fresh wave of resentment from children. Children may try to hide this in order to please the parent, but it is inevitably there. This resentment will need to be released in a safe place with a counsellor.

Effects of birth and childhood trauma

The strain of living with a step-parent, especially a step-parent who has children as well, leads the child to view them, and maybe relate to them, as rivals and home wreckers. They will often appear to the child as Cinderella's stepmother, or the wicked witch in Snow White, or the giant ogre that Jack met at the top of the beanstalk.

Raising an unarmoured child

As long ago as the 1940s, Wilhelm Reich, originally a student and colleague of Freud, began to study the causes and effects of armouring in young children. Current explorers in the area of psychosomatic (mind–body linked) symptoms confirm his investigations. Armouring is the permanent contraction of muscles into a fixed body stance, holding feelings and energy from expression.

Since so much of our inspiration and tools for exploration come from Reich, it is very interesting to review some of his findings. We have also catalogued (see page 72) some of the main feelings held in the armouring of the body.

Reich said that a newborn infant can be assumed to have an unwarped, highly fluid energy system. He posed the question 'What obstacles do we encounter if we decide to let only the interests of the child, and nothing else, determine the course of development?' From his extensive research he gave this preliminary list of the obstacles to raising an unarmoured child:

- Pelvic armouring of the mother reduces vitality of genital area and thus impedes full energetic functioning of the foetus.
- If the baby is startled, for example by being taken out of the bath too quickly, the tension can be held.
- If the mother is tense at times, the milk flow can be restricted, leaving the baby hungry and unfulfilled.
- Resentment from the mother can build up because of the time taken to care for the baby. This resentment is felt by the baby, causing emotional and then muscular contraction.
- The mother's guilt about not being a good enough mother, holding an ideal that the baby must be healthy and happy *all* the time, can cause a loss of deep contact with the baby for a time.
- Circumcision and the emotional need of family and friends to have it done cause emotional and physical shock.
- Racial, religious, cultural and national moulding – while child is defenceless – call into play stresses to maintain something that is not natural to the child.
- Contraction of the body due to lack of deep contact with the mother attracts chest infections, which, in turn, strengthen emotional and energetic blockages. The emotional and the physical causes then work together, causing cycles of sickness and contraction in the chest.
- An armoured parent will not feel or sense the child's problems.
- Many parents lack knowledge of emotional first-aid for baby's early armouring. Reich found that sometimes simply tickling would allow muscular holding to release, and a state of energy flow and well-being to return. We recommend Dr Frederick Leboyer's book *Loving Hands* as an inspiration for new parents to begin giving positive touch to their baby.

Reich considered that a complete program to enable an infant to function purely, naturally, without a build-up of armouring would concentrate on the development from conception to the fifth or sixth year. He was the first to outline a program that would include:
- prenatal care of the mother, including counselling, particularly on the use of her energy
- careful supervision of the delivery and first days of the newborn's life
- prevention of armouring in the first five to six years
- follow up, recording developments (especially of any armouring) till after puberty

Reich showed up glimpses of an ideal that would allow a child to develop perfectly, without stress, lacking nothing. It is a high ideal, but many are quietly working in a range of fields to move us closer to this possibility.

We know of several midwives who are helping mothers-to-be work with their own fears and armouring, in order to have more free-flowing energy. This freed-up energy allows freer emotional flow, which in turn allows deep contact with the newborn.

Since Reich wrote about the obstacles to raising an unarmoured child, we have been influenced by Leboyer and others who have transformed birthing techniques and environments.

Counselling help and practical home help for new mothers are somewhat dependent on community finances. We need to watch that everything possible is done to allow mothers the most restful time with their babies.

The women's movement has empowered many mothers to demand what they instinctively feel is right in the birthing place. It has encouraged them to be more informed about birth. All this allows for less anxiety.

ERC helps us deal with the effects of difficult births, of armouring that defends us from deep pain, and of the hurt inner child. Children are able to move through so much of their pain, and come to a quiet and sensitive state, or an excited and alive state – whichever is congruent with their true energy at that moment.

The good news is that children do respond well to the exercises that help them heal and grow.

Birthing games

Since the stresses of life are for the most part the direct result of the original painful experience of birthing, it is very useful to help children to contact and even re-experience these forceful unconscious negative energies. (A caesarean-born child, or a breech-born, would need the games modified to re-create their particular experience.)

The games can be pure fun. They can awaken memories of birthing trauma and provide an outlet for the release of perinatal energy charges. These games can be extremely healing, releasing energies locked in the system since birth, energies which may, in part, contribute to aggressive, passive and/or hyperactive behaviour. They can release parts of the body that have been in shock since the birth.

The games are created according to the principle that through re-enacting the traumatic experience in a manageable way, giving the body the experience again, the psyche can open to physical and emotional memories that need to be released. These games are presented in a spirit of fun, whereas many of the other exercises need a serious approach. We have seen children in individual and group work dive wholeheartedly into these games and emerge with a new sense of freedom.

It is sometimes difficult to entice children over 12 to participate in these games.

Here are some images for introducing birthing games:

- 'Be a turtle, with a mattress or large cushion for your shell, and have someone make it tighter. Feel the need to slip out. Repeat over and over.'
- 'Be in an egg. You are hatching. Peck at the shell. Push it open. Are you a chick, a turtle? what?'
- moth egg → caterpillar → cocoon → moth.
- butterfly egg → caterpillar → chrysalis → butterfly.
- acorn → seedling → sapling → oak tree → drop new acorns.

Birthing exercise

Leaving mother

Suitable for children aged 4 to 12 years.

Have crayons and large sheets of paper ready. Heartbeat music or gentle background music would be useful

1. Children lie down with eyes shut.
2. Guide children into imitating and feeling the energies of being angry, crying, laughing.
3. They then sit up and draw each of these expressions with crayons on large sheets of paper.
4. Each child holds up their drawings to the group and acts out each expression in front of the group.
5. Play some music. Children take some space and curl up into foetal position, tightly.
6. Say to children: *Make yourself so small now that you disappear!*
7. Ask them to wriggle out, making the original sounds to show how they felt as a baby emerging. This may be done several times.
8. Ask them to begin larger movements, remembering and/or imagining what happened after the birth.

Birthing exercise

Baby learns

Suitable for children aged 4 to 12 years.

1. Children curl up, breathe deeply.
2. Ask children to remember being in their mother's womb.
3. Tell them to feel themselves getting ready to come out, then moving out, slowly.
4. *Remember:*
   - *trying to hold your head up*
   - *trying to sit up*
   - *crawling*
   - *standing*
   - *walking*
   - *talking baby talk*
   - *growing up*

Observe what this means to them.

Integration exercise

Bringing new life into my world now

Suitable for children aged 4 to 14 years.

Have drawing and writing materials ready.

This exercise is ideal for use after new learnings, especially from birthing exercises.

1. Children form into groups of three.
2. Two children make a 'blockage', a wall – something for the third child to push through.
3. The child whose turn it is takes a moment to tune in with some deep breaths. They are invited to reconnect with their new learnings, and then bring these through the wall with them.
4. The children making the wall make sure the one breaking through has to squeeze through so that the whole body feels what is happening.
5. You can note, and possibly mirror back, which children fight their way through, which ones progress in a surrendered or resigned way, which ones have a gentle ease.
6. All take a turn.
7. Ask children to write or draw the new learnings or experiences that they brought through the wall with them.

CHAPTER THREE

Practical planning for ERC

Sometimes it is very difficult to keep firmly in mind
the fact that parents, too, have reasons for what they do
– have reasons, locked in the depths of their personalities,
for their inability to love, to understand,
to give of themselves to their children.

Virginia Axline, *Dibs: In Search of Self*, Penguin, 1971.

Counselling sessions

Structuring sessions

Counselling sessions with children and adolescents usually range in time from about forty minutes to about ninety minutes. This depends very much on the attention span of the child, their willingness to enter the work offered, their previous experience (those who have felt the benefits will be keen to work longer), and the time available to the counsellor.

A private and soundproof room is best. Unfortunately many counsellors in schools have a room close to the administration offices. A carpeted room is ideal. A good supply of well-made cushions for lying on, rolling around in, hitting etc. is essential.

The work space should be ordered. This helps a child feel safe, especially when there is much inner disorder.

Structure the sessions by breaking up the time with movement. Beware of too much sitting – have them lie down, sit up, stand, shake, move to another area of the room and come back.

Some basic stages

In planning individual or group counselling sessions it is important to include both emotional release exercises and the teaching of inner-life skills. Here is a suggested framework for ordering the sequence of exercises:

1 Finding hope, inner strength, and trust:
  - visualisations
  - Gestalt exercises
  - making resistance conscious

2 Self-exploration:
  - verbal questioning
  - relaxation
  - dreamwork
  - using body outline drawings – locating pains and blocked feelings

3 Emotional release processes:
  - drawing feelings
  - bioenergetics – to practise and give permission for release
  - guided focusing methods
  - exercises to trigger and release feelings, for example:
    – become animals – make animal sounds
    – speak to a spot on wall (shrink parents)

- draw face and direct feelings towards it
- imagine 'other' in chair sitting opposite
- express feelings to a mother/father stand-in (group work)

4 Integration:
- verbal sharing (including assessing further support)
- journal writing and mandala drawing
- sandplay
- relaxation and visualisations
- body outline drawings – compare 'before' and 'after'
- review of the session, possible links with past work

5 Support for creativity:
- hopes and projects for the future
- new directions, aims, intentions
- ideas for using energy positively

6 Homework:
Children are familiar with academic homework. It tends not to have very exciting connotations. However, suggesting exercises, new ways of working or new ways of being within a family, can be extremely supportive of the child taking responsibility for their own inner growth. Exercises that increase levels of communication between children and parents, or children and carers are the ideal ones. They should be fun exercises to some degree, and the setting of these tasks could become a regular part of the counselling session routine. (See also notes on integration on pages 18–19.)

Group work

Children going through a crisis or recovering from trauma often need peer-group support. Counsellors are usually so overbooked that group work is a practical and efficient way to begin working with children. Ideally this will be sympathetic ongoing group support where they can learn that it is okay to be vulnerable, to let the inner world out. The composition of the group should remain the same for each session – this helps to sustain trust and confidentiality and allows children who have dropped their defences to remain open to the group.

Advantages

Some children may experience feelings of acceptance for the first time. Acceptance from the outside helps recognition on the inside.

The presence of the group as accepting witnesses of inner processes makes inner exploration, tears, expressions of anger, etc. acceptable, not weird.

Group work facilitates the learning and practice of the skills of support. (If only we had grown up knowing how to be with someone who is going through an emotional reaction or a time of very deep feeling, rather than being afraid, keeping our distance or trying to calm them down.)

Leadership skills and confidence can develop from this group work, especially where individuals have the chance to lead small subgroups.

Structure

A group formed for inner work is most effective with about six to ten members. If it is necessary to work with a larger number, create subgroups that can easily form a bond and identity. Initially group work may be more effective if best friends are placed in different subgroups.

When adolescents share deep emotional experiences, when they go through the risk of exposing their feelings, they very quickly form close bonds. Many may fall in love with another member of the group. It is a huge learning to find that underneath they are all very similar. Privacy and continuity enable and support this tender relating.

We recommend that the group work with two facilitators. One can focus on the presentation to the whole group and stay tuned in to the general group energy and readiness. The other facilitator is free to move about and give individual support as needed. Facilitators should be clear on these roles.

It is also effective to have some adults in the group who have worked before, personally, with emotional release techniques. They need to be adults who are not afraid to release their feelings in front of others. This gives permission for the whole group to go deeper. It lets the children see that adults too carry deep problems and feelings locked away. It also contributes to narrowing the generation gap. Those adults who have shown their willingness to release pent-up reactionary feelings become the ones that the children trust and turn to later for help.

Group work varies in length of time. In a school setting where the group session is timetabled into a busy day it may run for 40 minutes and allow the exploration and integration of one exercise. In a retreat or workshop setting more time will be available, but the group will need many clear beginnings and endings as new work is introduced. Frequent breaks are essential. A rhythm of gathering together, inner focus, release work, sharing, integration, recording and relaxation, then a change of scene, pace or modality is advised.

Peer group sharing, especially during informal break times, is very important for adolescents to connect with each other at a deeper level. Plenty of breaks are recommended during group work. Our experience is that the level of their discussion with each other at these times goes much deeper than usual. They connect with each other more and the choice of topics moves on from clothes, schools and music towards the meaning of life.

To build an ongoing trust and readiness to undertake emotional release work, a group could meet regularly, say once a week. It is normal that, after the healing of a particular issue, a child's interest in the group may wane for a time. This is usually a sign of health.

Important issues

One of the most challenging situations for a facilitator in working with a group of older children is the high level of resistance that is generated in some participants. This can seem to slow the rate of work for the whole group, but the challenge is yours! Those that resist inner adventure and revealing of anything personal can actually mirror and even trigger your own resistance. You will know this if you experience a reaction to these individuals. Again, take back any projection of the problem. Clear yourself or become conscious of your own resistance. Suddenly then, they are not a problem. A creative new way emerges to support their real need at their level of readiness.

Resisters, non-participants, are actually the most fearful ones. Remember that under their fooling around, under their disruption, is their fear. Knowing this changes your own attitude to them. You need not be anxious or worry. Give them little attention, while always hoping and inviting them to participate. Their unconscious, deep behind its heavy guard, is slowly getting the message that it is safe to feel and reveal!

Practical planning for ERC

When working with school children, it is almost impossible for the facilitator also to be the one who is responsible for the children's behaviour to and from the workshop or group. Children will rarely open up with an authority figure. This is why teachers and parents often cannot help their own children as much as an outsider can.

Presenting exercises

Always work with the exercises yourself, experience them, before presenting. Is the language appropriate for the age group you are working with, and for their social/cultural backgrounds?

Set up the space and bring order into the work space, before beginning – preferably before children come in. Check you have all the materials before beginning.

Familiarise yourself with equipment before presenting. For example, it is amazing how often the volume control on the cassette player disappears when you are in the middle of an exercise!

Check music suitability before using it. Rewind tapes, and have other options ready.

Give a brief overview of the aim of the exercise before presenting. If you are doing partner work, choose partners before giving introductory instructions.

Always repeat your instructions at least twice. Then look carefully to see if you have been understood. Do you need to rephrase the instruction? If using background music, turn it down as you give instructions. Make it clear at each stage whether you want children to open or close their eyes and whether you want them to look at you or relate to each other.

Give time boundaries clearly, and give time warnings when it is nearly time to stop an exercise, or a section of it.

If you sense resistance in the children, get them to talk about it, make it conscious before beginning. This decreases it.

Talk to the children about:
- the need for confidentiality
- the aims of the work
- the occasional use of supportive touch

Planning: A checklist

Here are some planning questions for facilitators running group work:
- Are you clear on the aims of the group work?
- Have you planned how to express these aims to the participants?
- What are the main issues or themes to be addressed?
- Are the participants clear on what is being offered to them?
- Can your contracts or agreements on goals with the children take them as far as they need to go?
- Which child/children do you suspect might need individual support?
- Are you clear on role allocation? Who will focus on the group as a whole? Who will attend to individual needs?
- Are your practical preparations complete? All materials ready?
- What are your feelings about this group? Are there any reactions in you towards the children? Do you need to clear any issues before beginning?

Group sharing

For the child, the purposes of group sharing are:
- to enhance integration of inner work
- to give them the chance to hear themselves speak about their experiences, thus bringing clarity
- to give them the chance to proclaim new knowledge about themselves, to honour and confirm their inner discoveries
- to give them the experience of uninterrupted attention from facilitator and group
- to create an energy of bonding within the group
- to develop trust, thus allowing deeper work in the future
- to develop the skills of expression in front of a group

For the facilitator, the purposes of group sharing are:
- to check that processes are complete by listening to the voice energy and watching the body language
- to clarify any misunderstandings about the processes or the conceptual frameworks
- to check that there is group cohesion – are any members in reaction to each other?

Sharing methods
Children can:
- show their mandalas and drawings
- read written summaries of their inner work
- tell the story of their sandplay
- say whatever they would like to say
- say what is their new learning
- speak one sentence only about their experience in the group work
- mime the main thing that happened for them
- take a stance that shows their energy now
- use a talking stick, or an eagle's feather, or something to empower them as speaker and clearly designate that it is their turn
- answer or respond to a specific question; for example:
  - How do you feel right now?
  - What do you need to say when you get home?
  - Become the animal you found within again. Show us how it sounds and moves.

Evaluating group work

Here are some self-evaluation questions for facilitators running group work:
- Were you clear on the aims of the group work?
- Were you happy with the way you kept in touch with each other during the exercises?
- Was the role allocation clear?
  - Who focused on the group as a whole?
  - Who attended to individual needs?
- Was the division of responsibilities in presenting clear?
- Were you able to be flexible? Were you satisfied with your ability to flow with the group's energy and needs?
- Were you satisfied with your practical preparations?
- What issues for the children seemed to be left incomplete?

- What exercises do you think might be useful for this group next time?
- What things would you do differently next time?
- What is your general feeling about the group time allocation?
- Have you had any personal issues triggered by working with the group? How will you deal with these?

Dealing with projection and transference

A projection is a trait, attitude, feeling or bit of behaviour which actually belongs to your own personality but is not experienced as such; instead, it is attributed to objects or persons in the environment and then experienced as directed towards you by them instead of the other way round. The projector, unaware, for instance, that he is rejecting others, believes that they are rejecting him; or, unaware of his tendencies to approach others sexually, feels that they make sexual approaches to him. (F Perls et al., *Gestalt Therapy*, Bantam Books, 1977)

You may project your missing, buried or rejected parts or feelings on to the children in your care. It is as if they were a blank screen on to which your unconscious throws a reflection of itself. The children may have a little bit of what is unconscious in you, just enough for you to justify projecting all of your stuff on to them. For example, if you were never allowed to play, you insist that the children do; if you are desperately unhappy with your life, you presume the children are – you think you sense the unhappiness coming from them, rather than from inside yourself; if you are very hurt and therefore cynical about your own personal development, you will find that you always seem to attract cynicism from the outside, from the children.

Sometimes you can project your state on to others. For example, you may see the children as chaotic, overexcited or depressed – in some state that you believe is *theirs*. If you find a strong reaction to them, or a disproportionate interest in fixing them, you need to come home inside yourself and acknowledge that you are the one who is chaotic, overexcited, depressed etc. If this is not acknowledged you may continue to project it on to them. This owning back, this self-examination enables you to deal with the real cause *in you* and allow the changes necessary. When you have owned back the projection, you usually find that it is not long before the children catch on and respond to your new state!

Children will often transfer feelings that are really directed at a parent on to a facilitator. If the facilitator is not aware of the power of this phenomenon, and has not cleared his or her own parent–child issues, this can result in reactions. These reactions can then bring a counter-transference back on to the child. These would be feelings that originally arose in the facilitator in response to their own parents.

We may be able to recognise what children project on to us and see it as truly theirs. This helps us stay free of reaction. We may even be able to help them own their own inner energy.

If a child is not willing or able to feel the pain of some negative truth about a parent, if they are defended, they may insist that it is the facilitator who exhibits the parent's negative characteristics. What is negative in the parent is transferred on to the facilitator. (This is at least more healthy than the child taking on those characteristics themselves, and believing it is they who are bad, mad or unlovable.) Children transfer like this because they don't want to face up to parents. They have too much to lose. This form of transference is their defence.

If we are familiar with the idea of transference and its purpose for the child we can remain objective and help the child return to themselves and acknowledge what they are really feeling and who the feelings are really about.

Mirroring, reflecting back what they seem to be feeling, is very helpful here. For example, we might need to say: 'So, you are angry with me? Is Mum/Dad sometimes like me? Do you sometimes feel like this towards Mum or Dad?'

Disowned qualities and emotions are projected out, unconsciously, and then felt as coming to us (not from us). Most people have been taught to disown their feelings and essential qualities; for example:

- Excitement that is not owned is felt as anxiety – something 'out there' seems to be making us anxious.
- Desire and drive are felt as pressure.
- Aggression is felt as fear.
- Anger is felt as depression.
- Our own potential when not recognised is projected out and felt as overblown awe (hero worship).

Some tendency or trait which we refuse to admit in ourselves leads us to feel indignation at that trait (real or imagined) in another; for example, prejudices, snobbishness, prudishness, meanness etc. In other words, *we* are responsible for the anxiety, the pressure, the fear, the awe etc.

How can we tell if what we sense in another is really 'them' or our projection? Ken Wilber in his book *No Boundary* (Shambala, Boston and London, 1985) puts it like this:

> Those items in the environment (people or things) that strongly *affect* us instead of just *informing* us are usually our own projections.

Processing exercise on projections for adults

Dealing with a difficult child

Have ready tissues, cushions, strong music, drawing and writing materials.

1. Stand facing a wall and focus on a particular spot on the wall. Imagine that this spot is the difficult child.

2. Take some full breaths. Make an agreement with yourself that you will let yourself feel the whole truth of your feelings.

3. Begin to speak to the child (spot). Let your real feelings come through. Picture the qualities of the child that annoy you most.
   For example:
   - 'You are so . . . (obstinate, stupid, wild)'
   - 'You are so . . .'
   - 'You are so . . .'

4. Allow any anger to release. Put on some strong music if it helps you shout out any held-in energies.

5. Keep saying 'You are . . .' until something inside you recognises what has been happening.

> You will hear in your words a description of some aspects of yourself that you may not like, or have struggled against. You will realise, suddenly, that you are speaking to you.
>
> 6 Perhaps the words are 'You are so mean!' Keep saying this one sentence until you have really owned this part of yourself. It is this rejected part of yourself that the child has been mirroring to you.
>
> 7 Notice how you feel when you realise this. Often it is very funny.
>
> 8 Now that you have brought this part of you to consciousness, does it still feel the same? What is underneath it for you? Recognising this will lead to a transformation of this quality. What has it transformed into?
>
> 9 Draw the energy now and give yourself time to write about it.
>
> 10 How do you now feel towards the child who was so difficult?

Affirmations and goal-setting

Affirmations and goal-setting are often considered useful in some new approaches to personal growth and helping children attain self-esteem. However, while it may certainly be true that positive thinking has a beneficial effect, beware of artificially glossing over inner turmoil and lack of self-esteem with wonderful-sounding affirmations.

Thought has no lasting power over emotions. If it did we would all be well controlled and children would not repeat the outbursts that so often get them into trouble.

An affirmation may make a child feel good for the moment, but unless it has organically grown out of inner work, come from inside them, it really has no lasting power.

It is important to ask: Where has the affirmation come from? the ego? someone else's suggestion? the inner child? the essence? a perception of parents' or teachers' expectations?

It is more important for the child to find the right place within from which to set goals than to make lists and promises. From this place within they can sense the right direction, the right choice for them. They then do not run the danger of forcing themselves or moulding themselves (or others).

Feeling good about themselves through achieving goals set by the ego part or the hurt inner child, or by another person, is not therapeutic. It can, in fact, reinforce the imprint that 'I am no good as I am', 'I have to achieve in order to have value'. It is a superficial 'feeling good', and not helpful in coming to wholeness.

It is vital that goals, wishes, intents, steps, new directions are indeed set by the maturing part of children, not the hurt inner child. The inner child part, of course, has its own agenda and goals. Following these will lead to emotional regression and greater emotional dependency on others, even if actually gaining some outward approval.

How do you know the difference between the maturing part and the hurt inner child? If the focus of wishes or goals is to get something from the outside, be very suspicious! If goals centre around discovering more inner resources, they can be followed confidently. If the intentions are simple and straightforward, not complicated, they are more likely to come from the mature part of the child. If we try to live up to externally imposed goals, affirmations, 'shoulds', we are bound to create our own hell.

The agenda of the hurt inner child can be recognised through: the need to win, the need to get something right, the fear of emptiness or being alone, the making of plans that will create great struggle.

An emotionally mature or healed child can be open to a range of outcomes, is interested to learn from mistakes, is ready to face unfamiliar states of emptiness and can enjoy being alone. They certainly have efforts to make in both inner and outer life, but if these are a struggle it is fairly certain that the hurt inner child is actively lurking in the background.

ERC and schools

It is a deep satisfaction for the authors that many teachers are now successfully incorporating ERC work into their curriculum. We receive good reports on children's enthusiastic self-discovery, on the positive improvement in classroom morale and on academic improvement made by some struggling pupils who have begun ERC work. These advances have required great interest and dedication from the teachers and have brought many rewards and satisfactions.

There are many challenges for a teacher who wishes to introduce ERC and the inner-life skills into the classroom. Some of the challenges are:
- large groups
- limitations of the physical classroom
- timetable requirements – especially in high school
- apparent conflicts in the teacher's roles of classroom management and inner-work facilitator
- support from colleagues who may be fearful of the new work

Many teachers have reported that the most important element of successfully merging the range of ERC work with their traditional programs has been their own regular personal work of 'clearing' reactions and emotional problems. Through this they have rediscovered their initial joy as teachers.

Informal use of ERC in the classroom

One teacher who uses ERC for herself and in her work shares how she uses her knowledge in the classroom.

When a child becomes restless and disruptive and has ceased to learn or participate, rather than punish or get into 'authority mode', she takes a few minutes to help the child connect to what is happening within. The whole class sometimes stops and helps. It goes something like this:

TEACHER: Could we stop and help John? John what is this energy that is bumping Billy

	wanting to say? Do? (*To the class*) What do you think this energy is really doing?
CLASS:	It wants to play.
TEACHER:	Is that what it wants? Let it speak, John.
JOHN:	(*Acting out the energy a little through moving and bumping*) I want to play! I want to move. I want to jump up and down!
TEACHER:	Keep saying it and doing it, energy. John is listening to you.
CLASS:	Could we do it too?
	(They join in with the role-playing too.)
TEACHER:	We all have a part that is alive. Isn't that great? Feel this part in you. You can be with that part in yourselves now as we go back to our reading.

Note: In the recognition of what is wanting to happen – bringing it to consciousness – the energy is satisfied to some degree and is now a creative source. It is now more integrated and no longer driving John.

A large number of the exercises in this book can be loosely classified under the standard headings of classroom programs. Many work well in the normal classroom setting. The focus for classroom use would perhaps be the inner-life skills – the exercises that promote self-awareness, self-esteem, positive use of imagination, finding of hope and inner strength. Some ERC exercises are most useful for classroom management, enabling the release of frantic, chaotic or scattered energies that disrupt the class learning.

Many exercises include elements of artwork, drama, dance, creative writing, music and aspects of religious education/personal development.

Exercises which use **artwork**:
- The Little Person with the Radar Inside (page 66)
- My Belly Circle (page 68)
- Learning More from My Drawings (page 80)
- My Family at Dinner (page 81)
- A Visit to the Aliens' Home (page 82)
- Talking about Families (page 85)
- Modelling the Shadow Parts (page 86)
- Getting Ready for Emotional Release Drawings (page 90)

Exercises which incorporate **drama**:
- Breathing Games (page 92)
- Exploring My Sound (page 94)
- I Love a Tantrum (page 94)
- The Dragonfly (page 96)
- My Fireworks Display (page 97)
- Roaring at the Monster (page 97)
- Finding an Animal Language (page 117)
- Messages from the Sandplay (page 131)
- Inner Treasure (page 137)
- My Beauty Revealed (page 140)
- Tension and Surrender (page 163)

Exercises which encourage **creative writing**:
- Journal writing (page 72)
- Creative writing (page 74)

- My Inner Parts Go on a Journey (page 76)
- My Life as a Myth (page 77)
- The People in My Life (page 100)

Exercises which explore the use of **music**:
- Getting Ready for Emotional Release Drawing (page 90)
- See also Appendix 4, 'Choosing Music' (page 200)

Exercises which might be useful in **religious education** and **personal development**:
- What Would You Really Like to Do? (page 121)
- Questions for My Dream (page 144)
- Exploring the Conscious and the Unconscious (page 148)
- A Gift from a Wise Part of Me (page 152)
- Visualising Relaxation (page 160)
- Walking Meditation (page 161)
- At Home in My Hands (page 166)

Exercises which include **dance** and **creative movement**:
- My Fireworks Display (page 97)
- My War Dance (page 98)
- My Real Face (page 102)
- Am I a Puppet on Strings? (page 103)
- Moving in Slow Motion (page 164)
- The Sunset (page 165)

Release of agitation at school

A primary teacher uses these principles with her class

It was a windy day. The children were restless. They were picking on each other and inattentive. Some had become disruptive. The teacher, who was training in ERC work, told the class in a strong voice to stand up and quickly form two lines outside.

She marched them briskly down to the oval. At the oval they formed a large circle. They turned to face outwards from the circle. She invited them to let free – to the wind – whatever they needed to say. They could speak or shout as loud as they liked. All the irritations were to be expressed to the wind and carried away, and forgotten. The teacher joined in too.

They returned to the classroom and the rest of the day proceeded smoothly.

Encouragement for teachers

ERC work is congruent with the basic stated goal of education in most Australian curriculums: to develop the whole person. Most educators would now agree that traditional Western educational methods have focused too much on academic development. ERC can now help redress this imbalance.

Practical planning for ERC

Academic development depends on a certain basic level of emotional well-being. Students who are wrestling with inner conflicts find it much harder to focus on their studies. All reports on the use of ERC over a period of time in schools have shown that attention spans, and thus academic achievement, have improved.

ERC methods have a huge contribution to make to effective pastoral care. ERC exercises give counsellors, chaplains and teachers a new range of approaches that can deepen bonds with students and help both the student and the carer get beneath the surface to the root of conflicts.

ERC principles can contribute to more effective classroom management. (See the reports on pages 46 and 48.)

The ERC exercises and the basic tools of ERC can help to extend a teacher's methods. Since the exercises are experientially based, they support a discovery-based approach. They extend self-awareness and encourage language development both through the integration stages of verbal sharing and in the recording of journal work.

An understanding of the effects of past trauma, the influence of the hurt inner child, the concepts of conscious vs. unconscious and the methods of physical and emotional release all support students and teachers in understanding and releasing stress.

Teachers are particularly prone to stress from unexpressed reactions to students. Those who wish to lower their stress levels can learn to regularly trace back through their day to the major reactions, contractions, hurts or disappointments, and undertake a few moments of release work along with some informed pondering on their unconscious part in the stress. This 'return home' after a difficult day can 'clear' their energy so that they are ready to enjoy their home life.

Teachers wishing to implement this work should address these important questions:

- Has there been some clear collaboration with colleagues? It is ideal to present this work with at least two facilitators. One can follow the progress of the group and the other can attend to any urgent individual needs.
- Has there been communication with parents? Are parents prepared for the results that release work might have on children? Is there a way to obtain parents' understanding, approval and even enthusiasm for ERC work?
- Have boundaries been set? Exactly what sort of behaviour will you allow? Have you given the students a guide to how casual they may be during this time? Have your feelings about your authority been examined? Where does your authority come from?
- Have you considered the modifications necessary for doing the exercises with a large group? Most of the exercises in this book are designed for small groups. One simple way is to create subgroups that can begin to form a distinct identity. Sometimes half the group may participate at a time. In that case, will the others watch? Or will they have a different task?
- Is there back-up for referral needs? What if a child acknowledges through this work a deep and difficult inner conflict, and is ready to ask for help? Who can they go to? Is the school counsellor on side? What are the alternatives?
- How will you evaluate the work? A simple way, after an exercise or a series of exercises, is to have the children write down some words or phrases 'which best describe their responses to the activities'. The responses will give the teacher confidence to proceed and ammunition for encouraging colleagues and administrations. Evaluation also brings the intellect into a new relationship with the experiential work and opens students to integrated understanding.

ERC methods in the primary school classroom

A report from Sonia Dayspring, a primary school teacher who has trained extensively in ERC

Teaching a group of six- to eight-year-olds has given me the opportunity of exploring some inner-life skills and emotional release exercises with a primary school class.

The children in my class range from normally well-adjusted to abused and emotionally damaged, with more than half having difficulties in learning. These difficulties, especially of concentration, often occur after a period of individual writing or after an especially long assembly. At these times, and when I realise that what's happening in the classroom is not working, we move to the withdrawal room and I give opportunities for movement, sounding and coming home to themselves.

I often use bioenergetics linked with visualisation after presenting an initial stimulus for a theme or a piece of work, in order to let them explore their own experience. Then I invite them to draw, write, share orally with a partner or in the whole group, construct, model, paint and/or dramatise in a small group. Such holistic experiencing allows release, extension and integration of inner experiences.

The need for these particular children to develop their self-concepts is acknowledged and I am encouraged by the administration to do all I can in this area of the curriculum. This addresses the justification for bringing these methods into my planning.

Music, movement, free dance and making music with voice covers much of the bioenergetics and release work that is possible in such a setting. Drama accounts for the rest. Much of the language program, especially using a whole language approach, incorporates visualisation and imagination games, with myths and fairy tales, dreamwork and meditation. Opening children to their feelings, hopes and inner qualities is incorporated into human relationships education. The expression of this inner treasure can be in many aspects of the art program.

We use the withdrawal room when privacy, sounding, loud music, free movement and no distractions are needed. The oval, or way down the back of the schoolyard amongst the trees, especially on a windy day, can also be spaces for free expression. Sometimes we simply find our own space, or stand in a circle facing outwards and focus on a cloud, or a spot in a tree, so our expression is not directed at anyone else.

Much of the quieter work, relaxing, imagining and expressing ourselves, is achieved within the open, double-teaching space classroom, even though the two classes work totally separately. Spontaneous opportunities often arise, such as when the other class moves out of the room – I then excitedly take the opportunity for some inner exploration with the children.

What I do in the moment depends on the group energy and needs. Very often individuals are niggling each other or there's downright aggression. In effect, emotions are near the surface and clearing is needed. Often aliveness has been held down and the children are naturally wanting to move and reconnect with themselves. In the past I sensed this and went outside for physical games. Now I find inner focusing, after movement, far more productive.

Having a sound understanding of the principles and experience of the practice of ERC, I can spontaneously meet the moment and create new processes appropriate to our classroom themes and the present inner state of the children. In this I usually invite centring and inner focus into their bodies. I develop a movement progression, gradually awakening their bodies and invite sounding. After expression of their energy I encourage stillness and inner focus. I often support this with a visualisation to find strength, hope and/or inner treasure. Integration is supported by some form of expression and maybe sharing after, or later.

Becoming more alive myself through my own personal development work, and being more consciously responsive to the energies of the children, has brought a vitality and enthusiasm to my classroom practices. This generates an aliveness in the children, which is very challenging in a school environment where control is highly valued. My task is harnessing the energy into productive and creative activities. I find the children often are really focused and all can more readily work silently engrossed in a book.

My aim, as a facilitator of learning, is to foster independence in learning and self-reliant behaviours. Now there is an authenticity in how these are emerging from within each child in my class.

Inner-life skills exercises in the secondary classroom

Comments from Dorothy Bottrell on working with secondary students

It is important with high school students to articulate some basic theory and principles to meet their cognitive needs. For young people who have not given much time and energy to turning inwards, this kind of understanding is necessary groundwork. The experiences of schooling predominantly take them into their heads and this is what they expect when they arrive in the classroom. Cognitive explanation helps to develop the trust and confidence which are formative for this work.

Inner-life work in the 'regular classroom' should follow the ideals of formal curriculum processes in that it should be introduced according to students' needs, curiosity and readiness, and should be allowed to evolve at their pace. It should be introduced in ways that make sense of their experiences in other aspects of their lives. ERC has the potential to add the missing dimensions of whole person development which is supposedly the primary goal of education.

Support groups

Parents, counsellors, teachers, therapists and group facilitators usually need ongoing support for dealing with their emotional reactions to children. Great support comes from reading: new information and new approaches bring new energy. However, the most enriching support comes from a group in which each member feels enough trust to process their own emotional reactions, thus retrieving their original, happy self.

Parents can make contact with other parents who have had to deal with similar problems in their children. Concerned parents often gravitate towards support groups established through local schools, mental health associations, playgroups, local government agencies, etc. The authors can put people in touch with others who use the methods in this book.

Whatever form it takes, a support group is advisable for:
- *replenishment*. The group can bring extra energy, directly and in the form of ideas, approaches, release work, shared experience, etc.
- *enthusiasm*. The group can redirect your interest back to its original hopefulness.
- *positive feedback*. There is nothing to equal a simple 'Well done!' from peers.
- *ideas*. Practical methods, solutions to problems, alternative ways of looking at your problems, professional and lay advice.
- *personal work*. Releasing reactions to working with children – especially the suffering of our own inner child, which is always coming to the surface when we give lots of time to children, or are triggered by their issues. This is the most helpful activity of a support group.
- *objectivity*. The group helps you see things at a distance – the whole picture – not just the drama that overwhelms you in the moment.
- *a feeling of satisfaction*. Recognise again the good in what you are doing. There is a tendency to be so involved that you only focus on the current problems, the difficult clients, the yet-to-be-healed hurts.
- *overcoming any feelings of isolation or of oddness in working this way*.

The biggest gift you can give yourself is a support group, even a group of only two. You need regular meeting times and a set venue. The work of the group can range from informal sharing to an inner-work time led by a professional.

Parents and carers who have a particular worry could form a specific interest group to:
- talk about the problems
- share their worries
- process their reactions
- seek a wider view of the problems
- find some possible action together
- together seek professional support and advice
- hear how it was for others and share about their own adolescence or primary school years

It can be helpful to seek professional guidance for a support group. A facilitator can formulate discussion questions that will help the group move to a deeper level, especially around their own part in the problems. A facilitator can also help with the subject of projection, which needs to be understood in order for adults to be clear on how to support children. This applies most particularly to work with adolescents.

Successful support group participation – a checklist

- Find a qualified facilitator. On page 202 there is a list of contacts.
- Prepare yourself. If possible, before meeting with others to share problems or to work together, take time to 'come home to yourself' and remember why you need this group. This time to come back into a deep sincerity, to centre, creates a better starting place for relating to others.
- Affirm confidentiality. Groups must clearly affirm that nothing personal from any member's process will be shared outside the group. This is absolutely vital, and any breaches must be addressed immediately. This confidentiality is important in creating conditions that make

group members feel safe to open up. Great psychic damage, as well as social damage, comes from sharing personal details – both for the one talked about and for the one who talks.
- Allow vulnerability. Become more comfortable in sharing inner states, practise sincerity. You need a vulnerable type of attitude to really bond with a group and to get to the bottom of problems with children. Also begin to welcome feedback on others' feelings about you. This requires a very conscious willingness to drop the defensive, protective attitudes.
- Share any resistance. If you are aware of it, always voice any resistance to sharing your innermost feelings. Share any worries or concerns. These are a force, resistance is a force – and you need to integrate that force, not alienate it and make it stronger. You don't want to resist your resistance. Once resistance has been made conscious and is shared it seems to reduce. And, of course, then it won't hide in the background and spoil things, becoming the silent 'no' to your conscious 'yes'. Revealing resistance usually helps bonding in a group.
- Practise active listening. Begin listening to the feelings conveyed in the voice of whoever is speaking, not just the meaning of the words. This way your support will go way beyond just agreeing or disagreeing. Paying attention to others will test your compassion. Notice how long you can remain interested in another person. If you feel any irritation about listening to others' problems, ask yourself:
  – What is happening in my heart right now?
  – What is my inner child saying when someone else is getting all the attention?
  – How can I stay connected and alive within while attending to another?
- Mirror back feelings. The main value of a support group is the emotional support. This special type of support helps us open to new creative ideas for dealing with our problems. Therefore accept the feelings of those in the group and acknowledge them, rather than always try to do something about them, or give a helpful answer straight away. Through this there will emerge a feeling for them of: 'I am not alone in this.' If there is a leader, always ask before offering comments.
- Remember that we are mirrors for each other. Others may actually see some of us, but usually they see themselves – especially characteristics that bring reaction. If you really dislike something in a child you work with or in someone in the support group, you need to look within yourself and see if it is there also. Normally we arrange our lives to have only friends who will not mirror things in ourselves that we would prefer not to own or accept.
- Be aware of projected feelings. Watch to see if you project your own feelings and expectations on to the other participants or the leader, or have done this with your own children. Support each other in sorting this out. Strong reactions will usually show where projection has taken place.

  When we are not in contact with our feelings we can sometimes find that they are projected out on to others. This is an unconscious mechanism. What is really inside us seems to be coming to us from the outside. If we feel that someone has something against us, or that everyone is against us, we need to check out our reality, our perceptions of others. Does this feeling really come from within ourselves? This applies particularly to self-judgements – often you might feel that the support group members may be judging you – when really it is yourself.

  If we are informed by what we see in another, it may be really there. If we are affected, if we are in reaction, it may be a projection. So, what in our children affects us most? How much of that 'problem' is really just within ourselves?
- Watch your reactions. When we react, the problem is within us. Normally out of our reactions we try to change the other, instead of finding out what is going on in ourselves. Reactions are a major source for learning about ourselves. How does our body react? What trains of thought are

started? 'Over-the-top' reactions are a sure sign that our hurt inner child part has been activated. How many hundreds of times does this happen to us with our children: the outer children set off the inner child!

Begin to recognise emotional triggers. What in the others, the leader or your children, sets your reactions off? See how it is for other parents.

- Listen to your own hurt inner child. Is it demanding something? Is it impatient when others speak at length? Ponder if it is responsible for your prohibiting or restricting your children in some way? Share your observations with other adults.

Remember you are in the group to learn about yourself, to encounter yourself, since you are the main source of your problems. It is too easy to get busy dealing with others, arguing, trying to change them, trying to 'get your point of view across'. Encounter yourself. Watch your own inner child. Use your reactions for self-knowledge.

- Care for yourself. Make sure you take some time to come home to yourself in the group. Don't get trapped into offering support all the time, or covering your own needs by constantly giving, or living through others.
- Don't hold back. In a dedicated support group it is best never to 'sit on' an issue that is alive for you. This holding back can cut you off from others – particularly if the issue is connected with the group or someone in it. Always share what is happening for you, find the right moment to put out any reactions or reservations or strong excited energies. Once you enter the journey it is vital that you don't add to the internal load of things held down.
- Watch for tiredness. Holding down anger or rage uses up huge amounts of energy and is very tiring. Holding excitement and joy out of sight – as many of us have learned to do – is exhausting. When you realise what you have been doing you will see there is usually a need for a big release of energy. This leads to a new aliveness.
- Ask for support. It is vital to ask for support when something difficult comes up in your journey. Most of us operate from the unconscious imprint that there is no support – usually it is the inner child who learnt that. It is often easier, if you are used to having no support, to suffer something in silence and alone, than feel that there are others around who would like to support.

Recognise times when a support group can heal and when you need professional support to process your difficult feelings.

CHAPTER FOUR

■

Encouraging children to talk about themselves

■

Children are our finest teachers.
They already *know* how to grow, how to develop, how to learn,
how to expand and discover, how to feel, laugh and cry
and get mad, what is right for them and what is not right for them,
what they need. They already know how to love and be joyful
and live life to its fullest, to work and to be strong
and full of energy. All they (and the children within us) need
is the space to do it.

Violet Oaklander, *Windows to Our Children*, Center for Gestalt Development, 1988.

Beginning discussion

These exercises are suitable for individual counselling work, and also for group work with adolescents. For group work it is useful to have some music in the background to aid privacy.

Talking exercise

Talking about what is inside me

Suitable for children aged 6 years and over.

Have writing materials ready.

These questions are one simple way to begin to support children in sharing any painful memories or feelings. It would be helpful for the facilitator to revise the summary of the child/adult concept on page 57.

1. Talk about opposites.
   Tell me about any recent time, or time when you were younger, when you felt very:

   strong   weak
   brave   afraid
   friendly   lonely
   hopeful   hopeless

2. Talk about 'then' and 'now'.
   Identify a time when each child felt happier, and then talk about the differences between then and now. Note any emotions touched and allow these to expand if need be.
   - *What was the main thing you wanted then?*
   - *What is the main thing you want now?*
   - *What are the differences in your family between then and now?*
   - *Are there any differences in where you live between then and now?*
   - *What are the main changes in you between then and now?*
     - *your body?*
     - *your hobbies?*
     - *your feelings?*
     - *how you behave?*
   - Ask the children to journal the main differences and similarities.

Encouraging children to talk about themselves

Talking and worksheet exercise

Developmental milestones

Suitable for children aged 8 years and over.

Have ready sufficient copies of the pro forma 'Milestones' on page 195.

This exercise is very helpful both in starting children talking about themselves and in gaining a wider picture of the influences at work in their families. Older children can fill in the worksheet; younger ones can contribute what they know, with some back-up from parents.

The exercise consists in tracing back through time to explore the links between outer events and inner states, moods, symptoms and behaviours.

See the example on page 56.

Talking exercise

Breaking the ice

Suitable for all ages, with vocabulary modification.

Some simple questions to begin children opening up to you:
- Tell me how you see your image. How do you think others see you?
- What do you do in your spare time?
- What are your main likes and dislikes in music?
- Who are your main friends and enemies?
- What sort of home do you live in?
- Who lives with you there?
- What seems to be your main worry?

Milestones – 18 year old boy

Age	Family changes	Outer events	Moods, behaviours, symptoms
2 yrs	First sister born	Live-in baby sitter while mother in hospital	Withdrawn, uncommunicative. Said: "It was a sad time." Dad was always angry.
8 yrs	Third sister born. Mum in hospital 2½ weeks.	Live-in baby sitter. Unkind to children	Withdrawn, retreated into own fantasy world. In trouble with Dad a lot. Spends more time hiding. Began compulsive eating.
12 yrs	Move house. Separate room – away from sisters	Began new highschool. Live in new neighbourhood	Overweight. Spent much time alone. Increase in interest in typically feminine activities.
13 yrs	Mum starts her uni. course. Dad has new job – busier.	Children left alone more	Not wanting to join in family activities. Mood – withdrawn more often. Spends much time alone in room. Depressed.
15 yrs	Parents discuss separation	No changes	Boy taken to psychiatrist and on anti-depressants for 3 months. Only one friend. Compulsive masturbation. Half-hearted suicide attempt. Parents were not told.
16 yrs	Parents separate	Complete School Certificate. Mother, sister and boy do studies together	Enjoyed sharing study time for exams with mother and sister. Glad father gone. First girl-friend. More relaxed, but always worried.

The hurt inner child within children

> **A mother of a 10-year-old girl writes:**
>
> My daughter Selina, who is 10, goes into silence and will not cooperate. Recently it was dinner time and she was sitting on the floor, refusing to come to eat and refusing to talk. I sat near and said, 'I can see two people: I see Selina who is ten and I also see a little baby girl who is hurting.'
>
> I asked, 'Do you feel little?' She nodded. I asked, 'Is baby Selina hurting?' She began to cry and I said, 'I'd like to nurse the hurt little girl.'
>
> She crawled up on to my lap and sobbed for quite a while. When the tears ceased and she was coming out of the felt experience, I got her to hold out one hand and put on it the little one who had been crying. On the other hand we acknowledged the 10-year-old. I asked her to join her hands and feel both these parts of herself. Then I said, 'How do you feel now?' She slid off my knee and said, 'Like having dinner!'

The theory of the hurt inner child, the conflict between a child part and an adult part applies equally to adults and children. In children the hurts from the past are not as deeply buried and the defences, in most cases, not so fixed.

It may sound to some readers that we are advising more splits in the personality by using the child/adult (or hurt child/older child). In fact we are recognising a split that already exists. Using this concept to discuss the sources of behaviour, over-the-top reactions and recurring hurts leads to a great deal of inner freedom for the child. Understanding that there is a hurt part active inside allows them to separate from it. Recognising that it is not all of them that gets them into trouble restores some self-esteem. Their inner world becomes more understandable, less chaotic.

Understanding with their mind, and feeling through their processing, the truth of this inner split helps them be less identified with their problems – the problems are not *all* of them.

Clarification exercise

Separating my hurt child from me now

Suitable for children aged 12 years and over.

Have writing materials available.

Immediately after accessing and feeling the hurt of the inner child in a session the child works to show symbolically the separation they have made from this part of them that belongs to the past. Although this exercise has been written for older children and adolescents, it can be simplified for younger children.

1. The child who has just worked puts out the left hand and looks at it while briefly describing the experience. The child part is placed on the left hand; for example, 'You, little James, were never ever listened to. No matter how hard you tried to be heard, your parents only pretended to listen. They were too busy.'

2. Then the right hand is extended and what happens in life now that feels the same is acknowledged. In the case of James, it might be that there is still a part trying to get everyone to listen. There is admission that the part that feels hurt when 'they' don't listen now is really the hurt child still active in present life, still trying to make the parents listen.

3. Invite the child to bring the hands together slowly while admitting inside that the present feelings were those of the hurt child. The images of then and now are brought together.

4. When this is done and felt inside, the child separates the hands. At the same time, the separation inside is felt: the hurt inner child separating out from the present more 'adult', real self. It is this self that can know when the inner child is active and the cause of sadness. This image from the past is now able to be recognised and the true child can speak up now, clearly and strongly, asking for what is wanted.

5. It may be appropriate to invite the child who has worked to share with the group; for example 'Is there anything you would like us to listen to now?'

6. Give participants time to write down anything new they have learned about themselves. This recording is part of the integration process.

The separation from child to older child or 'adult' is keenly felt, understood and described by adolescents. See more about the hurt inner child on pages 168–170.

Working with the child/adult concept

An adolescent girl was dealing with feelings of anger and sadness after her parents had separated.

She was asked, 'What was really good for you *then*, when you were 3 years old?'
'We were all together.'
She was asked to draw the feeling of this.
She was then asked, 'What is really good for you *now*?'
'I feel good when Mum and my sister and I are happy together.'
Again, she was asked to draw the feeling.
She was then asked, 'Do these two drawings have the same feeling in them?'
'Oh! Yes! – I'm still being a baby, aren't I?' she volunteered.
She was then asked, 'Is there some other time *now* when you are happy and alive, and it is not this baby feeling?'
'When I'm dancing!'
She drew that feeling.
She was then asked, 'What's the difference between this one and the first two feeling drawings?'
'I'm by myself and I feel I don't need anyone.'

Hearing the inner child

A report from Margaret Thomson

Katie is 12 years old. Her mother is a single parent with three children. Katie had been to some workshops with me, along with other children. Her mother is also doing her own personal growth work.

Katie's mother noticed she was quiet and tending to stay close. There were also outbursts with her sisters. She came to see me. As Katie talked she started to cry. I asked her to take some deep breaths, and the tears flowed. She was a happier child after this.

She came to the next workshop. I asked how she was feeling now about her sister and her mother. She said, 'Mum is very busy!' It was obvious she was feeling unloved again. She started to cry and with some deeper breaths she went back to being the small child, feeling 'Mum doesn't love me enough!' She released the sadness of the hurt inner child. We did a 'child/adolescent' separation process. Katie now knows it is her hurt inner child that gets the feelings of not being loved, and that big Katie can love and be loved for herself. Katie is now a happy 13-year-old, and does not need any prompting to come along to workshops.

Beginning discussion exercise

My family, my life

Suitable as an individual or group exercise with children aged 6 years and over. If group work, children work in pairs.

Have ready sandplay symbols, drawing and writing materials, and perhaps a Polaroid camera.

1 Ask children to draw a large circle in their drawing book, and call it 'My Family'. They then place a dot at the centre, and call it 'Me'.

2
- *Close your eyes. Take a slow full breath and relax it out.*
- *Feel yourself coming home inside your body.*
- *Open your mind to a picture: your family. See them clearly.*
- *From the sandplay collection find a figure to represent you. Let it choose you. Don't think too much about it.*
- *Then choose a figure for each member of your family – as you pictured them in your mind.*
- *Place the figure for you on the dot at the centre of the circle.*
- *Arrange the other figures for your family on the page.*
- *Listen to these questions as you do this:*
  - *How close or distant from you will they be?*
  - *How do they connect with each other?*
  - *Are they facing, or turned away from you?*
  - *Are they inside or outside the circle?*
- *Talk about your family to your partner (or me). Things to talk about:*
  - *how you arranged the figures*
  - *your family relationships*
  - *each one, and the figures you chose for them*
  - *anyone who is not there on your page*
  - *how you would really like it to be*
- *Gestalt the figure called 'Me'. What qualities are represented? (See questions on page 140.)*
- *Draw the figures on to the page – or write a brief description of them. Or take a Polaroid photo.*
- *Write a few lines in your journal about the most important things you felt or learned from this exercise.*

Variations

If no sandplay figures are available:
- Use cut-out pictures from magazines as symbols.
- Children can draw stick figures, then cut them out and move them about on the page.
- Make pipe-cleaner figures. Children can be asked to talk about the people as they are formed.

Encouraging children to talk about themselves

Body awareness

The body remembers everything

I was dressing my 3-year-old daughter before the log fire. As I dressed her and we both felt the warmth I told her the story of when she was a newborn baby.

'I used to hold you to breastfeed you. You used to suck milk out of my breast. When you had had enough milk you would fall asleep and milk would trickle back out of your mouth. Your head would droop and be all floppy. I'd wrap you in soft bunny rugs and put you down gently to sleep on your side. You used to have the palm of your hand against your cheek.'

As I shared this story, her body responded and she gradually went back into the same position – on her side, on the rug, with palm against her cheek.

I could see, before my eyes, proof that 'our bodies remember everything'.

Using body outline drawings

Children's verbal language for expression of feelings, energies and muscular states is usually undeveloped. The body outlines allow graphic expression and sharing of inner states.

The completed outlines provide parents, teachers, counsellors, masseurs with a guide to the inner self-image and what the child perceives as his or her energy/mood flows and blockages. Being seen, sharing what is locked inside is usually a great relief to children, and the mere sharing can sometimes be enough to allow flow again. Often it is a surprise to the child.

It can be useful for children to explore specific parts of the body rather than the whole body and what is held inside. They could draw their own outlines, for example: trace around the hands or feet; draw oval shapes for the face or torso; draw circles for the belly or chest.

Never interpret body outline drawings to the children. From your own interpretation find questions that will draw out the meanings from the child.

The body outlines are:
- a diagnostic tool
- a short 'therapy' in themselves
- a way of objectifying progress (by using before and after counselling sessions)
- useful for review of a period of work
- a way of turning inwards to enhance self-awareness

The outlines can be used to guide children to an awareness of the full range of inner experiences, such as:
- emotional stresses and buried feelings
- muscular tensions

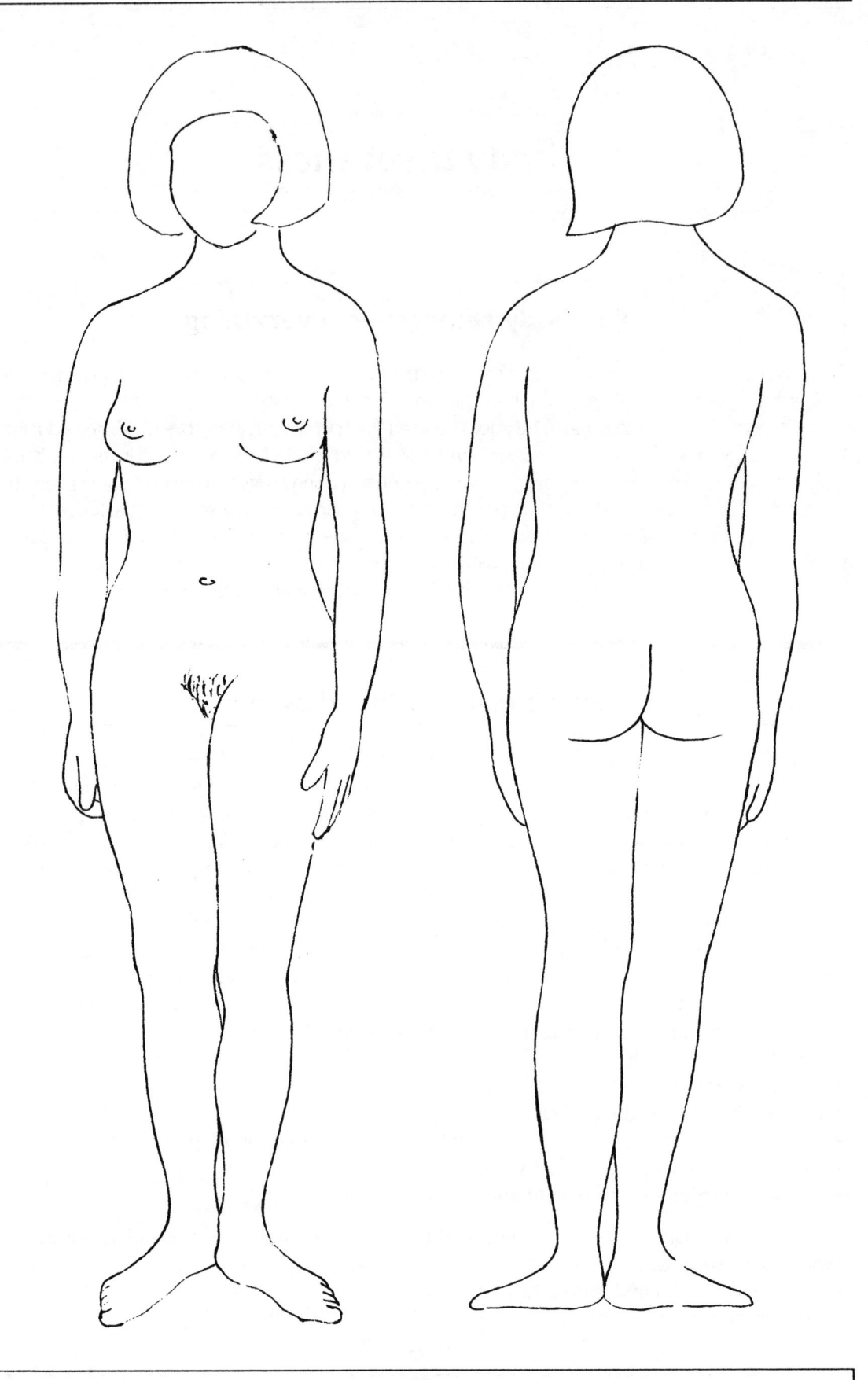

Emotional release for children

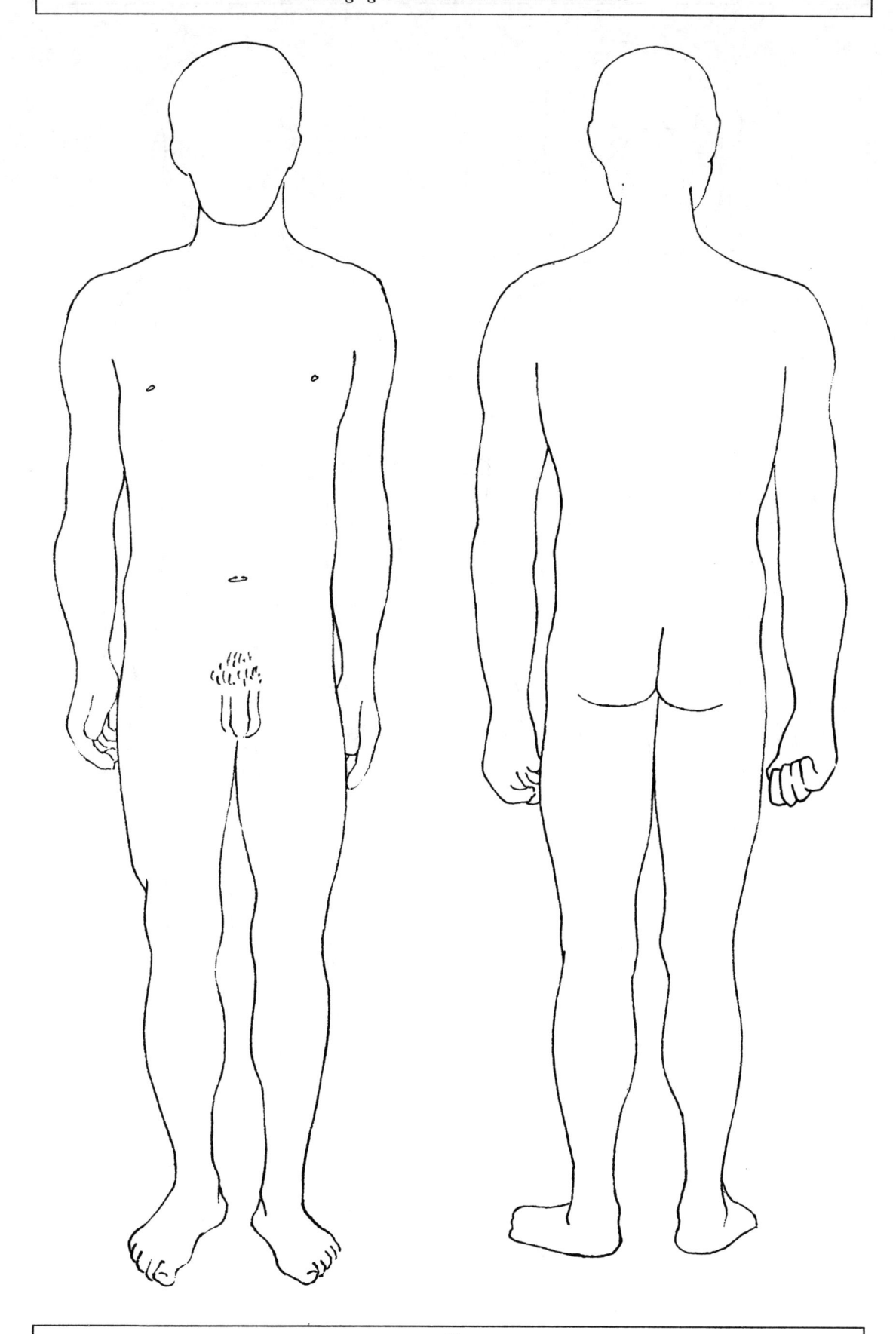

Encouraging children to talk about themselves

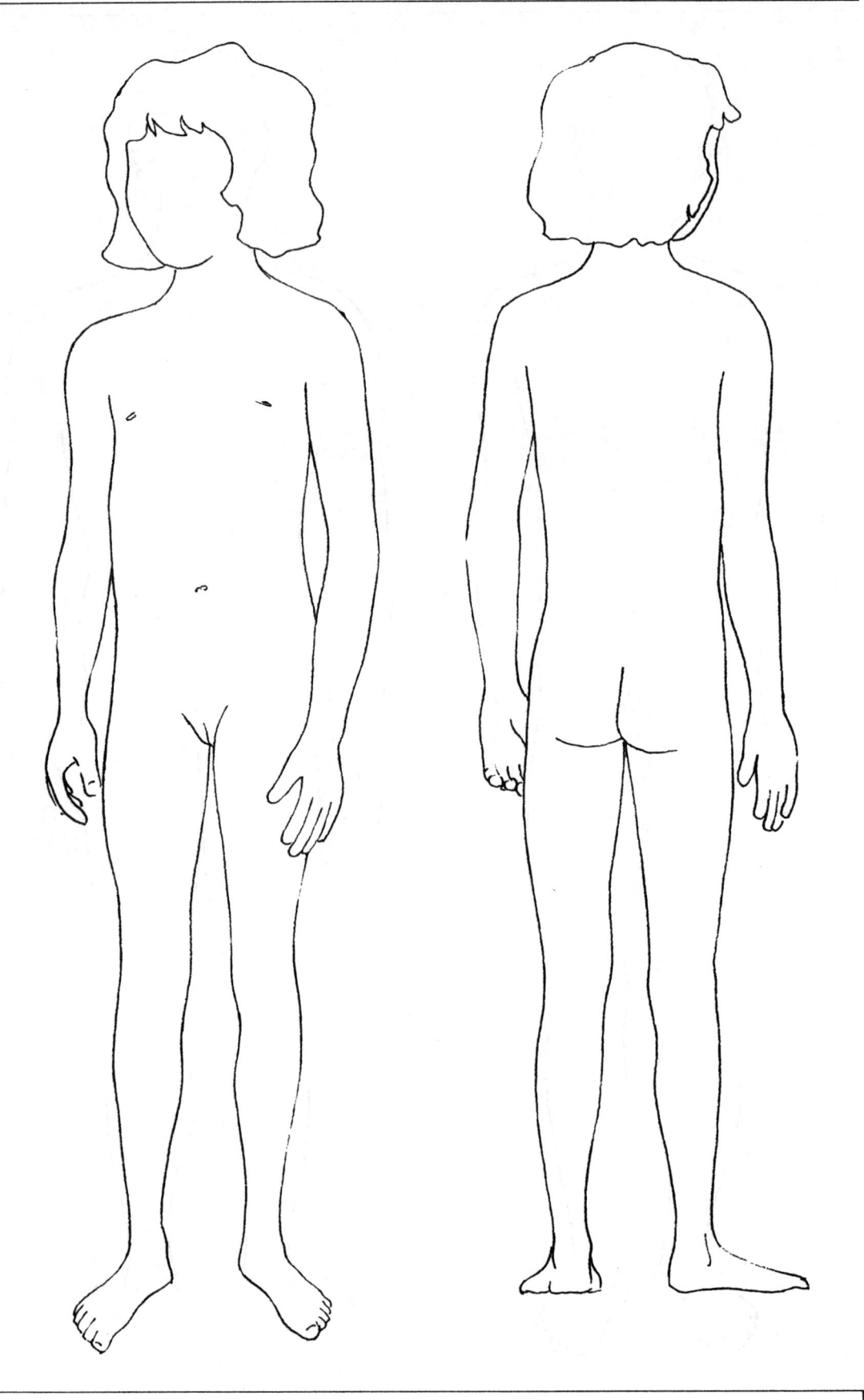

Emotional release for children

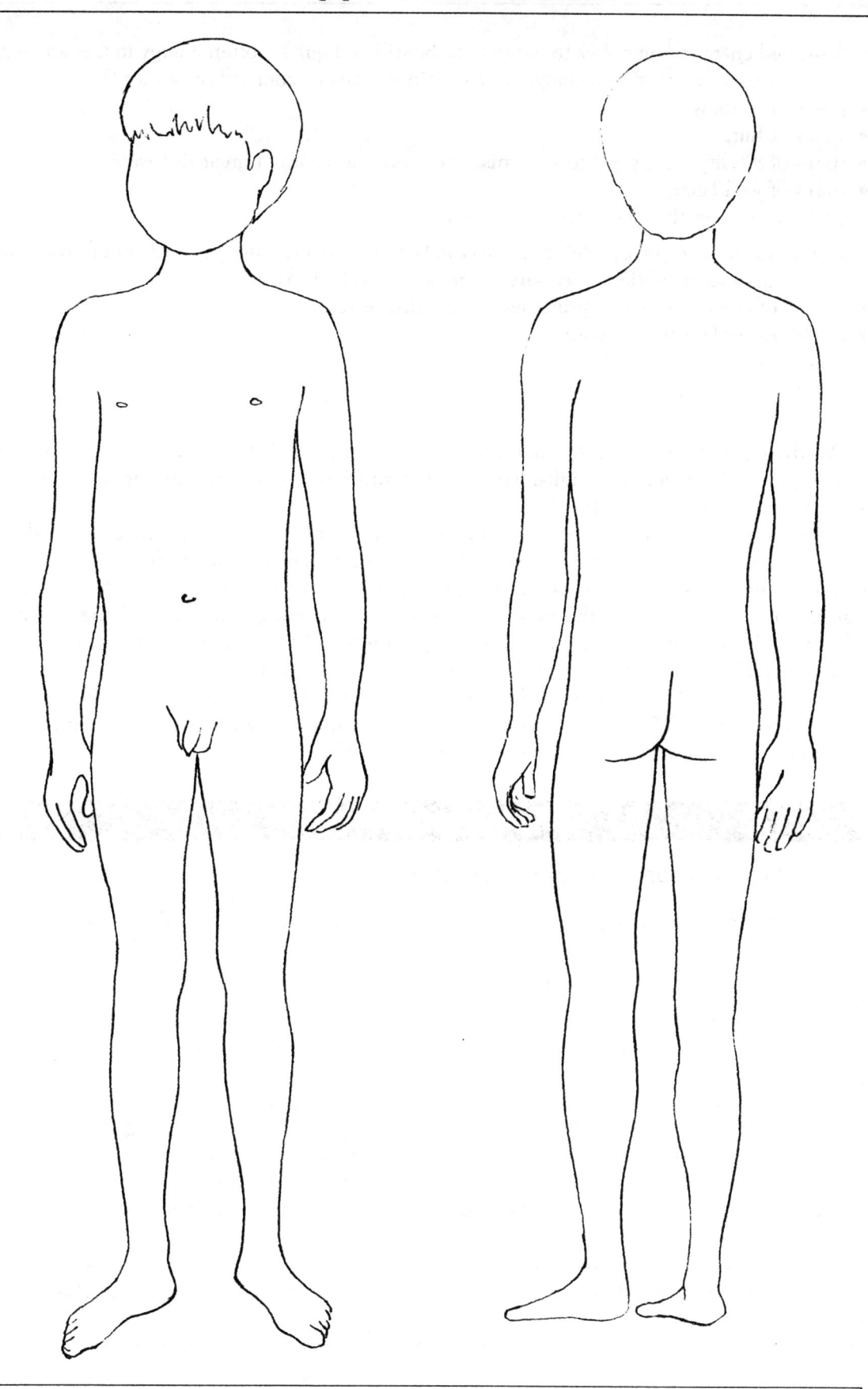

Encouraging children to talk about themselves

65

- frustrated energies – impulses to move or to be still and quiet – often energy in feet and legs (There may be a wanting to move, not sit still in class or counselling session!)
- states of softness
- states of hurt
- states of vitality – it's good to recognise these even in times of great distress
- states of well-being
- positive energies that have been 'swamped'

A wide range of crayons, pastels or paints can be used. Usually felt-tip pens do not provide the colour gradations or subtlety necessary. Expression can be through:
- choice of colours (observe: primaries or muddied tertiaries)
- brightness or faintness of colour
- solidity or fragility of strokes
- shading or outlining
- lines and dots

All these give an insight into the child's state. Usually the first outlines will contain little shading. As children become familiar with both the tuning in and the drawing out on the outline sheet the results will be much fuller.

Expression is not limited to the area within the body outline (as indeed our energies spread out beyond the skin). Children often have a feeling that their skin is not able to contain them. Their energy is bursting out and it is good to recognise it and mirror it back. Let them feel that it is natural. You could indicate the range of possibilities, including going beyond the outlines. Children who are carrying much inner pain may not want to do this exercise. You may need to guide the child's attention back inside a number of times – never forcing, of course.

You can learn also from watching the force used by the child in filling out the outlines. (How many crayons snap?) Mirror back this force – help them deepen the contact; for example 'They are strong lines. How strong or soft is this place in you?'

Self-awareness exercise

The little person with the radar inside

Suitable as an individual or group exercise for children aged 6 years and over; adolescents find it very interesting.

Have ready body outline drawings (see pages 62–65) and crayons.

The aims of this exercise are to improve communication skills; to locate problem areas in the body; to bring deeper self-awareness; and to bring relaxation and facility for turning within.

Although there are fifteen things listed for the internal 'radar' to find, for most children, between six and eight is quite enough. For smaller children, sometimes three things are enough to find the first time. Gauge the right number of things to find by the child's attention span. This exercise, with variations, can be done over and over, to cover all fifteen areas. As children become accustomed to doing it, their ability to sustain attention for more questions may grow.

1 Children lie down on cushions or carpet, close their eyes if possible, take a few deep breaths and relax.

Encouraging children to talk about themselves

2 Guide children to imagine a very little person checking through each part of the body: *A very little person with a torch is going to check around inside to see what is there, to see what they can discover. This explorer inside you is beginning inside your head, shining the torch around inside you. They know what is inside you. They move gradually from your head down through your body to your toes. Imagine them walking through a tunnel inside you.*

3 *Then the very little person returns to the control room in the forehead. There a radar is switched on. It can sweep through the body to find things.*
   The radar will sweep through and look for certain things. If it finds them, you turn over and draw them on the body outline beside you. Pretend that is a map of you.
   You will need to feel what colours and lines feel just right to describe what the radar finds.

4 Things the radar looks for:
   - coldness, coolness
   - heat or warmth
   - pain
   - sadness
   - happiness
   - anger
   - fear
   - weakness
   - strength
   - relaxed, free, light parts
   - tight, holding, tense parts
   - peaceful parts
   - parts you don't like
   - favourite part
   - place where an animal, bird or fish might be hiding

5 *Show the completed body outline drawing to a partner or to me and describe what you found. Consider showing it to your parent(s).*

6 *Gestalt the animal.* (See questions on page 140.)

7 You can draw out conversation that may enlarge on each child's self-awareness and some possible causes for what was found. Take some time to draw out connections between what was found in the body and what is happening in the child's life and the emotions about that. For some children, the connections will be made themselves, in the session or later.

Points to consider
- If you know there has been some sexual abuse in a child's background, change the imagery to be less threatening. The child's sense of personal privacy and safety could be better supported by having them visualise their own 'witness' or 'inner watcher', rather than a little person inside them. The emphasis could be on the fact that this observing part loves them and wants to help their healing to happen as quickly as possible.
- It is usual for children who have had to close down their perceptions and defend against abuse to have great difficulty in finding things to draw on to the body outline. This simply means the exercise could be repeated many times, as a support for them to re-connect to their body. It would be good to start with very clear physical sensations first; for example 'Is the carpet/floor cool or warm underneath you?' 'Are there any parts of your legs that are not touching the carpet as you lie there?'
- Older children who are new to this type of work may respond with repeatedly flippant answers. Their symbols may give silly, amusing or apparently irrelevant messages. Bear with this and move on if the exercise seems too threatening, but do not be disappointed. Try again another time when their need to defend is not quite so strong.

Emotional release for children

Body awareness exercise

My belly circle

Suitable for children aged 8 years and over.

Have ready drawing books and crayons.

1 *Prepare a large circle in your drawing book.*

2 *Lie down and tune in to your belly. Feel what it is like on the inside of your belly. What colour does it feel like in there? Are there shades of darkness and light?*

3 *Draw this now in the circle, imagining that the circle is your belly.*

4 *Lie down again. Put your hands on your belly to help you tune in again. Feel inside. What shapes and lines are in there? Is it the same in the upper part as the lower part?*

5 *Draw that now, on top of the first colour(s).*

6 *Look at your drawing. Find three words that go with what you have drawn.*

7 *Lie down again. Imagine you have a microphone now, with a chord going into an amplifier. Rest it on your belly. You have earphones too and can hear your belly speaking to you. What is it saying?*

8 *Write this down, beside or under the drawing. Sometimes it might be in picture language.*

9 *Share what you discovered in your belly with me or the group.*

Variations
Similar exercises can be easily created from this model for exploring in the chest, feet, face and hands.

Body awareness exercise

My face mask

Suitable as an individual or group exercise with children aged 8 years and over.

Prepare a page with four oval shapes to represent faces. Have crayons ready.

You describe particular situations and events to children and ask them to make the face that goes with the situation. They might make a real facial expression or a mask face, a pretend face.

1. With each face, ask the children to slightly exaggerate the expression, then feel their face with their hands, before drawing the expression into the oval shapes. Each time they feel their face they take note of: the forehead, the eyebrows, the eyes, the cheeks, the lips, the jaw, and consider if the tongue is involved. They then draw the face.

   The situations and events:
   - *It is shortly before Christmas. You are with your grandparents, whom you like. They are talking about good children getting presents. What face would you show them?*
   - *You are in the playground at lunchtime. The gang you usually play with suddenly tell you they don't want you around, and they run away. What shows on your face?*
   - *You are in the classroom and your worst subject is just about to start. The principal comes in asking for a child to deliver a message around the school. They want someone reliable and trustworthy. You also know that the principal gives nice little rewards. What is on your face as they look around the class to choose someone?*
   - *It is the end of a boring weekend at home. Mum or Dad has just said that they are going to go and do something really exciting and they are thinking of taking you. Then suddenly they decide not to take you. You have to stay at home. What happens on your face?*

2. Ask children:
   - *Are some masks and some real faces?*
   - *Can you find a word or phrase for each expression?*

3. Share how you felt with each face.

Massage and body awareness exercise

Stories in my body

An individual exercise suitable for children aged 6 to 14 years.

Have ready a mattress or cushions for child to lie on, and drawing book and crayons.

The aim of this exercise is to allow a child to become aware that there are lots of stories in the body. There is no need to take any clothes off for this exercise.

1. *Today we are going to help the body tell us a story. To do this we will do a special kind of massage.*

2. *Lie down on the mattress and start taking big breaths.*

3. *Imagine a big wheel as you breathe. As the wheel comes up you pull breath in – as the wheel goes down you allow the breath out. What is your wheel made of? Maybe it's in water. The wheel goes around very smoothly – so does your breathing – no stops and starts – it just keeps going round and round.* (Demonstrate with the sound of your own breath.)

4. *As you breathe, let your body go very loose.*

5. *I am going to massage you now – let me know when we get to a place that feels sore or that doesn't feel good.*

6. When the child indicates a place, ask:
   What story does this sore part have to tell you?

7. Use some questions to encourage; for example:
   - *Does it know how it got sore?*
   - *What pictures can you see in your mind right now?*
   - *Are there any people or animals inside you?* etc.

8. When the story finishes, ask:
   How does the sore place feel now?

9. If still sore, ask more questions; for example:
   - *Does it have more to tell?*
   - *Does it want to cry or be angry?*

10. Depending on the time available, either finish the process when one part feels better or move to one or more other places.

11. Invite the child to do some drawings of the stories found, or act out any animated parts of stories.

Self-awareness exercise

Painting the body

Ideal for children aged 4 to 12 years; possible with older children if a firm group bond has been established. Good as a group exercise; can also be done with individuals. Needs to be done outside in warm weather.

Have ready a good quantity of water-soluble finger paints or ochre clay, a groundsheet (or something to protect the floor or ground), a full-length mirror, a Polaroid camera, soapy water, old towels.

The aim of the exercise is to enhance self-awareness through recognising feelings and sensations in the body, and to express these feelings with displayed markings on the body.

1. *Sit in a circle.*
2. *Take a deep breath down into your tummy.*
3. *Close your eyes and feel inside your body.*
4. *Is there a feeling somewhere inside, which would like to come out? (Give time for inner connection.)*
5. *Really feel this feeling calling to you, 'Let me out, Let me out!'*
6. *Can you imagine a shape, a colour, for this feeling?*
7. *Imagine this feeling coming into your hand.*
8. *Now put paint on to your hands and make the marks on your body that want to come out and be there.*
9. *Breathe deeply and let the feeling out from inside into your hand. Let your hand choose the paint and put the feeling on the outside of your body.*
10. *Keep doing this until the feeling is all out.*
11. *Look in the mirror and see how it feels to be all out.*
12. *Dance how it feels now.*
13. *Line up to have your photo taken.*
14. Hose down the children, or provide warm soapy water, old towels.
15. When children's hands are clean, get them to write an explanation of the markings on the body.

A guide to feelings locked in the body

This brief guide can help you formulate questions to encourage children to tell you what has been happening in their lives.

forehead:	Not wanting to know something. Not wanting to see the truth.
eyes:	Sadness, tears, shock, not wanting to see (a memory).
jaw:	Anger, words held in or bitten back.
neck:	Control, not wanting to surrender.
shoulders:	The weight of controlling or nagging adults. Carrying too big a responsibility.
chest:	Grief, longing.
arms, hands:	Expression, creativity. Holding back from hitting out. Wanting to reach out.
diaphragm:	Deep sobbing.
belly:	Fear.
buttocks:	Anger, rage and hate.
outer thighs:	Power, strength.
inner thighs:	Sexuality, sensuality.
knees:	Flexibility, resistance to growing up.

Journalling

Journal writing is a process; it is very alive. It includes our thoughts, our feelings and records of what we find within our body and psyche. It comes from our realisation in the moment. When it is really alive there are changes as we write. Things become clearer. Feelings transform.

The mind's function is to integrate, to bring things together, to link up realisations and combine felt experiences with intelligence. Thus we can sort out what is going on inside us, record what we observe, review where we have been, resolve present issues and clarify future directions.

Journals are places to record dreams for later work. They support a sense of journeying. They are like an inner counsellor. In them we can dialogue with parts of ourselves. Journal writing is a way of giving ourselves inner space. Journals are private – so we can be truthful. As a tool for reflection they help us deal with reactions and prepare for important and clear sharing with others.

Journals allow our poetic side to emerge – most of us normally hide this side. They support reflection time to reassess our life's direction, to review the journey.

Younger children can use drawings, body outline drawings and photos of sandplays as visual records.

Journal exercise

Are there messages in my mandalas?

Suitable for children aged 12 years and over.

For an introduction to mandala drawing, refer to page 79.

This exercise is intended to be used after a period of intensive inner work.

1 Spread out your mandalas in chronological order.

2 Which ones seem incomplete and could be extended off the page? Imagine what would be there, then allow it to be drawn, using extra paper.

3 Look at the strong and the light colours and lines. Consider what the possible meaning of those could be.

4 Are you more comfortable with mandalas of feelings and not body-oriented ones or image ones? Or the other way around?

5 Ask yourself if the drawings are predominantly about:
- the inner child
- the body
- the unconscious
- special memories
- deep feelings
- energy
- the spirit
- current relationships

6 Look for repetition of: colours, themes, shapes, moods, symbols.

7 Are there any clear divisions, splits, or strong connections in the drawing?

8 Is there a progression, sequence or a transformation?

9 Are the boundaries being broken? Is the energy contained? unbounded? outside? inside?

10 Are there clear masculine/feminine energies? doing/being? active/receptive?

11 Is there a recognition of birthing imagery? For example whirlpools, tunnels, foetal or baby-like shapes.

12 What were the main learnings and messages in your mandalas?

13 What does the series say to you right now?

14 Take some time to research the symbols.

15 With clear symbols or images, Gestalt, say 'I am...' (See questions on page 140.) Are there some energies still to be re-owned?

> **A child's journal entry**
>
> 4.10.93
> I came home from school and after a while I felt bad. I wonder what happened? I had a great day at school. When I came in I was bouncing. I said 'Hi' to Mum. Something happened inside me then. I know that's when I changed.
>
> I thought about this for a while. I went back in my mind to when I came home. Mum was so busy, she didn't look up. She spoke but she didn't see how great I am. And she said 'Change your clothes', as though my clothes are more important than me.
>
> That made me angry and sad. Now I know when it happened I feel better. I'll go and see what Mum is doing now.

Creative writing and storytelling

Creative writing is a way of uncovering aspects of the child's inner world, hidden feelings and troubling current life situations. As well as uncovering these issues and preparing the child to talk about them, the symbolic resolutions of the stories can be very helpful for the child.

The facilitator begins a story. It can be set in the present, but usually there is more freedom for the child if it is a setting that is distant in time and space: 'Once upon a time . . . long, long ago, in a far off place . . .'

In verbal storytelling the facilitator may guide the story, mirroring elements from the child's current stressful situations, and including known ways that the child deals with these. Each take turns at developing the story. There is encouragement for the child to have the hero do anything – no limits! With older children, stories can be written, the child and facilitator alternating sentences or paragraphs.

For example:

FACILITATOR: Once upon a time there was a deep dark cavern, and in it lived . . .
CHILD: a ferocious beast with shaggy hair (child expands)
FACILITATOR: And every morning the beast set out to search for . . .
CHILD: people to eat.
FACILITATOR: Nearby in the forest lived a brave and handsome . . .

The story continues, being guided towards any areas the facilitator feels the child might need to explore. They write down the main parts of the story.

The child becomes each of the main characters, maybe dialoguing between them.

Music could be used to help the child dance and move as the characters, and own the energy, the feelings that are ascribed to each.

For younger children you might need to make up a whole story to help them explore current issues.

Bedtime stories

It is best not to leave children in their heads at bedtime. It's helpful to arouse the imagination, but also to use touch, stroking to bring the awareness down into the body. This may be difficult if you have several children, but they can become accustomed to waiting their turn. Remember the quality of sleep relates to how well the brain, feelings and body disconnect in sleep. The more the child is in their body, the quicker and more deeply the let-go takes place.

Scriptwriting

Children can be given a list of characters and asked to write a radio or television play script. Usually archetypal characters should be included, for example king, queen, magician, witch, fairy, dragon, warrior, etc. In reading out or performing the scripts the child is able to express feelings and ideas that would normally be censored or blocked from their awareness.

Discussions after the script readings can link up similarities and differences with the child's own life. This gives a structured time for the facilitator to draw out the child in sharing more of their inner and outer life.

Myth-making

Myths are stories out of which groups of peoples live. These stories touch the hearts and minds of the group so that the whole group is moved to live in a certain way. The characters and symbols that appear in the myths across many cultures are to a great extent the same.

In most cultures there is a warrior/hero myth. The story teaches and leads people. It moves them to live out the truths in the myth. In the warrior/hero myths there is always a great deed to be performed: leaving home, security; meeting a blockage, obstacle or challenge; using a higher power, magic or special helper; achieving the task and sometimes rising to a new world or higher state.

We are all connected individually to the power of myth via the collective unconscious. Giving children an opportunity to experience this universal energy personally can be very simply done, and is very empowering.

Emotional release for children

Scriptwriting exercise

My inner parts go on a journey

Suitable for children aged 10 years and over.

Have writing materials ready. Access to sandplay symbols is a help, but not essential. If no sandplay equipment is available, have drawing materials ready.

1. *Lie down, relax, and take a few deep breaths.*
   - *Find a part of you that you don't like very much. It can be a part of your body, or a part of your character. Think about this, then jot down a note about it.*
   - *Find the part of you that you like best – part of your body or character. After getting a clear picture of it, or thinking about it clearly, jot down a note about it.*

2. *Get a sandplay symbol, or do a quick drawing, for each of these two parts of you. Give these two parts names that seem to go with them. They can be real people's names, or silly made-up names.*

3. *Lie down again. Clear your mind.*
   There is going to be a story. Where will this story begin?
   - *in the mountains?*
   - *along the coast?*
   - *under the sea?*
   - *a long time ago?*
   - *on another planet?*
   See what picture pops into your mind, then write it down.

4. *There will be the rescue of a stolen treasure in the plot. Find a symbol, or do a drawing, of the treasure. What is the main quality of the treasure?*

5. *Give an example of a script – how it is set out, the list of characters, the scene, the action or stage directions, etc.*

6. *Write a short script that is a dialogue between these two parts. The plot of the script will go something like this:*
   'These two parts have to go on a journey together to find and rescue the stolen treasure. What helps them succeed? What hinders them?'
   It must have a happy ending.

7. *Read out your script to a partner, or to the group. Or, better still, be the 'director' of the play and get two actors to read the parts. If you are reading it out yourself try to use a different voice for each of the characters; let yourself really be each character.*

8. *At the end, become the director again, if you have been playing the parts. Talk about ways the script is similar or different to your life.*

Creative writing exercise

My life as a myth

Suitable as an individual or group exercise for children aged 10 years and over. It can be simplified to work with younger children.

Have ready drawing and writing materials; rhythmic, tribal music.

This exercise is a way of mining the unconscious for the raw materials of the personal myth. The language of the unconscious is images. So we encourage the opening to whatever images present – no matter how irrational, or way out they may seem.

1. The children work in pairs. One partner lies down. The other has a note pad and biro ready to write down what their partner says.

2. The facilitator – or the other partner – asks those lying down to open to the images that come – the first ones – and describe them, to be noted down:
   - the setting: a mountain top? another planet? a forest? heaven, or home of the gods? ocean cave? desert? the underworld? etc.
   - the atmosphere: turmoil? disintegration? panic? an aggressor? a problem? a dark shadow force threatening? peaceful? calm?
   - the hero: masculine or feminine? appearance? character?
   - the journey or the search: to find an answer? a power? the magical weapon? a key to a riddle? a wise old man? the earth mother?
   - unexpected support: from something normally overlooked – an animal? a spirit? a servant?

   (Stress that there is no need to try to tie the story together at this stage. Keep returning to the images that appear spontaneously.)
   - the big clash: or the transformation, or the reunion
   - the happy ending, the world renewed, order restored

3. The listening partner jots down notes that will be used later.

4. The pairs swap roles.

5. Each child then spends time alone weaving their story together – either verbally or in writing, discarding anything if necessary. Let any new material appear. Let the story take its own direction. Allow the child to keep dropping away from logic. Ideally the child is just the scribe – the myth has emerged from within.

6. After writing, the child draws a picture of the main part of the myth.

7. The child then tells the story, from memory if possible.

Visualisation exercise

Going ahead of mother duck

Suitable as an individual exercise for children from 4 to 10 years.

The aim of this exercise is to help a young child to separate from Mother, to learn there is choice – to be alone or together.

I am going to tell you a special story. You are going to be part of the story. Listen carefully and imagine yourself in the story. Close your eyes.

Imagine a beautiful river. There are lovely green trees right up to the edge of the water – it feels very peaceful here. Imagine how that would feel.

You are a baby duck swimming with your mother. Usually mother duck swims in front. Today you are in front. This is a big adventure, you are the one deciding which way to go, you have the choice.

The whole river is in front of you. You swim right out into the middle with your duck brothers and sisters following and mother duck at the back. You are feeling very free. It is great fun being in front.

Then you see an interesting place, and you swim towards it. There is a willow tree hanging low over the water and there are reeds growing there. You swim between the reeds and you are under the tree. It's like a cave and you are having such fun swimming between the reeds. It's great.

It's so much fun you don't even notice mother duck isn't there. She is a lot bigger than you and couldn't fit in the place. You keep swimming there among the reeds under the cool green trees.

After a while you swim out into the open river again and there is mother duck waiting. Now she swims in front again. This feels good too. It felt good swimming in front and having that adventure. Now it feels good swimming behind mother.

Questions

These can be asked after the first reading or after the story is repeated:
- *How did it feel swimming in front?*
- *How did it feel choosing where to go?*
- *How did it feel back with mother?*
- *Is there a different ending you would have liked?*
- *Are there any times in your life like this story?*

Drawing

Mandala drawing

'Mandala' is a Sanskrit word meaning 'circle' in the ordinary sense of the word. In the sphere of personal development work it denotes circular images which are drawn. The mandalas are drawn at the conclusion of personal ERC work. They give an opportunity to express the conscious and the unconscious reality of a person's psyche at the time.

Because the mandala drawing is within a circle it encourages the person to give the mandala a point of reference – a centre, a base – around which energy revolves and explodes and flows.

There is a definite distinction between emotional release drawings and mandalas. Mandalas are a way of completing a session, a process. Emotional release drawings are a process in themselves or a strong step in release. Mandalas are kept for review and contemplation – even after two or three years a mandala review can be very helpful. Emotional release drawings are best thrown away as soon as they are finished with, for one emotion is quickly replaced by another.

It is not unusual for mandalas to show splits or divisions, often expressed as light and dark areas. Often the mandala will be an expression of a child's innermost essence.

Drawing a mandala is therapeutic in itself. It can bypass the usual mental process and allow many aspects of the psyche to flow together. The more the mandala is 'allowed' rather than planned, the more it has a healing effect.

Mandalas are drawings of deep feeling states, states of resolution, and recordings of what has appeared from the unconscious. Sometimes a child will want to draw without the structure of a circle. We simply call this a completion drawing.

Drawing exercise

Preparing for mandala drawing

Suitable for all ages.

Have drawing books, crayons and plates for drawing circles ready.

This exercise is a simple way to prepare children for mandala drawing.

1. Have children rest in a relaxed position, eyes closed.
2. Play some beautiful music. Let them soak it in.
3. Ask them to draw (in the circle) how the music made them feel.

Life-story drawing

Consciously or unconsciously, we express our emotional states when we draw. These states are often very clear in children's drawings.

Simple Gestalt methods can be used to allow these states to become conscious and thus able to move, evolve or clear. Through Gestalting, children can re-own energy, especially if it is something usually considered negative or unacceptable, dark or ferocious. Normally we/children might be afraid of the dark side, but actually the fullness of our energy depends on all the parts that were pushed down and disowned being re-integrated.

Drawing exercise

Learning more from my drawings

Suitable for children aged 10 years and over. Works best with individuals or very small groups.

Have ready drawing materials.

1. Begin with an open invitation for a spontaneous drawing, then ask the children to do two more; for example:
   - *your home now or when you were little*
   - *your family, with everyone doing something*
2. Point out that drawing skill is not being tested. Your approval remains positive no matter what the outcome.
3. Check the questions presented for the Gestalt work (page 140). (Remember all aspects of the drawings are parts of themselves and must be considered and allowed to speak.)
4. Adapt these to the children's vocabulary and specific drawings.
5. Children may talk generally about the drawings first.
6. They then become the elements and the people.
7. The process may be completed with more drawing:
   - the past
   - life now
   - the future

Life-story drawing exercise

My family at dinner

Suitable for children aged 8 years and over.

Have ready drawing books and crayons.

This exercise aims to help get children talking about their family.

1 *Lie down, or sit comfortably so you can fully relax.*

2 *Go back in your mind to:*
   - *last weekend*
   - *or the time when you were a baby*
   - *or when your were . . . years old*

3 *Get a picture in your mind of your family at dinner time:*
   - *See who is there.*
   - *Where do they sit?*
   - *Are they all in the same room? same house?*
   - *What sort of food did you eat?*
   - *Was it a happy time? a quiet time? a noisy time?*

4 *Now draw the picture; draw as much as you can remember. It does not matter if you are not a good drawer. You can use stick figures if you wish.*

5 Draw out conversation about the family and the dynamics of their relationships, based on what the child has drawn. Look particularly for:
   - who is missing
   - what is drawn clearly, what is faint or peripheral
   - the placement around the table (if there is one)
   - the child's preference, if it could change anything

Possible next steps
- Draw in cartoon-style bubbles, and write in what each person is thinking.
- Role-play each family member. What are they really wanting to say?

Variations
- A similar format could be used with the title: 'My family on Sundays'.
- The child could visualise going through a family photograph album and talk about each photo. See where in the album the child comes. Are there many photos of the child?
- The child could visualise and then draw the positions of family members when they are all watching television. The child could do another drawing of the preferred arrangement.
- In group work, the child could imagine a family snapshot – say on Christmas Day – and use group members to do a living photo. Depending on the age of the children involved, another step could be assigning brief scripts to each family member in the photo, and making a short play.

Visualisation exercise

A visit to the aliens' home

Suitable for children aged 6 to 14 years.

Have ready drawing books and crayons, with science fiction or outer space music in the background (see page 201).

The aim of this exercise is to prepare children to talk about their family and home.

1 Children with eyes closed.
   You are in the most modern, fast, space ship. You are travelling at almost the speed of light, out of our solar system. Life has been detected on a planet in the next solar system. That is where you are going now. Now you are arriving on this planet. You are with the very first people to meet the aliens and see the planet. See the landscape of this planet in your mind. Let yourself make up what it looks like. Now the huge doors of the space ship are opening. You find you can breathe on this planet. See the aliens that have gathered to greet you. They are friendly. They signal for you to follow them. They take you to their home. Have a good look at it. See where it is. What is it made of? What does it look like? Now you meet their family.

2 *So that you can tell all your friends, and the scientists back on Earth about it, you will now draw the alien family and their home. Draw it as well as you can.*

3 Questions to ask – note particularly, and draw out, the differences from and similarities to each child's own home:
   - *Tell me more about what their homes looked like.*
   - *What are the main differences from your home?*
   - *What were their precious things?*
   - *Talk about their family. How was their family different from or similar to yours?*
   - *Did they have pets?*
   - *Was there anything in their home that you would like to have?*

4 Record any new insights about each child's own family and home.
   Note:
   - relationship with parents
   - relationship between siblings
   - is child's ideal, or 'actual', represented?
   - is the home hostile or friendly?
   - what is missing from the aliens' home?
   - around which aspect was there noticeably either 'positive' or 'negative' feelings and energy?

Encouraging children to talk about themselves

Energy release exercise

There's a zoo in me!

Suitable for children aged 6 to 14 years.

Working with this exercise in a group brings a helpful energy of enjoyment, but for deeper work and follow up – which usually needs to be immediate – individual work is necessary. The ideal situation is several facilitators working with two or three children each, combining into a large group and then separating for more intimate sharings.

Have crayons and body outline drawings ready.

This is an exercise for children who may appear very shy or resistant.

1 Children can lie down, or stand.

2 *Take some powerful breaths.*

3 *Imagine that you are a zoo, and there are animals and birds and fish inside you.*

4 *Feel inside yourself. What animal, bird or fish lives inside your head? See this creature in your imagination.*

5 *Now draw it on a body outline drawing, on the head. (Pause)*

6 *Make the sound, see the animal, feel the animal in you.*

7 *Now, what animal is in your face?*

8 Continue guiding children to find animals, birds or fish in their chest, arms, belly etc., depending on their attention span.

9 This can be followed by Gestalting the power of those animals. (See questions on page 140.) It is great fun!

10 Watch carefully. Are they thinking the response or feeling it? Do they sense it in their bodies? Sometimes children will 'play an old tape', especially if they have been with several counsellors. Be cautious if the response is too quick. The new life comes only with felt connections with a part of themselves.

11 After drawing and Gestalt work, perhaps the children (or facilitator, if children are young) could write down some characteristics of the animals, and then talk about similarities with their own characteristics.

Working with clay

Working with clay is another way for children to stay in touch with their inner world. The actual sensual contact with the malleable clay engages the child's interest and brings body and mind together in a way that also allows feelings to arise.

You can simply ask the children to make something that shows how they are feeling. Or you can choose directions or starting points in relation to the child's current energy or a specific problem. For example, with a child whose parents are separating, have them make all the figures involved, describing each as it is formed. Ask the child to play out these questions:
- 'How close do you want to be – to Mum? to Dad?' etc.
- 'Where will you place your brother? your sister? the baby?'
- 'Make the picture how you really want it to be.'

Mirror back the feelings detected as the child works, the aim being to assist the child to connect with their inner truth. Encourage expression and release.

Plasticine, beeswax and cold candle-making wax are also popular with children and can be used instead of clay.

Clay modelling exercise

My mask face

Suitable as a group exercise for children aged 10 years and over.

Have ready clay and a board.

1. Children each make a clay mask of their face.
2. Invite them to journal what they see in their face.
3. At a later time when the mask is dry, they take turns at standing in the middle of the group circle, holding up their mask over their face. Ask them to speak and move in the way that the mask makes them feel.
4. Then all look at the mask together and share the main features they see.

This exercise can support owning back and recognition of parts or features not previously known.

Clay modelling exercise

Talking about families

Suitable as an individual or small group exercise for children aged 8 to 14 years.

Have ready some clay and a board.

The aim of this exercise is to help children become more aware of themselves within the family, to talk about this and to claim their unique self.

1. Ask the child to make quick figures of:
   - father
   - mother
   - siblings
   - self

2. As they work help them to feel the kind of person they are making:
   - big/little?
   - strong/weak?
   - soft/tough?
   - bully/understanding?
   - gruff/gentle?
   - talks to me/doesn't care about me?

3. Each child arranges the figures how they experience the family group, how they feel about the group, how they feel the group relates to them.

4. Talk about:
   - Mum, Dad and child – notice distances, closeness, towering over, facing or turned away and let child tell what this means to them
   - Mum and child
   - Dad and child
   - child and siblings

5. Each time allow/encourage the child to express how they feel in this situation.

6. They may need to squash someone, throw the figure, change the order, stamp on, etc.

7. Allow them to continue until the energy is expressed and transformed.

8. They complete by dismantling all and constructing a figure of self *now* and placing it anew in relationship with Mum, Dad and siblings.

Clay modelling exercise

Modelling the shadow parts

Suitable for children aged 8 to 16 years.

Have ready clay and a board.

1 Children stand up.

2 With eyes closed, take big breaths and look inside yourself.

3 In there you will find a very big, strong, powerful, character. This part of you is not frightened of anything. This part of your can attack, fight, defeat all your enemies.

4 Have a good look to see if this character has hair, claws, beak. Is it more like a person or an animal? Get the feel of this one.

5 Now make a model of this character – give your model the feeling you have of this character.

6 Let yourself act out this character – move like it, strike, sign, command, direct, sound like it.

7 Talk about how this part of you acts in your life.
- Is it active? or hiding?
- When might you need it?
- Why did it learn to hide?

Modelling of shadow parts – such as angry dragons, frightened rabbits, etc. is a wonderful and enjoyable way to draw children out in describing their inner life and it assists them to identify parts that can be troublesome.

CHAPTER FIVE

Emotional release processes

It is not true that 'time heals'.
Time itself most certainly does not heal.
If you resist the process, all that time will do is
push the grief deeper into the unconscious, to grow there
like a cancer until one day, maybe many years further on,
it can no longer be contained.

Heather Teakle, *My Daddy Died*, Collins Dove, 1993.

Introduction to processing

We present here an array of exercises structured to support children in working back through the past to the imprints at the base of their difficult emotional patterns. We call the use of these mechanisms, within the counselling room, processing. Some children are very defended against the unpleasant memories and feelings in the unconscious. However, it is when these memories are accessed and felt that healing really begins.

Through owning their feelings totally, we support children to work back through the past to the imprints at the base of their negative or difficult patterns of behaviour. For most children it is these patterns from the past that are contributing to dysfunctional and destructive behaviour in the present. These old feelings can then be worked with, fully felt, expressed and released from the system.

We help children to distinguish clearly between acting-out feelings – being run by them – and processing them. To process is to acknowledge any current reactive feelings and, in a safe place, to allow them to emerge fully, feel the connection to the past, have full expression and move on in life. To process also implies that after the release has cleared there is a new positive state, from which new purpose and creativity flow.

The effectiveness of processing methods usually depends on the facilitator's skills and experience in creating trust and being able to mirror what is happening so that it can be more deeply felt.

Each process may have a specific aim. Generally there is an aim to assist the child to feel fully what seems to be too painful now and was too painful to feel in the past. These more directly confronting methods can take the child into issues that seem to be current and expose the fact that they really belong in earlier childhood and sometimes even birth.

The aim is to mobilise all that has been held in. Quite often the accessing and expression flows in this progression:

frustration or depression → anger → rage/hate/disgust → grief → sorrow → love and tenderness → connection to new energy and essence

Guidelines

- A child should not begin to process feelings with the person who has triggered off the reaction. Face-to-face resolution may come later.
- Eyes are the strongest support for expressing locked feelings. 'Put them out through the eyes', we often say to encourage expression. Always have the child say who they are seeing in the eyes; for example, 'You never listened, Mum!'
- Be ready to help the 'dumping' (disowning and displacing of feelings) move into owning of feelings; for example, go from: 'You make me . . .' to 'I am feeling . . .'
- Use words, sounds and movements to help release what has been locked in.
- Everything depends on strong breath.

Emotional release process

- Assist the child to drop below the content and reasons, below the story, the external event, down to the feelings.
- Mirror the feelings.
- The process finishes when the energy has transformed into its opposite, the over-reaction is cleared, and there is separation from the past hurts.
- If the issue remains unresolved, recognise this. Do the 'now and then' process – see page 58. Realisations and insights will not necessarily come all at once.
- Encourage the child to watch for the trigger that caused the reaction in future.

Conditions for supporting processing

How do you set up a room in order to help children open to past and present emotions that need to be released?

There should be no bright light. Close curtains, dim lights, so that their eyes can relax. This also helps the focus be turned within; there is less connection to the outside world.

Music in the background supports privacy – in both individual and group work. It may need to be strong to support anger release, or gentle to support grief expression.

The work space should be delineated (a mattress and/or cushions can set the boundary). It must be safe (a mattress and/or large cushions make strong expression safe) and ordered. Order, tidiness and beautiful impressions help to make the space psychologically safe for clients to go into their inner chaos. You may need tissues (most of us fear crying, although we begin to recognise the need for it).

A bond with the support person must first be established, for example through verbal sharing of fears, or through giving the child time to be there, to arrive there, to move into the ERC gently.

Confidentiality should be discussed, and be assured. This also connects with soundproofing: can others hear what is being said, or shouted?

The 'three rules' regarding not harming self, others, or the environment must be discussed with the child:
- You may not hurt anyone.
- You may not hurt yourself.
- You may not hurt the surroundings.

During group work make time to help the supporters; for example:
- Give clear instructions.
- Give a firm supporting hand on the back from time to time.
- Provide occasional eye contact to indicate that all is well – especially when the person being supported is expressing strong emotions.

Have anger-release equipment ready:
- large cushions to hit
- a towel to wring or beat out
- paper to rip
- drawing book and crayons to express with

Designate a definite beginning and a definite conclusion to the processing time. This may relate to entering and leaving the counselling room, or the area of the room designated for processing.

Expression exercise

Getting ready for emotional release drawing

Suitable as a group exercise for children aged 10 years and over.

Select four or five pieces of music that express different energies, moods, or emotions; for example, strong drumming, gentle flute, militaristic, flowing orchestral, hot rock, relaxing New Age (see page 200). Have ready drawing books and a good selection of crayons.

The aim of this exercise is to get a flow going in children's drawing expression, overcoming negative beliefs about drawing (if these exist).

Part one: Drawing music

1 Children stand, take a few deep breaths, close eyes and open ears.

2 Play a piece of music to the children.
   - *Feel its effect on your body.*
   - *Does it make you want to move?*
   - *Feel its colours.*
   - *Does it affect your mood? How does it make you feel?*
   - *Where does it dance in your body?*

3 After each piece, get children to draw quickly, using whatever lines, colours, shapes, images they feel go with the music. Encourage them not to think about it, just to do it!

4 Children form into groups of three and look at each other's drawings. They see how many are similar, how many are different.

Part two: Drawing feelings

5 Children lie down and take some deep breaths.

6 Ask them to remember a recent sad time (or fearful time).
   - *Is there any of that feeling in you now? Where in you?*
   - *Find its colour. Is it a pure colour, or mixed?*
   - *Find the lines or shapes that go with that feeling.*
   - *Let yourself draw, let it flow out rather than plan it: let your hand and the crayons do it.*

7 Ask them to remember a recent time of happiness (or courage, or strength).
   - questions as above

   Opposites are usually picked for emotional drawing practice. Present the negative feeling first, especially in classroom work, unless this exercise is to be followed by stronger release work. For counselling work it may be right to end this exercise with the negative if further exercises are to follow.

8 Children share again in same group of three, talking about these two drawings now.

Eye-to-eye processing

Eye-to-eye processing, using the eyes of another, or a drawing of a face with clear, large eyes, is one of the most effective and dramatic processing methods. The child sits opposite someone (or a drawing) who represents a person they are angry with, afraid of, or have some strong tension with. The child then begins to speak as if the person was actually there in front of them, and is supported to express in words, sounds and movement how they really feel.

This method helps the child confront unexpressed thoughts and feelings that have been held inside, or have begun to erupt in destructive ways. This method is often used in group work when there has been some bonding and familiarity with release work. It is confronting and should be introduced gradually. It is generally suitable for children over the age of 8 years.

This simple method is ideal for current upsets that have a charge out of proportion to the event – even if we don't know what the upset is about or why there is so strong a reaction. The strong reactions, of course, are an acting over again of something from the past. Eye-to-eye processing can lead naturally to the inner child's issues, the unresolved, unsatisfied needs from earlier childhood.

Using eyes as a focus allows a temporary regression. How many times were we told as children: 'Don't be such a baby!' 'You're acting like a child!' 'Be a man!' 'Grow up!' 'You're a big man now!' 'You're too big to cry!' Processing is a time for being the baby, for being non-rational. This regression enables the deeper layer of needs to be fully felt, so that in the return to the present the child finds the issue simplified, not highly charged, and the need for further acting-out gone. The need to win is dissipated.

In an ongoing group situation the fact that one of the group is asked to volunteer to be the 'eyes', to receive the projections, creates a deep mutual understanding. It may seem hard on children to take this load, but they do learn quickly to separate out, knowing that what is being said at them is not really to them personally. We have generally found children to be willing to act as support eyes.

Energy release work

Releasing shallow breath patterns

The main and initial way emotional pains are held down from consciousness in childhood is through lowering the general excitement in the system through decreased breath, through letting breathing become shallow. The body knows how to automatically reduce lifeforce flow by reducing breath. Feelings, energy, lifeforce all operate together.

By simply increasing the breath flow we can increase the possibility of emotional flow. Shallow breath has become habitual in most of us. Full breath can be allowed and encouraged as a beginning in reclaiming the fullness of our emotional life, then in the releasing of our own unique and wondrous lifeforce. This principle is at the core of the effectiveness of modern breath therapies. It's a simple reversal of the neurotic breathing pattern.

When asking children to take a deep breath – as we advise in every exercise – be sure to also say 'and let it out'. Sometimes an obedient child will keep holding until this permission is given! Many breathing disorders originate from an inability to exhale – for asthmatics, exhaling is particularly stressful and should be monitored. Some of the feelings that tend to be held in the chest include: grief, sadness, longing and fear. They will sometimes be activated when strong and full breathing is included in an exercise.

Vary the ways of giving the instruction to take deep breaths so that it does not become boring or mechanical. Emphasise relaxation on the out-breath. For example, when the child is sitting or lying down, you might suggest one of the following:

- Put your hand on your chest. Is it tight or willing to expand?
- Take a big breath and let it out.
- Make your chest huge with a breath.
- Put your hands on your rib cage and feel what happens as you empty all your breath out this time.
- Take a breath in through your nose and let it out through your mouth.
- Take three fast breaths.
- Take a big breath in through your right nostril and let it out through your left.
- Take a big breath very, very slowly.
- Take a breath like you were a balloon being blown up. Now let it out as if someone suddenly let the balloon go!

Breathing games

Here are some games to introduce the use of full breath in the ERC work.

The feather
Children form a circle and sit down facing the middle. They imagine a feather lying in the middle. They try to blow this imaginary feather to the other side of the circle. Then the facilitator puts a real feather in the middle, and they repeat the exercise. It seems like magic when it rises up in the air.

The young tree
Children gather in a circle, facing the centre. One child volunteers to be a young tree, standing in the centre. The group becomes the wind, blowing the tree, making it sway and bend. Then they blow the tree one at a time, so that the direction of the breeze keeps changing, flowing around the circle. Several children take turns at being the tree.

The horse
In a circle, children gallop around the room (all going in the same direction). They are told it is a very cold morning, and the horse is snorting very strongly, so strongly that they can see the breath. They become the snorting horse, galloping over the hills.

| Emotional release process |

The rabbit
Children become rabbits jumping around the field enjoying their lunch. Suddenly a fox appears. They freeze, holding their breath, then they dash home to their burrows, and sit panting for a while.

Other suggestions
- Be a whale clearing its spout.
- Become a dragon breathing fire.
- Blow up some large imaginary balloons.

Breathing exercise

What is in my chest?

Suitable for children aged 8 years and over.

Have ready crayons and drawing books.

1. *Children lie down and relax.*
2. *Feel from the inside what it is like inside your chest. Is it tight? Elastic? Moving a lot or a little? Describe it.*
3. *As you take a big breath in, vibrate your hand on your chest – side-to-side and up and down. Now, as you breathe out, groan loudly. Do this three times.*
4. *How does it feel in there now? Is it the same?*
5. *Draw how it feels in your chest. Find the colours and lines that go with how it feels.*
6. *Talk about your drawing.*

Reversing controlled sounding patterns

Allowing children to make sad, angry or fearful sounds about inner pains is important in releasing the energy held in with emotional hurts. The secondary pain of not being allowed to express hurts has been in many cases the key to deepening repression. It can be very difficult to get this sounding mobilised. Children are just as resistant to therapy as most adults – often more so.

It is necessary to check if you are uncomfortable with sounding, if you will be unconsciously preventing children's sounding out despite your conscious intent.

When a new energy has been released or received and we attempt to proclaim it, live it in some way, the energy in the sound we use is a good gauge of our wholeheartedness. You can hear yourself, or a child with whom you are working, be totally connected and full in their proclamation – or you can hear held-back energy, hesitation, apology. At these times a simple reminder is often enough to encourage the child to allow the new.

Hearing ourselves is therapeutic. Hearing ourselves express verbally, sing or even hum actually revitalises the brain. Many children who have never talked much may need to be encouraged to do so in order to hear themselves.

Emotional release for children

With sounding and sharing comes an increase in self-esteem, a stronger sense of self, and mobilisation of energy and feelings. Sounding exercises are also a good support for shy children and those fearful of sharing and expressing themselves.

Sounding exercise

Exploring my sound

Suitable for children aged 6 years and over.

Have some strong music ready.

The aim of this exercise is to free up children's ability to express sound and give permission for expression in group work.

1. Children stand in a large circle.

2. *Make a groaning sound. Put your hands on your belly; now let the sound come from there. Make a groan from deep in your body.*

3. *Now make a roar.*

4. *Say 'Yes!', and nod your head at the same time.*

5. *Say 'No!', and shake your head.*

6. *Turn out from the centre, focus on a spot on the wall, tell off everyone you don't like, tell them what you don't like.*
   (Loud music in the background.)

7. (Continue music in the background.)
   Now just say any words that want to pop out of your mouth. Don't think about it, just let them come.

8. *Now try for a positive sound. What would that be?*

9. *Form pairs. Face your partner eye to eye. One says 'Be quiet!', the other says 'No!' Then swap words.*

Energy release exercise

I love a tantrum

Suitable as a group exercise for children aged 8 years and over (although adolescents may resist!).

Have ready mattresses (one between three children), cushions, journals and biros.

This exercise is really a game that helps children feel freer with their emotional expression and release. It acquaints them with some of the tools of emotional release work in a non-threatening way. Children work in groups of three.

Emotional release process

Part one: 'I Want!' – 'No!'

1. Two children elect to play the part of parents. They stand, one at each end of the mattress. They take a body stance that reflects a feeling of 'No!'

2. The other child plays the part of a child, and kneels in the middle of the mattress facing one of the 'parents'. The body stance is one of 'Please!'

3. Start the game by counting to three.

4. On the count of three the child in the middle begins to ask for all the things they want. They must keep asking. They can't stop asking until this part of the game is over.

5. The children playing the roles of parents exaggerate the denying aspect. They are allowed to respond to the child only with the words 'No!' or 'Definitely not!'

6. The child in the middle will turn from parent to parent, asking and asking, being told 'No!' continually.

7. At a signal from you – perhaps a drum beat – the child in the middle will throw themselves down on the mattress and perform a tantrum. Encourage thumping of fists, kicking of legs, crying out, etc. It may take several rounds for the children to get the permission and feel free enough to really enjoy the tantrum.

8. Each of the three has a turn.

Part two: 'I Want!' – 'Yes!'

9. The set up is the same.

10. On the count of three the child in the middle again asks for everything they want. This time the 'parents' will say only 'Yes!' 'Of course you can!' 'Yes, as much as you want.' etc.

11. Pause for a moment. Ask the child in the centre to feel what it was like hearing 'Yes!' all the time. Talk about this for a moment.

12. Each of the three has a turn at being the child.

Part three: Completion

13. At the completion the three children sit down together on the mattress and discuss:
    - how it felt hearing 'No!' all the time
    - how it felt to throw the tantrum
    - how it felt to be told 'Yes!' to everything
    - how these feelings are similar or different to their real life
    - what things they know the parents really should have said 'No' to

14. Children could then take time to journal their experience and their findings.

Energy release exercise

The dragonfly

Suitable for children aged 6 to 12 years.

Have ready drawing books and crayons.

The aim of the exercise is to release held feelings and energy through exaggerating the holding until they become too big and have to come out. This exercise is ideal for children who are holding down feelings (either negative or positive) and energy, and therefore becoming dull, tired, bored, argumentative etc.

1. *I want you to imagine it is a bright sunny day and you are out in a beautiful garden with a lily pond.*
2. *You are a big dragonfly now. You are very powerful and can fly fast and far.*
3. *What colour are you, dragonfly? Imagine your colours.*
4. *How fast can you fly with your powerful wings? Show me.*
   Children fly around the room.
5. *Now drop down on to the floor. Lie flat out with arms and legs straight.*
6. *Suddenly you are caught in a big spider web. It is very sticky and holds you by the wings. The more you wriggle the more you get stuck. Feel your wings held tight.*
   Encourage the wriggling, sounding, struggling.
7. *You take deep breaths now. Your power builds and suddenly you are free. You have broken the web.*
8. *Your breath, deep again, helps you feel the free flying. Stand up now, feeling your power and freedom – let it be free!*
9. *Draw a picture of your free power.*
10. *Talk about any feelings you may have at times that are like the dragonfly's.*

Emotional release process

Energy release exercise

Roaring at the monster

Suitable for children aged 4 to 12 years.

The aim of this exercise is to relieve a depressed mood, to move energy when it is flat (especially useful if children are bored or tired and inattentive). It is useful if children are scattered and there is a need for focus. It helps timid children begin to open up and make a noise, and works best as a group exercise.

1 Children stand in a circle.
2 *Take three big breaths in and make a big sighing noise on the out-breath.*
3 *Then imagine there is a really scary thing, a creature in the middle.*
   Children describe how they see the scary thing.
4 *Then in a really big voice, yell, roar, scream or whatever is needed, to get it to go away.*
5 *Keep the noise going until the thing goes, or the energy changes.*

This exercise is great to lead children into another process that depends on aliveness.

Bioenergetics exercise

My fireworks display

A series of exercises to release held energy and armouring, suitable for children aged 6 to 11 years.

face	*Imagine the worst food, something you hate eating. You've just eaten ten of them. How would your face be? Exaggerate it. Let the sounds come. Shout out the name of your food.*
arms	*You are a karate expert. See your enemy in front of you. Punch out, with your arms, at your enemy (include sound).*
legs	*You are a kick-boxing expert now. This is the final competition. If you win this one you will be world champion!*
legs	*It is the middle of summer, the temperature is 40°. You are at the beach on hot sand with no shoes. It's a long way to the water. Let your legs move. Let the sounds come.*
whole body	*You are a firecracker. You are very small and on the count of three, you will be lit – then you explode. What sound, colour and movements will you make?*

Now rest, be still for a while and feel what it is like inside you.

Bioenergetics exercise

My war dance

Suitable as an individual or group exercise for children aged 8 to 14 years.

Have ready some powerful drumming music.

This exercise is a preparation for processing; it can be both preparation and integration, or arousing of strength.

1 *Stand still, eyes closed. Take some big, deep breaths.*

2 *Imagine you are all Native Americans. You all belong to the same tribe. You are going to war against another tribe. But first you must prepare yourself by performing a war dance.*

3 Dim lights low if possible, and play music.
 Open your eyes. Imagine there is a blazing fire in the middle of the room. Take your position around the fire.

4 *Begin the dance by moving around the fire making frightening and scary faces. Include the tongue. Include sounds or a power chant.*

5 *Add powerful arm and leg movements (arms swinging, legs stamping).*

6 *Let your dance movements get bigger and faster. Remember the sound.*

7 *As you move around the fire your whole body starts to shake.*

8 *You are now ready to be a warrior.*

9 Either proceed to processing with this energy, or have the children lie down and be still, and invite them to let the power fill them.

Energy release sequence of exercises

Using up potentially disruptive energy

Suitable for children aged 8 to 16 years.

Have ready some loud music, towels, pillows, drawing books and crayons.

This sequence allows release within structured boundaries. The stopping and starting of the parts of the exercises provides both a yes to free expression, and a containment. The sequence aims to help children focus their attention within – after release of holding – and shift from disruptive, automatic release to interest in self-discovery and self-awareness. Ideal with groups.

Part one: Sounding out the negative words

1 Take children on a short jog to an open space outside – such as an oval (or imagine this and act it out indoors).

2   Form a large circle and arrange children facing outwards so that their words will not go to anyone specific.

3   Invite them to shout out the things they really want to say, anything they are not allowed to say. Imagine the wind carrying these words away. (If indoors, use some loud music to represent the wind and to give privacy for expression.)

Part two: Bioenergetics games
4   Working in pairs, children perform the following activities:
    - *Jack in the box*. Children take turns at pushing each other down – hands on shoulders from behind. The one being pushed down suddenly springs up and breaks free.
    - *tug of war*. Use a rolled towel to use weight and strength. At first children think either *no* or *yes* while pulling, then after a while they speak the words out loud.
    - *standing hand-to-hand*. Children gradually mobilise their strength, activate as many muscles of the body as possible, from feet up to hands, push on the other. After a while they add growling sounds.
    - *punching*. Children take turns at holding a pillow while the other punches it. After a while they are asked to try to laugh at the same time.
    - *kicking*. Children take turns at holding a pillow while the other kicks it. Words or phrases can be added after a while, such as: 'I'll get you!'

Part three: Role-playing active then quiet things
5   *Become an ant, a bee, a humming bird, a happy yappy puppy.*

6   *Form a circle, hold hands and together become a rough sea, make the sounds.*
    Other options for role-playing active things: a school of fish being chased by a shark, soldier crabs scattering as people walk along the beach at low tide, a beaver building a new dam in a hurry.

7   *Become a snail, a lizard lying in the sun.*

8   *Become a still lake just before sunrise. Be the lake for a while. Go inside yourself as the lake. What colours are there? What is it like in your chest? In your belly? See what is around you.*

Part four: Being the lake
9   *Draw yourself as the lake.*

10 *Share with a partner what it was like to be the lake.*

11 *Gestalt the lake: find your qualities as this still quiet lake.* (See questions on page 140.)

Reactions to parents

Journal exercise

The people in my life

Suitable for children aged 6 years and over. Note that young children may need some assistance with written expression.

Have ready copies of the pro forma 'The People in My Life' on p. 197.

This exercise involves children filling out a form. It will help children find and extended language to describe relationships with, reactions to and problems with the people around them. It will help them – and a parent, teacher or counsellor – pinpoint the source of difficulties. It may help children in realising that they need to speak out about some relationships.

Notes
- A possible next step or seventh column, leading into emotional release work, might be headed: 'Say it to them as if they were here now.' Make this an encounter, possibly using a drawing of a face as a trigger.
- Within column 5, be aware of children's first reactions. Is it the real feeling underneath? Are there real things that do actually need to be said – in real life?
- If a child has difficulty with column 6, try breaking it down into two parts:
  – Say something you like about them.
  – Say something you don't like about them.
- If there are obviously significant people who bring a strong positive or negative response, consider asking a child to become the person, to Gestalt it, in order to learn more (see page 140 on Gestalt work).

Emotional release process

The people in my life

Person	1 Their colour	2 Their shape	3 Animal like them	4 Their big problem	5 What I would like to say to them	6 How I feel about them
Dad	brown	☁	slug	lazy	Wake up!	Scared and sad
Mum	pink	○	duck (mother)	none	Thank you for my lunch.	Good
Sister – older	black	∿∿∿	bat	bossy	Leave me alone.	Scared and angry
Brother						
Sister – younger	red (hair)	☺	rabbit	messy	Goo-goo.	Glad.
Brother						
Stepfather						
Stepmother						
Stepsister(s)						
Stepbrother(s)						
Grandmother	purple	∿	hen	–	I love you Gran.	Good. Warm.
Grandfather	dark green	○	hippo	lonely	I love you Granpa.	Good. Warm.
Teacher	yellow	□	snake	angry all the time	Leave me alone.	Tired
Best friend	red	–	kangaroo	–	Hi! Brett.	Good.
Worst enemy						
…………						
…………						

101

Visualisation exercise

My real face

Suitable for children aged 8 to 14 years.

Have ready white, round paper plates (2 per child) and crayons.

1. Children sit with their eyes closed.
2. *Take three large breaths in and out and let your breath keep going.*
3. *Imagine you are a clown. See what you look like (in particular your face), what you are wearing.*
4. *Draw your clown's face on a paper plate as you keep breathing.*
5. *Eyes closed again, imagine yourself in a circus. See yourself performing tricks and being funny. Hear the crowds laugh. The performance comes to an end. Crowds go home. You are now in your dressing room, taking off your make-up or funny face. You no longer have to be funny or perform. You can show how you are really feeling.*
6. *As the make-up comes off, what is the face you see?*
7. *Draw your real face on a paper plate.*
8. *Think about these questions, then tell me your answers:*
   - *Are there any times in your life when you have felt that you had to perform? pretend?*
   - *What is the main difference you can see between the faces?*
   - *Do you know what's happened to make you feel these ways?*
   - *Have you felt like this before?*

Drama exercise

Am I a puppet on strings?

Suitable for children aged 6 to 14 years.

1 Stand with your eyes closed. Imagine you are a puppet. Strings are attached to your arms, legs and head. They hold you up and control you.

2 Somebody is at the other end of the strings. Who is it?

3 This someone is going to make you do something you don't like:
  - What is it?
  - Act it out.
  - How does it feel?

4 Now is your chance to say no.
  - Let your body, face, hands say no.
  - Exaggerate it.
  - As you stamp, shout out your no.
  - Let yourself see who you are saying no to.

5 What does the 'no' want to do with the strings?

6 You no longer have strings, you are no longer a puppet. Feel that.

7 You are free to do what you want. Imagine what that is.
  (Perhaps act it out now.)

8 Talk about:
  - all the things you would do if you were free
  - any reasons you can think of for being stopped or controlled
  - what you might need to say to somebody who controls you

Exercises for adolescents

Many of these exercises can take an hour or more for half the group to work. They may be more suitable for workshop or retreat situations where time structures are not so limiting.

Talking exercise for beginning group work

Getting to know each other

Suitable for children aged 12 years and over.

Set up the room with two concentric circles of cushions in pairs. The number of cushions is to coincide with the number of adolescents in the group.

This exercise is used when beginning group work with adolescents. It is a simple way to ritualise first meetings, to begin to break the ice.

1. Members of the group choose a partner, then sit opposite each other. If they have not met before, they introduce themselves and make sure they know each other's names.

2. Give them a list of questions (see below) to talk about with each other.

3. Before each question they must become still, close their eyes, take a full breath and feel what is going on inside themselves. When they have had a moment of inner contact they leave their eyes closed and are given the question. They wait and see what presents itself in their mind, then ponder the question for a moment. When both are ready to talk they open their eyes and share.

4. After each sharing the children in the outer (or the inner) circle stand and move on to the next cushion on their right.

5. Vary the number of questions to suit the time available and the interest level. If there is time they can choose a partner to meet with from their own circle as well.

6. Sample questions:
   - *What things annoy you the most in your life now?*
   - *What is your strongest or best quality?*
   - *How many brothers and sisters do you have? Where do you come in the family?*
   - *What things make you sad? What things make you most happy?*
   - *Is there anyone in your life you are afraid of?*
   - *How do you feel about being in this group right now?*

Emotional release process

A meeting exercise

Symbols of my life

Suitable for children aged 12 to 19 years.

Have ready sandplay symbols, drawing books and crayons.

1 Children prepare a large circle on their drawing books.

2 *Visualise your life at these ages, see the setting, remember the feelings that went with these ages:*
   - *baby*
   - *toddler (3 or 4 years old)*
   - *child 8 to 10 years old*
   - *now*

3 *Select a sandplay symbol that goes with each age.*

4 *Arrange the symbols in the circle on your drawing book, in the way they relate to each other.*

5 *Talk about these stages of your life. Share with a partner or small group.*

6 *Draw the symbols on to the book.*

7 *Write a word under each that sums up the main feeling about each stage.*

8 You may recognise one stage that shows some problems or brings up a negative response. This symbol could be worked using the Gestalt method (see page 140).

Emotional release exercise

Focusing with deep breath – current problems

Suitable for adolescents aged 14 years and over.

Review 'Conditions for Supporting Processing' (see page 89). Briefly review the child/adult concept (see page 57). Set up mattress and cushions, have ready drawing books, crayons, journals, biros and tissues.

This process is designed for older children and adolescents to help them release some of the power of current emotional hurts.

1 *Tune in, remember a current problem or emotional hurt.*
   Get the child to talk about it with you.
   Draw the person who caused the hurt, or the situation, on the right-hand side of your drawing book – call it now.
   Draw it large, with a dark crayon.

Emotional release for children

2. Tune in, remember your parents when you were smaller. Talk about how you felt about them, their qualities, how they treated you, etc.
   Draw their faces on the left-hand side of the book — call this then.

3. Set up the book against the wall. Sit on the mattress, opposite the drawings, with some cushions in front.

4. Breathe deeply, look at the drawings, the now and the then.

5. Open to these layers inside you:
   - understanding — go through the reasons, the rationalisations
   - reactions — especially any resentment, anger, fear, hate, whatever the real feelings were, let them be expressed now; if you feel that someone is to blame, 'blame' them
   - find the hurt — underneath all this is the hurt; feel it and put it out in simple words, as if you were talking to the people concerned right now, as if they were here

   Give children time to drop into deeper feelings and the underlying energy. Since much of the real feelings around a hurt of emotional problems will have been 'rationalised away', it may take time and assurance for them to re-emerge.

The following three steps (6–8) may be too complicated for younger children. Simply allowing some release may be quite enough for them. In that case go to step 9.

6. Note any similarities between the hurts of now and then.

7. In what way has the hurt inner child been struggling? Trying to get it right? Trying to correct the past? or win? or keep the survival mechanism going?

8. What was the young child's defence or survival mechanism? withdrawal? exhibitionism? secretiveness? self-blaming? etc.

9. Recognise when it is time to rest, when the energy for the exercise has reduced. Then get children to lie down, allow any deeper feelings or memories to surface. Ask the children to share these, or simply lie still and quiet with the new energy, knowing how it feels to have contacted and released feelings.

10. Draw the new energy, record insights, journal about the process and any hoped-for future behaviours.

11. Invite the children to share all this with you.

Emotional release exercise

Exploring unconscious feelings towards parents using 'The Gateway' questions

Suitable as an individual or small group exercise for adolescents aged 14 years and over.

Have drawing books and crayons ready. Set up cushions, mattress facing the wall. Give a brief overview of the process.

This is an ERC routine to reveal an inner child part that may be insisting on something from the past. It is to help older children and adolescents come into their true inner strength. This strength is found through releasing the opposites of strength. Two main triggers are used for focusing: pictures of parents' faces; and questions based on 'The Gateway':

> The Gateway
> Through the gateway of feeling your weakness lies your strength.
> Through the gateway of feeling your pain lies your pleasure and joy.
> Through the gateway of feeling your fear lies your security and safety.
> Through the gateway of feeling your loneliness lies your capacity to have fulfilment, love and companionship.
> Through the gateway of feeling your hopelessness lies true and justified hope.
> Through the gateway of accepting the lacks in your childhood lies your fulfilment now.
>
> Eva Pierrakos, *The Pathwork of Self-transformation*, Bantam, 1990.

This exercise can take a long time – sometimes one hour or more. If there is no limit on time, and the mood of the group feels positive, the other half of the group then work. Allow integration time and a break before swapping roles. If time is limited, the other half can work next time you meet.

1. If doing as a group, choose pairs and decide who will work first.
2. Read 'The Gateway' to the group.
3. Children draw faces of parents: large, quick, strong colour, clear eyes.
4. Prop drawings against the wall. Children sit opposite.
5. Stress to group that this is an exercise to open to the positive by clearing out the old negatives, old beliefs, old grudges, against parents.
6. Invite the ones who are working first to share with their partner any resistances, how they feel now.
7. Talk about noise in the room that may result from emotional release during the process. Warn that it may bring up some fear.
8. *Close your eyes, take six strong breaths. We'll come back to breaths during the process to help release emotions. Encourage your chest to open.*

Emotional release for children

9 *First Gateway: Read out the first line of 'The Gateway', then say:*
   In a moment open your eyes and tell your parents about your feelings of weakness *now, and from the past. Let any memories or pictures come to your mind and tell your parents about them. Talk to them as if they were here now. Tell them all your feelings.*

10 If a child cannot speak directly to faces, have them speak out the feelings to their partner first, then repeat to faces.

11 It might be good to have children stand and shake off the old feelings, then sit and breathe deeply again, ready for the next phase.

12 Second Gateway: Read the second line, then ask children to tell parents about any *pain* now or in the past.

13 Continue through the Gateways. The sequence may be too long for some children. (If necessary, leave out Fifth Gateway.)

Note:
- Watch for a need for expression in the hands — clenching? rubbing?
- Encourage deep breath throughout the process to unlock deeper layers.
- If emotions flow, partners may be invited to put hand supportingly on the child's back.

14 After the last Gateway, children lie down, feeling any *belief* about themselves that came from parents.

15 Let them rest and integrate, then share insights with partner.

16 Children write down learnings, and/or draw to express feelings and new energy.

Emotional release exercise

Body focus – tight and angry parts

Suitable for children aged 14 years and over.

Prepare photocopies of two body outlines for each child (see pages 62–65). Have ready crayons, mattress, cushions and tissues.

1 Children talk in pairs about how they deal with anger in their lives.
2 *Lie down.*
   - *Tune in to your body, just gathering information about how it is inside, not trying to change anything.*
   - *Look within for any parts that are tight or angry.*
   - *Check through from head to toes, looking for any parts like this.*
   - *Draw the tight or angry parts on to the body outline.*

3 Focus on the part(s) and get children to dialogue with them:
   - *Tune in to the parts.*
   - *Take six very full breaths and relax them out.*
   - *Let the parts answer through you. The questions are for this (these) part(s):*
     – *Do you have a movement, or a sound? How would it be if you were allowed to make these?*
     – *Does ... (child's name) hang on to you? Let yourself speak to them now.*
     – *Why are you there?*
     – *Who might have caused you?*
     – *Do you want to say anything to them?*
     – *What animal are you like? Express yourself as this animal.*
     – *Is there any help you could ask for now?*

4 *Visualise the tight or angry part(s) spreading out now. Let them flow out to become energy for your whole body.*
   You or the partner could stroke or massage to help with this spreading out of energy.

5 *Rest. Connect now with how it feels inside you.*

6 *Here are some questions for the new energy, the new feeling inside you. It does not have to answer. It may wish to stay quiet and still.*
   - *What colour are you?*
   - *How big are you?*
   - *Are you in parts, or all of the body?*
   - *Are you bigger than the body?*
   - *Are you a moving or still energy?*
   - *Do you have a purpose?*
   - *Is there any image or symbol that goes with that purpose?*

7 *Draw the energy, the way it feels inside now, on to the second body outline.*
8 *Journal what you have learned and experienced, especially if there was a purpose.* The supporting partner can journal about the feelings activated by their support role.
9 The children share the learnings with you or their partners.

Focusing exercise

Finding the positive in trapped body energy

Suitable as an individual or group exercise for children aged 14 years and over.

Photocopy two body outlines for each child. Have ready crayons, one mattress per pair.

1 Children choose partners and decide who will explore first.

2 The partner who is working first lies down on the mattress, relaxes and takes some full breaths.

3 *You are going to search inside your body to find any alive or excited parts. Begin by feeling your body on the mattress, feel its weight, feel what part of your back touches the mattress. Now slowly move your awareness down from your head to your toes. You are looking for alive parts, warm parts, tingly parts that stand out from the rest. When you find some part like that find the right colour, the right lines or shapes or shading, and draw it on to the body outline.*

4 *Now lie down again and tune into that part. Put your hand on the part if you can, or get your partner to put a hand there to help you feel it.*

5 *These questions are for the part. We are going to give it a chance to speak, to reveal itself, and you will learn a whole lot more about yourself. Let the part answer. Lend it your voice. Speak so your partner can hear. Take a big breath between questions.*
   - *Are you still or moving? radiating? sparkling? or a bit stuck?*
   - *How big are you? How far do you spread?*
   - *Do you have a texture? What do you feel like?*
   - *Did somebody else start you off, or do you belong to the person you are in?*
   - *Does the person you are in listen to you? Do they notice you?*
   - *Is there something the hand that is resting on you can do for you? Is there some movement you would like?*
   - *Is there a way that the body part that contains you would like to move? Let it happen now.*
   - *Is there a picture that goes with you? Send that picture to the mind of the person you are in.*
   - *What is the gift you contain? What is your name?*

6 *Take time to feel the energy now. Draw on to the second body outline what it feels like inside now.*

7 *Draw any picture that the energy presented to you.*

8 The other partner now works.

9 Encourage group discussion on creative ways of using this energy.

Emotional release process

Visualisation exercise

No stone unturned

Suitable for adolescents aged 14 years and over.

Have ready drawing book, crayons, journal and biro.

1 *This is a review exercise to see what else you may need to focus on in your inner work.*

2 *Lie down now and relax. Close your eyes and take a few deep breaths and relax them out.*

3 *I want you to imagine you are walking beside a river, up near its source. You are walking over and around pebbles, rocks and boulders. These are along the edge of the river as well as in it. The water is gently flowing over the pebbles and around the boulders. Along the bank are many stones: smooth ones, rough ones, coloured ones. Under some of them lie pictures of the important inner work you have done over the last . . . days/weeks/months.*

4 *Imagine yourself stepping forward, going upstream along the bank. Come to an interesting stone now. Bend down and turn it over. Look at the picture underneath it. It is a picture of some important things you have learned about your life, about yourself. What do you see? Look at the picture for a moment, then quickly draw the stone on your art pad and sketch the picture you saw. Maybe write a few words as well.*

5 *Now continue the walk.*

6 Children turn up three or four more stones, and record what was found. They are invited to feel the satisfaction from dealing with all these issues.

7 *You come to an odd-shaped stone that is a different colour. This is the last stone left unturned. Underneath it is a picture of the thing you have avoided or given up on dealing with. Lift it carefully and slowly. Let it reveal the picture of what you have avoided so far or given up on. Draw it as carefully as you can and write a little about it.*

8 *Notice how you feel now that you have admitted this, faced this issue and do not have to use energy avoiding it.*

9 *Share what was under the last stone with a partner or with me.*

> ### Discussion and journalling exercise
>
> ### Dealing with anger
>
> Suitable for adolescents aged 14 years and over.
>
> This exercise consists of two lists which can be used in individual or group work. They can be photocopied and handed out to groups of three or four adolescents, with instructions to read them through and discuss. They provide starting points for discussion.
>
> **Some old ways**
> - Dump out all the anger, explode, then withdraw, become embarrassed?
> - Hit and punch, hurt and destroy, then feel bad about myself?
> - Talk and talk and argue, then give in, or make peace, apologise?
> - Talk and talk and argue, then give in and go away, withdraw?
> - Push the anger down inside, close off, withdraw, stay alone?
> - Tighten up my body, hold it all in, resent people, then hate them?
> - Pretend I am not angry, then gossip, hate, or pretend I am a saint?
> - Squash my aliveness?
>
> **Some new ways**
> - Find the hurt or sadness under the anger, be vulnerable?
> - Find my support person to help me 'process' the anger, release it, then go and find the person(s) who made me angry and say what I need to say, clearly?
> - Learn to find what I really wanted, and ask for it?
> - Draw, dance, go for a strong walk, play basketball (kill the ball)?
> - Stay alive, find the power under the anger, use it for me?

Work with anger

Anger work is one of the most feared areas of ERC – often feared as much by facilitators as by children. This is because most of us fear our own conscious and unconscious anger. We have learned to hide or deny it. Releasing it safely in the processing room and personally experiencing that it is really power, strength, etc. denied, prepares us to support children to release the surface level and reclaim themselves.

Under all negative feelings are other feelings. The energy of anger holds so much of our potential: strength, authority, aliveness, assertiveness, sense of self. Anger is often the reaction to these qualities being suppressed. Deep under most anger is hurt or sadness.

When we try to control anger or suppress it, we eventually find that it either oozes out caustically, explodes out destructively, or implodes, sometimes affecting our health.

Emotional release process

'I was so angry I pulled Mum's tree out.'
An 8-year-old boy drew this dragon as part of his sandplay. This is his 'attacking' dragon. He made the sound of the dragon. After twenty big breaths and sounds he eventually felt his anger coming from his belly. It was no longer the dragon's – it was his!

Sequence of bioenergetics exercises

Reclaiming the energy of anger

Suitable as an individual or group exercise for children aged 10 years and over.

Have ready strong rhythmic music (see page 200), large pillows (one per pair), crayons, drawing books, journals and biros.

Read through the descriptions of the bioenergetics exercises on pages 116–117, practise them and demonstrate each one as it is presented.

1. Play the music and give these instructions:
   Listen to the rhythm of the music. Feel it inside you. Now dance with the music, feel the rhythm of

Emotional release for children

it and let your body move with it. Take some big breaths, breathe as if you could take the air right down to your belly and hips.

2. Tell your inner child part that it is safe now to show the truth of what is inside. Whatever feelings might be hidden inside can come up now in this safe room.

3. Now dance out this expression: 'I am furious!!' What do your fists do? Pretend you are an actor. What do your feet want to do? How could you do a furious dance?

4. Face the wall. Imagine a spot in front of you. Open your eyes wide and start making growling sounds at the wall. Good, now imagine the main people in your life standing there in front of you. Find something that you want to tell them off about, and say it loudly. I will turn up the music so no one will hear you.
Turn music up for a minute or two.

5. Now look at me. We will do the 'Get off My Back!' exercise (see page 116), saying the words loudly: 'Get off my back! Get off my back!'

6. Find a partner for this exercise. One of you hold the cushion up in the air like this. The other starts punching. Let the punching bring your strength up from your legs and back. Now swap. Let yourself make noises as you punch.

7. Drop the cushions over by the wall. Everyone shake now. Shake like you have ants running all over you and you want to get them off.

8. Form a large circle facing into the middle of the room. Every second person step back. The others try kicking with all your strength up in the air. Now step back and let the others try. Let yourself make sounds as you kick.

9. Move out of the circle formation. Take space throughout the room. Imagine you are standing in the middle of your own circle. Close your eyes. Put your hands on your hips. Begin rocking your hips and bottom forward and back. Take some big breaths down low in your belly.

10. Follow me, walking around the room in a big circle. Walk briskly and let your hips sway. It feels silly, but try to let your hips go up and down as much as possible. Take big strong steps.

11. Come back to the partner you had before. Stand in front of each other. Feel the strength in your body. I want you to show each other how strong you are, let your strength show. Let's see who looks the strongest. Look around the room now.

12. Close your eyes now. See if your imagination can show you a picture of something that is strong like you. Watch inside your mind. Is there an image or a symbol of something with energy like yours now? Wait for it to come to you. See it clearly in your mind, see every detail.

13. Quickly draw this image.

14. When you have drawn the image, stand in front of your partner again. Take turns at becoming this image. Describe what you are like. Pretend you are it!

15. Take a few minutes to write down in your journal what it felt like doing these exercises, what were the main qualities of the image you had at the end.

Emotional release process

Opposites exercise

The giant and the little people

Suitable as a group exercise for children aged 6 to 14 years.

The aim of the exercise is to allow children to feel their positive and negative parts, and to know it is normal to have both.

Part one: Visualisation
1. *Lie down on the floor in a comfortable position – feet and arms unlocked, head flat on the floor. Relax the body from your feet through to the head.*
2. *I want you to imagine there is a cartoon being played out inside you.*
3. *In this cartoon there is an army of little people on one side and a very big giant on the other. The army is hiding amongst the trees and can't be seen. The big giant is in his castle. The army sneaks up closer and closer, until they are all around the castle where the big giant is asleep. They climb the walls of the castle, being very quiet.*
4. *All of a sudden the giant wakes. He rushes out and captures all the little people. They are powerless. Feel how it feels to be the little people.*
5. *The giant locks them away in his dungeon and throws away the key.*
6. *Feel how it feels to be the big powerful giant. The giant is very happy and goes back to sleep.*
7. *Come back into this room now. Let your eyes open.*

Part two: Action!
8. *Who would like to be the giant? The rest of us will be the army of little people.*
9. Children act out the story, taking turns until all have a sense of both energies.
10. Children discuss how it feels with both energies, then the times in real life when they let these parts out.

The bioenergetics exercises which follow were developed from Reich and Lowen's work, to help get energy flowing and to unblock specific parts of the body. By mobilising physical energy, they also mobilise emotional energy. They can render a child more vulnerable to feelings, so should be done in a situation of support, where emotional expression is fully allowed. They are especially effective for depressed children and those with deep locked-in anger. Generally a sequence will begin with the face and work down the body.

You should participate in these exercises with the children to model them and to enliven yourself. Be prepared to act and look very silly!

Emotional release for children

Sequence of bioenergetics exercises

Waking and releasing anger and strength

Suitable for children aged 6 years and over.

These exercises are simple and fun – however, adolescents will rarely let themselves appear foolish and join in wholeheartedly.

Encourage the strong use of sounding – use the voice to open up emotional flow and release. As in all emotional release work, the breath must be full. Have a towel per child ready.

1. *shaking*. With powerful breathing, children 'go crazy'.

2. *follow the finger*. Children roll eyes, keeping head still, to follow a finger which is describing irregular circular patterns. The finger is about 30–40 cm from the eyes. Tell children, 'I bet you can't keep up with my finger.'

3. *crazy person*. Children hold eyes wide open and roll them in wide circles, several times in each direction. Usually done with children lying down on the floor.

4. *face mask*. Children make their face a mask of fear then anger, let it exaggerate – move between the two.

5. *shouting*. Children shout out everything they want to say, for example tell off everyone they feel angry towards, send it out to the wall.

6. *gibberish*. Children shout out continuous, meaningless nonsense.

7. *tongue*. Children poke it out, stretch it, make circles.

8. *Superman*. Children expand their chests and make themselves look like Superman, Superwoman, Wonderwoman or the Hulk (or some current muscular hero). Then they alternate with looking like a puny weakling. Focus on expanding and relaxing the chest. Helps break down breathing inhibitions.

9. *get off my back!* Children make hands into fists, and bring them up in front of them so that their forearms are parallel, one above the other. Their elbows should be out at right angles to their torso. They then move their elbows back so that their chest feels open and it feels as if their shoulder blades are going to meet. They do this more quickly and then add the words: 'Get off my back!'

10. *jumping*. Children move around the room with feet together, knees bent.

11. *Jack-in-the-box*. From a standing position, push the child down, really give the sensation of being squashed down. Then when you take your hand off their head or shoulders have them spring up suddenly with a shout.

12. *the axe-man*. Children stand with feet firmly apart, knees bent. They curve their back so that their bottom feels like it is pushed back. They clench their hands together and raise them above their head. Making a great sound, they chop down as if there was a chopping block in front of them, tilting the pelvis forward at the same time. They repeat and then do it quickly.

Emotional release process

13 *the fly swat*. Children fold a towel in half and then in half again, and hold it at one end, checking that there is a clear space all around. They place a cushion on the floor in front of them and imagine that a nasty stinging insect or huge blowfly is on the cushion. With all their strength, they hit it with the towel. They pretend that they keep missing, so hit and hit, finding the sound that goes with that.

14 *tantrum*. Lying on the floor or a mattress with cushions under feet and fists, children take a few big breaths, then begin hitting with right fist and left foot, alternating with left fist and right foot. They increase the speed and sound until it looks (and feels) like a tantrum. This can also be done in a standing position: they begin to jog on the spot, increasing the speed (facilitator claps or beats a drum) until they reach a tantrum pace. They then begin screaming!

15 *stillness*. If the exercises are over, the children simply lie still and feel what is going on inside them and what images are in their mind. If emotional release processing is to follow, go directly into that now, without the stillness.

Anger exercise

Finding an animal language

Suitable as an individual or group exercise for children aged 10 to 19 years.

Have ready drawing books and crayons.

This exercise is designed for children who often exhibit traits of anger, but may not have specific, obvious causes, and who may not be in touch with their anger at the counselling time. The exercise may awaken many feelings – make sure there is plenty of time at the end for completion and integration. Work with anger will often open underlying layers of grief.

1 *Think of someone you are (or were) angry with or afraid of.*

2 *Do a large, quick drawing of their face. Make their eyes strong and use a dark crayon.*

3 *Do a quick drawing of how you feel about this person: lines, colours, shapes.*

4 Present some bioenergetics exercises to awaken anger (see previous page and above):
  - the axe-man
  - punching
  - get off my back!
  - the fly swat

5 *Sit and look at the face. Prop it up against a wall and sit opposite.*

6 *Take six slow, deep breaths.*

7 *Think what you would really like to say to this person.*

8 *Whisper it.* (Give permission to say 'bad things'.)

117

9. Become a large black dog. Get down on all fours. Speak to the person in dog language. Say what you would really like to say – as the dog. (See note a below.)

10. Become a tiger, the largest, most powerful. Feel your claws, your teeth. Talk in tiger language.

11. Stand up. Become an enormous elephant. Express yourself as an elephant – sounds, actions.

12. Stand up, stretch, feel your energy and feelings now. Let your energy and strength and feelings be all through you.

13. Do another quick drawing of your feelings and energy and power.

14. Write down anything you now need to actually say to this person (or needed to say in the past).

15. Share with a partner how you feel now, and how you felt doing the exercise, and any changes you noticed.

16. Is there another step needed now for integration or completion? What conversation might children need to draw out any stirred-up feelings? Consider: journal writing, working with a symbol for their power, further emotional release.

Notes:

a If a child has difficulty becoming the dog, tiger or elephant, get them to choose their own power symbol from either their own imagination or from the sandplay collection (if you have one). Some examples children have chosen: dagger, witch, monster, dragon, dinosaur. Then let the symbol make sounds, do actions on their behalf.

b By step 10 or 11 some children may let the tiger rip up the drawing or the elephant may throw it away or stomp on it. They may sometimes need silent approval from the facilitator to do this.

c For steps 8 to 11 in group work, it may be helpful to have some background music to provide a sense of privacy.

d If resistance is noticed at step 2 or 3, stop to discuss it. Draw out any underlying fear so that the resistance is reduced.

Emotional release process

Anger and grief exercise

What does your heart long for?

Suitable for children aged 10 to 19 years.

Have crayons, white paper plates ready. Play soft, sad music in Part 2 (see page 200).

Part one: Releasing the anger
1. *Think of a person whom you are frightened of, angry with or don't like. Let yourself be in touch with those feelings now.*
2. *Draw this person's face on a paper plate (make the face look any way you wish).*
3. *Feel into what you'd really like to say to this face. Whisper it.*
4. *Let an image come of something very powerful. Say what it is. Become this powerful thing. Let your whole body be it. Describe yourself.*
5. *What does it want to do or say to the face? Let it do it and say it now!*

Part two: Connecting with the grief
6. *Lie down. Curl up.*
7. *Breathe deeply.*
8. *Place your hand on your heart. Can you feel it in there?*
9. *Imagine yourself travelling into your heart.*
10. *Ask your heart: 'What do you want or really long for from this person? (the person you were angry with or afraid of). Only your heart knows this. Let your heart speak to you.*
11. *Tell your partner/me the answer to this question: 'Does your heart get what it longs for?'*
12. *Allow any grief to release. Give permission for this.*
13. *Once the hurt has been felt, ask: What is the feeling in your heart now?*
14. *Children do mandala drawings and engage in further discussion.*

Processing exercise

Riding the magic carpet

An individual exercise suitable for children aged 8 to 16 years. Have ready one mattress per child.

The aim of this exercise is to create a situation of safety for a child to express anger and learn that breath, sounds and movement do bring release and allow depression to lift. Depression and the strong feelings and energies are closely linked. Depressed children are actually suppressing something. Often it is strong anger or grief. Sometimes it is pure excitement. When we find what has been suppressed and allow it safe expression the depression lifts.

1. *I want you to lie on the mattress. Take deep breaths. Let your body go floppy and melt down into the mattress.*

2. *Imagine you are a genie on a magic carpet. Picture yourself as this genie riding it through the sky. This is a beautiful place, up here in the sky. There are soft clouds and you can ride your carpet over them and through them. Allow yourself to really experience this.*

3. *You are powerful and strong. Soaring here above the earth you can look down and see everything. Down there you see someone being unkind or hurtful. Maybe there is someone you'd like to speak to, to tell off. Remember you are strong and powerful. You can do this now.* Encourage sound and allow time.

4. *Now come back to being yourself. Is this person someone in your life now or very much like someone in your life now?*

5. *I'd like you to sit up and look into my eyes.*
   Pretend that I am this person and it is safe to say everything you haven't said, anything at all. Just allow the words to come and use any movements, too. Kick, punch, anything. Let your body do what it wants to — it knows.

6. Watch for the energy change, then ask:
   What are you feeling now?

7. Allow for dancing or drawing that feeling.

Emotional release process

Anger exercise

What would you really like to do?

Suitable for children aged 8 to 14 years.

This is an exercise to help children find their own motivation for projects and decisions.

1. Pretend you are a puppet, with long strings that control you.
2. Close your eyes. Take a big breath and let it out.
3. Feel your body pulled by the strings, held up by the strings. Try moving a bit. Feel the strings holding you back.
4. Who is holding the strings? Who in your life controls you? Imagine someone up there who directs you.
5. Now imagine they are making you do something you don't want to do. What is it? Tell me about it.
6. How do you feel about doing it? Is it something you have to do a lot? How do you feel about being made to do it?
7. Now think what you would like to say to the puppet-controller. Now whisper it. Now say it out loud.
8. Let yourself say a big no to being told what to do. Show me how your body goes when it says no?
9. Take some very big breaths, let your body get very strong. You are changing from a puppet into a human.
10. You are strong now. Tell them that you do not want to be a puppet any longer. Feel your new strength. Now break the strings!
11. Feel your body free now. How would it move? What would it like to do, now that no one is pulling the strings. Feel inside yourself. What would you like to do?
12. Do it!
13. Follow-up discussion would include the appropriateness of doing this at home, at school, etc. – how can we do what we want and please others?

CHAPTER SIX

The world of symbols

An emotional disturbance can be dealt with...
by giving it visible shape.

C G Jung quoted in Ruth Ammann, *Healing and Transformation in Sandplay*, Open Court, 1991.

A basic postulate of sandplay therapy is that
deep in the unconscious there is an autonomous tendency,
given the proper conditions, for the psyche to heal itself.

Estelle Weinrib, *Images of the Self*, Sigo Press, 1983.

Sandplay

Like the ocean, our unconscious is continually washing up treasures. This is an inbuilt mechanism in the psyche that if acknowledged, listened to, attended to, will bring us to personal healing and then beyond that to individuation.

Sometimes it seems as if the ocean tides inside us stay out for a long time. There are sometimes vast stretches of bare sand. Sometimes there is a king tide. More is washed up from the depths. The storms of life can be the best times to discover the treasures spread before our feet as we wander along the shore. We have to be quick, sharp-eyed. The waves wash up what seems like rubbish, or empty shells, deceptive symbols that can speak of great inner treasure. Then just as quickly the waves begin to bury them again.

Visualise a medium-sized room. All around the walls are shelves, like bookshelves, but filled with figurines: tiny people, animals, fish, birds, trees, buildings, military equipment, miniature household items, model cars, trucks, buses, flowers, jewels, skeletons, funny things, frightening things, endearing things, religious items, primitive dolls – the list goes on and on. And in the middle of this storeroom of symbols from our unconscious is a table with a sandtray, similar to the ones we may have used in kindergarten. It's time to play!

The symbols on the shelves can represent parts of ourselves. Sometimes we will choose symbols to represent themes about which we are already conscious. At other times we simply allow the symbol to call us. As we look at the shelves we feel that some of the symbols reach out to us. We might feel greatly repulsed or attracted – that's usually a clue that that symbol is important for us. This is the unconscious speaking and this is the main purpose of sandplay. We simply take the symbols that call out, and start to arrange them in the sand – a little like playing on the beach. We probably will not realise it at first, but the symbols call out to us because something inside us resonates, recognises itself in them. We may even begin by arranging the sand, heaping it into hills and valleys, rivers or coastlines.

The process is a little like working with dreams, but the symbols are outside us, ready to be selected, not stored away in the unconscious. However, our unconscious emotional state – if we allow it – selects the symbol figures, arranges them and sorts itself out. In all of us there is a constant inner movement to make sense of our inner and outer worlds, to come into harmony with all the parts of ourselves. Working at the sandtray facilitates this sorting out and exposes much that was unknown to us before. Creating a congruence between the inner world and its external expression is therapeutic.

Sandplay is a wonderful way of exploring our inner world. A lot of transformation can happen at this level, as the figures are related to and arranged in relation to each other. It is very non-threatening. Inner changes are allowed which might remain hidden in a traditional counselling session.

Most adults and children look on sandplay as a bit of a lark at first, and because of that they move into it easily. They soon begin to contact the deeper parts of themselves. It is very good for clients with poor verbal skills, or those who are very shy.

Our method of using sandplay has evolved from the Jungian model. It has incorporated Gestalt work and gained great freedom and further healing power through the methods of ERC.

The *elements* of sandplay therapy include:
- the hands of the child
- the sand
- the sandtray
- the symbols
- water
- the child's personal mythology and unconscious
- the facilitator/observer
- the environment, the counselling room

The world of symbols

The sand, symbols, tray and water become a malleable tool that can take on the contours of the psyche as it is constellated at the time. Sandplay functions as an integrative tool since it brings together body, feelings and mind. Through the sandplay picture the child can release the old and embody new understandings. Sandplay is used to resolve personal problems, reclaim forgotten qualities, open to inner guidance and direction, expand self-knowledge and explore personal mythology.

The play aspect is vital. Sandplay brings up less resistance than more confronting processes. The look, the texture and the smell of the sand often bring up a link in our memory to a happy time at the beach. The feel of the sand can evoke childhood memories. There is a link to being beside the ocean – which is so often a symbol for the unconscious – and carefree times. Sometimes it can bring up a lack of these times.

The client uses hands to shape the sand. Through the moving hands energy can be released. Fingers flowing through dry sand leave ripples. Wet sand can be shaped into hills and valleys. For the child, being connected to the sensations of their hands means that they come home to the body more. Through this inner connection more material from the unconscious can reveal itself. The body awareness allows the analysing mind and its diversionary tactics to be left behind.

The sand is changeable – it is solid matter that has been transformed and has almost become liquid. This allows for stories to unfold, change. The inner transformation that takes place during a sandplay session can be represented visually: the old giving way to the new.

The sand can be dry, soft, or wet and clinging together. Dry sand can be blown, creating delicate formations. When water is added it turns darker and begins to take on the quality of earth. It becomes firm and can easily be formed or shaped. It can represent the dark, mysterious depth of the shadow side; it can represent a surface on which the whole psyche is spread. Touching the sand can sometimes also evoke emotions about touch.

The sandtray is a safe place to explore the issues that the unconscious is ready to release. Within the boundaries of the sandtray the child makes a visual representation of the inner world.

The sandtray becomes a sacred space, a different reality from the everyday world and everyday concerns.

To support this, the sandtray and the symbols are not treated as everyday toys, but dedicated to exploration of the inner world. The sandplay equipment is set up specifically for inner work – this makes it different from the sandpit at school, the bath at home, or the toy box under a child's bed. All these can provide space for the unconscious to work out some of its issues, but the dedication of the sandplay to inner work gives the unconscious security, permission and encouragement to open up.

What has been unknown, out of sight, can become clear as children arrange the symbols. Through the symbols they can explore their psyche, their ego, even touch their essence. What was inside can be externalised, brought to consciousness for exploration.

The human search for wholeness has always drawn on myths. Myths link us to the archetypes, to the collective unconscious. Sandplay allows us, and the children we work with, to discover and develop personal myths. What has been abstract becomes more concrete. Then there can be a link-up between personal healing and the collective unconscious. A transformation, a healing, can take place, and this might manifest at a later time in another sandplay.

The child's unconscious only presents what the child is ready to deal with. The facilitator respects this fact, and never pushes the child, expresses their own conclusions or interprets.

The facilitator is a co-journeyer, one who supports the child's wish to explore. The facilitator must already be clear about their own personal need for inner work, for journeying, so that there is no projection on to the child. Support for the child will be to feel the inner work as an exciting journey rather than just problem solving.

As has been said, interpretation is not part of our method. The vital role of the facilitator is to support the emergence of meaning from within the child. The effectiveness of the sandplay does not depend on the facilitator's or child's intellectual understanding of the process, although many clear insights will be evident.

The facilitator directs the child to draw or journal and share the learnings at the end of the session, perhaps drawing out any particular implications for their current life. Provision of a drink and perhaps a small snack at the completion of the session is a normal part of the facilitator's role.

The facilitator is responsible for creating a supportive environment. The work room must be clean and orderly. The symbols on the shelves must be presented well, grouped in themes. Water should be available, either in a sprayer to wet the sand, or in a jug to create rivers, lakes and ponds.

The sandplay method

Sandplay is used for:
- the exploration and resolution of a specific crisis
- dealing with the surfacing or triggering of an old hurt
- acting out what is not acceptable in real life
- providing an overview of the present direction of the inner growth
- giving space to find the best in themselves, to allow self-esteem
- gathering data about the child's unconscious self-image
- giving space for integration of disowned aspects/energies
- connecting children to their personal mythology, their personal symbols, their own fairy-tale world of hope
- providing a language for expression of the inner feelings, hopes, divisions, urges
- (for those too threatened by the counselling process) verbalising real feelings. They can begin simply by playing!
- (for those who are used to operating on a thinking level) helping to break through to the intuitive and feeling levels.

Sandplay equipment

The tray
- The height should be suitable for sitting or standing at. The tray should be on a stand with castors, or be light and mobile.
- The ideal size is one that enables the child to take in the whole tray without having to move the head or eyes, that fits into their field of vision. Suggested size: 75 cm × 55 cm × 15 cm (outside measurements).
- Do not use particle board, as it will swell if it gets wet.
- Use Estapol or sealer along the inside so that the water does not seep through.
- Paint the bottom blue to represent water.
- Three-quarters fill with sand.

The shelves
Shelves should not be too high – children must be able to see all the symbols.

The symbols
Suggested categories of symbols are:

mystical	religious	the sea
mechanical	buildings	precious stones
household	food	rocks
snakes	horrible things	animals, wild
animals, domestic	people – adults	people – children, babies
nature	fighting	bridges
birds	jewels	containers
flowers	trees	transport

Jug and sprayer
For wetting the sand.

Small brush
For dusting the sand from objects before returning them to the shelves.

Presenting the process

Allow for progression, change, freedom, absorption into the child's own world.

There are *no rules* for the child, apart from respect for the materials, and the child is always right in their choices and arrangements.

The facilitator, although vital to the process, is neutral.

According to the perceived needs for the counselling session and the facilitator's intentions, different suggestions could be given for beginning the sandplay; for example:

Make a picture or story:
- about your life
- about you when you were little
- about what is going to happen
- about yesterday
- about all the people you know
- about a pretend story with you in it
- with all your favourite things in it
- with all the most frightening things

Meeting the sand
The child sits or stands in front of the sandtray, eyes closed. They then bring their hands slowly into contact with the sand. Ask them to share any memories, talk about how it feels. Encourage them to move their hands – see what they want to do. Ask if there is a story that goes with the hands meeting the sand.

Mixing the sand
For those hesitant or new to sandplay, pour some water over the dry sand and ask them to mix it in. The movement will soon engage their interest, ready for the next stages.

Forming the sand
The child allows the hands to make shapes and formations. If necessary, the child may spray or pour water in to hold the sand in shapes.

Is the formation abstract? an expression of feelings? an actual scene? a story?

The child may talk about what they are doing *or* be silent – and talk after; *or* they may choose not to talk at all. This must be accepted. The inner transformation can take place even if you do not know what is going on.

Adding symbols
Invite the child to choose objects to add to the tray.

Advice for facilitators

- Refer to the pro forma 'Sandplay Report' (page 198).
- Momentarily drop all that is known about the child.
- *Be* with the child – physically and mentally, mostly silently.
- Watch the choice of objects and the way they are chosen:
  – Is there any charge (strong attraction or repulsion)?
  – Do they think about the choice or grab it immediately?
- Be aware of the development of the story.
- Bring a presence, a focus that will support the child's acting out of the story and help their own focusing.
- Judge when the story is finished: feel the energy change. Some do not want to stop; others might stop suddenly as an avoidance.
- Have the story told, allowing any changes or developments in the story.
- Try to recognise the symbolic level but *never interpret*, never tell the child what it is all about, even if it seems very clear to you. The child's realisations and connections are of no lasting use unless they come from within.
- Notice any apparent inconsistencies and jot down questions for later.

Observing the process

- As all symbols used represent energies within the child, see what qualities of the item chosen relate to the child.
- Consider the meanings of the symbols:
  – what they symbolise to you
  – what they might mean to the child
  – what their traditional, collective meanings are
  – what the child says about the items
- Watch the placement of the objects:
  – what is in the middle?
  – what is at the edges?
  – what dominates?
  – what items are separated?
  – what is buried?
  – what is in water?
  – what is on the hills?
  – what is under attack?
- Note if the child works from only one side of the tray, or moves around.
- Sense the child's energy, especially the bodily force while the choosing is going on.
- Watch the way the child moves, the force with which the items are placed in the sand; for example, brutally. Is the energy aggressive? lethargic? flowing? hesitant? Are you being checked for approval?

- Watch the child's facial expressions, body posture, energy/mood changes as the story unfolds and feelings begin to emerge.
- While watching, keep track of your own personal reactions and assumptions, to avoid projecting your own story on to the child's work.
- Themes can emerge that give clear directions for future work and reveal special care needs. Some typical themes to watch for:
  - nourishment
  - relationship
  - family disintegration
  - personal disintegration
  - loneliness, separation
  - recognition of treasure
  - self-worth
  - death, fear of death, death of the old way
  - order and well-being
  - masculinity/femininity
  - power

Supporting integration

- Ask the child to tell the story. Some may not wish to, and this should be respected.
- Gently probe a little deeper; for example:
  - 'I wonder where he came from?'
  - 'I wonder if they like each other?'
  - 'I wonder what that frog is croaking about?', etc.
- Encourage expression of:
  - movement; for example 'Show me how that moves.'
  - sound; for example 'I wonder what sound that would make?'
  - emotions
- If emotions have been triggered by the process, go with them, encourage full expression through mirroring the feelings. Then the sandplay is really finished and has done its work!
- Never make a connection for the child. Always lead indirectly until there is realisation for the child.
- Relate the qualities of symbols to the child's own body.
  - 'Where does this powerful black horse live inside you?'
  - 'Where can you feel his power?'

Simple Gestalt work with sandplay figures

If you notice a particular attraction or repulsion for one of the figures in the sandtray, or you suspect a deep symbolic meaning in a figure that seems to be ignored, you can deepen exploration with this short process. Gestalting can also be used if there are only sand formations and no figures have been used.

The world of symbols

Gestalt exercise with sandplay figures

Messages from the sandplay

Suitable for children aged 6 years and over.

1 Have the child sit in front of the sandtray. Leave the figure where it is.

2 *What do you like about this figure?*

3 *Now, I want you to become this figure for a little while. Feel yourself as it. Take a breath, and let your body change to take the shape of the figure.*
  - *What is it like?*
  - *Tell me what you feel like.*
  - *Describe yourself: how big? how little? colours? shapes? energy?*
  - *What do you want to do? What sound do you want to make?*
  - *Take another big breath. How do you move? Do you have a message for . . . ?*

Often the figure will symbolise some aspect of power or energy that the child has split from. By becoming it, they can become more themselves, own the power.

Concluding sandplay

- Reinforce the energies:
  'You have lots of strength!'
  'Part of you *is* a dragon! (or king, princess, army etc.)'
- Encourage the child to let go the past, affirm the *now* and recognise hopes for the future.
- Recommend certain constructive actions, games, tasks.

Emotional release for children

Sandplay report

Date: **10·11·98** Facilitator: **Patrica Rowan**
Child's name: **Joseph Niewenhuys** Age: **8 yrs**

Presenting problem: **For no apparent reason Joseph is unable to read out aloud in class now. He has been able up until now. He is also going to his room and curling up and 'wingeing' when his brothers get rough with him.**

Process initiated by: **His mother**

Pre-assessment: **Joseph seems very withdrawn – insulated.**
  body reading: **Shoulders hunched forward as though protecting.**
  reported body sensations: **There may be some – he is not aware or can't tell.**
  emotional state: **Controlled fear.**

Opening directions to child: **To play in the sandpit for a while. He might want to make hills or mountains or have it all flat. Showed him the blue bottom of the box for water. When he gets the sand how he wants it, tell me. I then invited him to look at all the symbols to see what ones he'd like to put in the picture in his box.**

Choice of objects: **A fawn, crocodile, flamingo and dinosaur, trees, a bridge.**

While choosing: body energy, posture, attitude, etc. **Became more involved, even excited**

During sandplay: expressions – facial, posture, emotional: **Posture straightened up – facial expressions were varied and congruent with his identification with the looks of the various symbols. His main evident emotion was excitement.**

Main themes noted: **Soft and strong as in fawn and crocodile, and flamingo and crocodile.**

Significant spatial relationships in sandtray: **The two opposites were close to each other and in both cases the soft was on one side of the river and the strong on the other.**

Child's insights: **Initially I didn't ask.**

The world of symbols

Facilitator's insights and observations:
Joseph was relating to the soft more than to the strong.
story: _____

unconscious meanings: **N/A**
body movements and sounds: **N/A**
emotional expressions: **N/A**

Integration processes used:
- ☑ Gestalting
- ☐ drawings
- ☐ body stencils
- ☑ dance, movement, sounding
- ☐ eye-to-eye-processing
- ☐ dialoguing with parts of self
- ☐ dreamwork

the process: We played at being the crocodile and faun, dinosaur and flamingo. At first Joseph was reticent about being the crocodile and dinosaur. Gradually he entered into it. When he was in the midst of wanting to devour the faun I asked, "Who would Joseph like to eat at home?" "My little brother," he answered. I said, "Instead of eating him what could you say from the crocodile place?" "Don't do that" he said.

Outcome: His strong was OK now. His withdrawn state had gone. He had finished work and was ready to go play.

Follow-up recommendations: _____
- stories: _____
- visualisations: _____
- games and dance: _____
- massage: _____
- dreams: _____

Special care recommended: Whenever he begins to withdraw Mum could invite the crocodile or dinosaur out to speak.

Child's comments at completions: I feel good.

Facilitator's evaluation: He has let himself be strong — needs support.
- body posture: More open
- energy state: Alive
- emotional state: Clear

Endings

When the sandplay story or picture is complete, consider:
- Has the action led to integration?
- Has the play been complete in itself?
- Does it require any analysis, extension or discussion?

Resolution may have taken place at an unconscious level and nothing more may be required.

Talk about what the child sees in the objects; for example:
- the qualities or traits of the objects or characters
- groupings and arrangements of objects
- relationships between the objects

Encourage the child to:
- speak to each object in the sandplay, especially if they are animate objects (animals, people)
- become each object and answer back as the object
- create a dialogue between the objects, developing a story line, possibly including themselves

Recording and analysis

- If appropriate, write down the child's stories for them to keep, or have them write it down. Some may want to keep it and illustrate it, later, alone.
- Complete the details on the 'Sandplay Report' (see page 198) for yourself.
- Take Polaroid photos of the sandtray and give one to the child to keep.
- Keep a reference file of photos and reports to compare past sandplays, particularly themes and recurring symbols.

Dismantling the sandplay

Children (and adults) never take down their own sandplay, but are told that this will be done. To do so would be to dismantle a part of the psyche. It is preferable to leave the final picture intact in the new structure of energies felt within.

Linking activities

Some of the following activities may be considered if conflicts persist. Depending on the child's attention span and interest, they can be done immediately after a sandplay or on another day.
- Have children explore similar themes through fairy tales.
- Have children read or tell their stories to others and show drawings. This can deepen the imprint of the symbols that have arisen from their own imagination (unconscious).
- Have children act out or dance the story, or actions of the main symbols.
- Link body outlines to the story; for example:
  - 'Where inside you is this battle?'
  - 'Is there a treasure inside you? Where?'
- Use visualisations and role-playing (as a hero from a known adventure) to deepen the feelings of worth.

The focused method

The focused method is for children with either very scattered attention or a very short attention span. Too wide a choice, instead of giving freedom, increases the scattering of attention, and is sometimes threatening.
- Close blinds and doors to eliminate any outside disturbances.
- Offer child distinct parts of the symbol shelf to choose from or direct them to only one shelf at a time.
- The child selects the symbols and then sits at the tray.
- From this settled position the child arranges the figures or plays with them.
- Encourage the child to stay on the chair and keep the focus on the tray.
- Keep refocusing attention and restating the initial direction.

Frequent reviews of appropriate sandplay room behaviour will also give children security. For example, remind children to treat the figures with care and to remember why they are doing the inner work.

The directed method

Sandplay is usually play, with very little direction from the facilitator. However, at times you may use it as a tool in order to help a child face an issue or open to positive parts of themselves. Sometimes you will play around with a theme or a task or a story that becomes the starting point. You are pointing the psyche in a certain direction. The sandplay exercises which follow (see pages 136–137) are directed sandplays. They are best used after the child has already established the basic method.

Sandplay with different age groups

While we can never expect specific outcomes, nor want to limit a child, we do recognise several broad categories that relate to children's ages and development.

2–5 years
- Child often uses no words.
- Child seems lost in the action.
- There is a lot of action.
- Child is often happy to play with sand alone, without symbols.
- Child often finishes suddenly.

6–9 years
- Child will make stories with symbols.
- Child will sometimes verbalise the story and invite the facilitator to respond. (Mirror, rather than agree or disagree. See page 204.)
- The stories will come from the unconscious and so will deal with situations in symbolic form.
- Child will not easily make conscious connections between the inner and outer life.

10–13 years
- All of the above points may apply for this age group.

Emotional release for children

- Child may want to take great care and spend a lot of time creating the picture, to get it exactly as they want it.
- Child is more likely to want to release emotional energy in the play; for example, roughly burying a symbol which represents an authority in their life.
- Child may want to play out a whole scenario from their life and to make it come out right.
- Sometimes, when emotions are raw and strong, a neat, tidy, beautiful sandplay will be made. The child cannot yet allow the raw, strong part of themselves to come to the fore.
- The child will sometimes volunteer the connection with their inner life at the end of the sandplay.

From 14 years

- From this age upwards the sandplay will be much the same as any adult would make.
- There could be an emphasis on the new interest in sexuality.
- There could be themes of separation, power, futurism, relationship.

Sandplay exercise

Journey to the new world

Suitable for children aged 8 to 16 years.

Prepare sandtray(s). Have drawing materials ready. For group work, children work in pairs.

The aim of this exercise is to support children in claiming inner treasure, to gain self-esteem.

1. *Visualise yourself as an explorer, crossing the ocean back in the days when the maps of the world were not finished. People still believed there might be an edge to the world and explorers could fall off if they went too far. But you are brave. You are leading your crew on this search for treasure in the new world.*

2. Children go to sandtrays and form the landscape of the new world.

3. Children go to sandplay figure shelves. They select symbols for the treasures that they will discover in the new world.

4. The symbols are arranged by the explorer child in, on or under, the landscape of the new world. Then one by one the explorer finds them.

5. Children talk with you or their partner about each of the treasures – what they mean to the child, why they are treasures, what their main qualities are.

6. You, or the child, can select the three most important treasures to Gestalt. (See page 140 for Gestalt method.)

7. The child will draw the three treasures and write briefly what they learned about the new world inside them.

The world of symbols

Sandplay and visualisation exercise

Inner treasure

Suitable as a group exercise for children aged from 8 to 16 years.

Bury an assortment of beautiful items (e.g. crystals) in the sandtray. Have ready cushions, journals, writing materials.

1 *We are going to take a special journey – crossing over water to a deserted island. On that island, one special treasure is waiting to be discovered by you.*

2 Invite the group to make a large boat with cushions.
Imagine sailing on the ocean . . . boat is rocking gently . . . excited about discovering this treasure . . . suddenly the waves get bigger . . . clouds become dark . . . rain starts to pour . . . the wind howls . . . the boat is being tossed from side to side . . . thunder . . . lightning. You want to go back home, but something in you wants to keep on going . . . suddenly the rain stops . . . clouds drift away . . . sun comes out and starts to dry you . . . water becomes still and the boat drifts ashore to an island. You see the sand dunes (sandtray) where the treasure is buried. One special treasure is waiting for you. Find your treasure.

3 *When each person has found their treasure, find a partner, sit together, close your eyes and hold the treasure in your hands. Let yourself become the treasure.* (See page 140 for Gestalt method.)

4 *What is one special quality about you? Share with your partner.*

5 *This special quality or treasure is always in you. Write about it in your journal and draw the treasure.*

Sandplay exercise

Family portraits

Suitable for children aged 8 to 18 years.

A simple process to begin exploration about family relationships.

1 *Make four pictures in the sand about your family.*
2 *Set out the tray like this, marking dividing lines in the sand:*

4 Future	3 Present
1 When a baby	2 When a small child

Child stands at section 1 to begin with.

3 Child selects sandplay objects to make four pictures about each period of their life, beginning with 'When a baby'.

4 Encourage child to talk about each picture, either while it is being created, or after.

5 Ask the child to note any similarities and differences, and talk about these.

Working with the whole child through sandplay

Report from Patricia Nolan

A mother began working through the Gestalt process, to bring more clarity and aliveness to her life. Soon after beginning her journey she was able to practise her new skills in moments of fear, blockage of her life. She could see her children more clearly and was able to recognise life and non-life.

One of her sons, whom we will call Andrew, was displaying quite a lot of fear at school. He couldn't read aloud in class and would sometimes be unable to perform other tasks which teacher and parents knew he had done already. Here was a 7-year-old child whose academic life and physical movement was being affected by an underlying fear.

This is an approach taken during a counselling session. It is one which produced signs of improvement throughout Andrew's psyche.

While Mum had a cup of tea, I showed Andrew the sandplay tray and all the small figurines. He was excited and listened well to my directions:

'First of all you can make the sand how you want it. You can have it all very flat or you can make it bumpy. You can make rivers, you can have hills or you can have a seashore with the sea.

'Then you can look along the shelves. See on the top one there are . . . (I mentioned the category) and on the next shelf there are . . . (We went along each shelf.) You can choose ten items after you have fixed the sand how you want it. Then place the ten items in the box how you want them.'

He worked quite quickly and then joined Mum and me. We had a chance then for him to tell me a little about his brothers and sisters. An older brother who is 9 is his preferred companion and a younger brother and sister, 5 and 3, are loved, yet a bit of a bother. 'They do quiet things.'

Returning to the sandtray we saw a huge angry dinosaur towering over a beautiful deer. A river divided the box in half and a fierce alligator lay in the river. The other objects, namely turtles, flamingos and a monkey, seemed to be in juxtaposition with the alligator and dinosaur. Power and strength were alongside fear and gentleness.

I asked which piece he liked best and he chose the deer. I asked what was special about it and he readily volunteered, as he stroked it, 'It's gentle.'

'How do you think this gentle part feels about the dinosaur?' I asked. Andrew quickly shifted the deer to the other side of the river and said, 'That feels better.' A similar sequence happened around the alligator and the turtles.

By this time, Andrew was open to the process and I felt that he would be able to role-play the alligator/dinosaur and be the deer/turtle. Through this he could express some of these energies which live within him – and are on the way to consciousness.

I suggested, 'How about we play at being the alligator and the turtle?'

'Yes,' he replied. 'Mum can be the flamingo.'

So Mum joined in and the alligator (Andrew) roared and snapped and we were frightened turtles and flamingos. Then we changed roles and Andrew, the turtle, hid and trembled.

'Now, how about you be the dinosaur, Andrew?'

He began clawing and punching at me, the deer.

'Can you tell me why you want to hurt me?' I cried.

> *The world of symbols*

> 'You get on my nerves,' said Andrew, the dinosaur, as he continued to punch the pillow I held.
> 'And who in Andrew's family gets on his nerves?' I asked.
> 'Willy!' he cried (younger brother).
> 'Could Andrew the dinosaur tell Willy that, and not punch him?' I asked.
> *'You get on my nerves, Willy,'* said Dinosaur in a big voice.
> 'How does that feel?' I asked.
> 'Good,' Andrew replied.
> We ended the session and Andrew was off to play. Later, he wanted to visit the duck pond outside. It was an excited energy that suggested this, and then just as quickly fear came and stopped him.
> I asked, 'Who could help you to go on your own?'
> 'Alligator,' he said and ran off happily.
> Two months later, Andrew was still using his alligator energy and the fearful wimpy energy had not shown itself.

Gestalt work

Gestalt psychology was developed by Dr Fritz Perls and others in the USA during the 1960s and 70s. The principles of Gestalt psychology that we find most useful in working with children are:

- An unresolved feeling, memory, attitude, energy, trait or quality (aspect) of the child which stands out is in the *foreground* of their unconscious.
- Working with that aspect to bring about release, resolution and integration means that it recedes into the psychological *background*.
- Aspects which are prominent in the foreground, though not recognised, are easily *projected* on to suitable symbols, objects or people; for example, for a teenage boy, a need to own strength and manliness might be projected on to a movie or sports star, such as Arnold Schwarzenegger or Michael Jordan.

A simple way to integrate or recognise the aspect is to *role-play* it.

Totally becoming the symbol, person or thing of the projection, brings new awareness and integration. Hence, to really understand dreams, fantasies, crushes, repulsions, fixations or attractions, get the child to become the thing or the person.

The qualities the child (unconsciously at first) is attracted to or repulsed by are actually within the child.

To effectively Gestalt the symbol, the child needs to:
- be relaxed
- have their awareness focused in their body
- allow movement, sound, expression

Integrating symbols

Having found a symbol, from dreams, fantasies, from nature or sandplay work, use this exercise to re-own the full meaning and energy.

Basic Gestalt exercise

I am ...

Suitable for children aged 8 years and over.

In group work, work in pairs.

1 To the child who is working first, you say:
 Let yourself totally become the symbol. Feel your body changing; change your posture if it helps. Take some full breaths and feel how it is to be this symbol.

2 The support child asks the following questions slowly, giving their partner time to feel the answers. The child working first answers these questions as the symbol would.
 - *What are you? Begin your answer with 'I am ...'*
 - *What do you look like? Begin your answer with 'I am ...'*
 - *Feel inside. What are you made of? What is inside you?*
 - *Do you have a particular sound or movement? If so, demonstrate it.*
 - *Do you have a particular intention?*
 - *Do you have a special function? What are you for?*
 - *Do you have a message for ..., or anything you would like to say to him/her?*

 The support child writes down the message.

3 Pairs swap over when they are ready.

Gestalt exercise

My beauty revealed

Suitable as an individual or group exercise for children aged 8 years and over.

Have ready drawing books and crayons.

This exercise is most successful when there is a beautiful garden. We use it with children who believe an old imprint of low self-esteem.

1 *Go outside. Look around in all directions. Look up and down the garden.*

2 *What stands out as the most beautiful plant? What is the part of the garden that you like best?*

3 *Draw it carefully. Then come inside.*

The world of symbols

> 4 *In pairs (if a group), Gestalt what you have drawn. Begin: 'I am a . . .' (rose, ivy, vine, pine tree, etc.)*
> *Describe yourself, slowly.*
>
> 5 *Breathe deeply as you describe yourself. Feel the energy of being this plant that you have drawn.*
>
> 6 *Is there a special message for you (the person) from you (the plant)?*
>
> 7 Refer to the basic Gestalt questions on page 140 to extend the exploration with this exercise. It is good to draw out any parallels the child may feel between the life of the plant and their own life.
>
> 8 The fruit of a complete Gestalt is the experience of a new inner state *now*. So encourage the child to identify and experience this new state.

A group exercise for older children

What do they think of me?

Suitable as a small group (four to six children) exercise for children aged 12 years and over.

Have ready sandplay symbols, journals and writing materials.

The aim of this exercise is to enhance group interaction and self-image. It is only suitable for groups that have been together for some time. You will need to take care that the differences between image, or what others see, and what is really inside a child are clearly drawn out.

1 Children sit in a circle and silently look at each other for a minute.

2 Then they go to the sandplay shelves and choose a figure that in some way makes them think of each person in the group – including themselves.

3 They come back to the circle and place the figures on the floor in front of them.

4 Each child takes a turn at trying to guess which figures the other children have chosen for them. It is good if they can say why they think it was chosen.

5 Then each child tells them the actual one they chose and also tells why, if they can.

6 Each child collects the figures that were chosen for them and arranges them either in the sandtray, or in a large circle drawn on a blank page in front of them.

7 They then journal or talk about: 'What others see in me, and what is really there.'

Dreamwork

The two fundamental points in dealing with dreams are these: first, the dream should be treated as fact, about which one must make no previous assumption, except that it somehow makes sense; and second, the dream is a specific expression of the unconscious. (C G Jung, *Man and His Symbols*, Dell Publishing, 1968.)

Another consideration we face when working dreams is, in Jung's words, 'Consciousness naturally resists anything that is unconscious or unknown.'

When a child brings a dream to an ERC session, hold the above within. These fundamentals must become innate. You don't think of them as you work, yet you are aware of:
- recognising the resistance from the conscious level
- giving the feeling that you don't know what the message is, and yet it is good and important, and 'Yes' it can be discovered.

Dreams open us to the content of the unconscious. Within this content are various confluences, the centres of which can be the wounded parts, or complexes, repressed emotional material, positive undeveloped abilities, directive energies and more... When working a dream we try to help the child stay very true to the dream. Should a child begin releasing and following a theme for which the dream is only a starting point, we can allow the process of this and at the same time know we will at a later time come back to the dream. We prefer to use other processes to access these 'tender spots of the psyche'. Dreams have special significance and specific functions of their own.

Exploring dreams

The first step in exploring dreams is to want to dream, and to remember them, especially the 'big' dreams. Every now and then, when children are going through a significant growth period or big outer changes in their life, they might have a big dream. These are usually dreamed in their deepest sleep. The other dreams, however, are important too, and hold great richness for day-to-day living.

Children and adults can develop the habit of asking themselves, 'Have I dreamed?' as soon as they wake. Parents can help children by asking at breakfast time, 'Did you dream?'

The second task is to write the dream down. Children may need you to do this for them. The writing is a way of making sure they remember. It also helps the child to begin to open to the message. As you write, look for symbolic language; for example, 'The bear was swallowed.' The word 'swallowed' might have a charge. In writing for a child, a parent could ask, 'Did that feel a bit scary?'

The world of symbols

Drawing or painting the dream image is also a way of letting the dream speak. While drawing or painting the dreamer is staying close to the unconscious, and perhaps the feelings will be felt or some clues to the message will emerge.

Having someone to listen to the telling of the dream is also helpful. As the telling proceeds the dreamer might hear words, phrases, descriptions of aspects of themselves that strike chords of recognition. A child might get quite excited or sad or simply experience a connection rather than notice. The energy of the dream will be activated and this conscious expression is part of the resolution and integration. When this happens there is a shift of energy within the body and there is a knowing.

Gestalting the dream is the principal tool to use. In the writing of the dream it is useful to make a note of every symbol, animate and inanimate. Fritz Perls says that the most important dream symbol to Gestalt is the missing one; for example, the missing steps in a staircase.

- Begin with the symbol that holds the most charge for the child.
- Ask the child to become this image.
- Have the child use breath and movement and sound.
- Let the symbol describe itself.
- Find a place in the body where the symbol resides, from where it can speak.
- Keep checking: 'and . . . (name of child) is listening to you, river, snake, tree etc.?'

When there is an energy connection between what is being said and the person receiving the message there will be relief or relaxation or free-flowing life. Work every symbol if time permits.

Sometimes if there appear to be contentious symbols in opposition to each other the child can be encouraged to make up a dialogue between them, changing roles until resolution is achieved. Often, if the child is in the dream the main symbol can dialogue with him or her as in the dream.

Finally, when the message of the dream has been received, and the child is in a completion state, it can be good to let the new be integrated into the body through dance.

Dance is also an avenue for exploration. The Gestalt can happen by choosing the three most significant symbols, and by dancing each one separately, until the child is expressing the qualities, the truth the symbol offers. The child can then dance each one, allowing them to flow one into the other so that the dance becomes a whole unit. The child does this dance several times until the overall message is received.

Some dreams do not need to be worked. They actually achieve the energy shift and insight as they occur. Children (or adults) who don't find the expression of anger easy in their waking life can break through this fear in dream, and shout or kick and be very free in their expression. The next morning the whole nervous and muscular systems will feel relaxed, and there is a gladness or some equivalent feeling state. We are not saying that the dream holds only the energy shift or the intellectual insight on waking. More could be gleaned by working the dream, yet sometimes the gleaning could be pushing. Why not enjoy the gift of the new of that morning?

If the underlying message of a dream that doesn't need to be worked is important, it will recur. Children often have recurring dreams. The most common of these are to do with fear:

- nightmares – being chased by monsters, big adults or in some way being threatened;
- falling dreams – feeling a failure or getting 'down to earth' could stimulate these dreams;
- flying dreams – these are mostly indications that life is too much and there is a desire to get relief by getting up out of the mess.

In the early phases of a child's life it is wonderful if they can be helped to find meaning for some of the big problem feelings they might have. Their dream is often this helper. The dream when Gestalted can release emotions and even give them certainty about their goodness.

Dreamwork exercise

Questions for my dream

Suitable for children aged 8 years and over.

The following questions are a starting point to connect the children to the precious energy. Let the questions grow, change, enlarge.

1 *Tell me your dream, or the part you remember.* You may have to question them further to extend their remembering.

2 *Which part of the dream do you:*
   - *like best?*
   - *hate most?*
   - *find most frightening?*

3 *Which thing do you remember most clearly?* Listen for the part with the most energy, hear it in the voice.

4 *I want you to become that thing. Close your eyes, take a big breath and let it out again. Start saying 'I am a . . .' and tell me:*
   - *what you look like*
   - *what colour, shape, size you are*
   - *what you are made of*
   - *what is inside you* (Each time they must say: 'I am . . .')

   Remember you are the thing. Have you any special feelings? What are you for? What are you doing?

5 Allow expansion of the dream/story. It may go into another story.

6 Allow movement and acting out of the energies:
   - *What do you really want to do?*
   - *Where do you really want to be?*
   - *What do you really want to say?*

7 Allow emotions and encourage the breath.
   What is the message of your dream?

8 Open to a clear learning and celebrate!

Samples of children's dreams

A 6-year-old boy began to have nightmares. His mother or father would go to him and all he would know was that he was alone and frightened. These dreams recurred every time there was significant friction between his parents. They had considered separating, but not told the child about their feelings. It was at times when this was likely to happen that the nightmare came back. He was knowing something true at an unconscious level, and was terrified of being left alone.

A 9-year-old girl awoke sobbing. Her father came to her and held her while she sobbed. It seemed that in her dream some terrible thing had happened to her. When she came through this release she explained that in her dream her mother had trodden on her pet grasshopper. The tenderness of this child's psyche was devastated. Perhaps her mother had been harsh, or 'trodden' on her the day before.

Both of these children were fortunate to have parents who could, as it were, hold the child's psyche safely, while they experienced themselves in these difficult times. Many parents would try to cheer the child up, tell them that the events of the dream were not true; 'It's only a dream!' This approach cheats the child of the growth, the treasure.

Dreams can be a source of guidance

A case story from Patricia Nolan

A young girl (14 years old) ran away from home, was picked up by police and taken to a children's home until some resolution for her dilemma could be worked out. She had set out initially to find an uncle who had been a happy part of her early life. Unfortunately he had died and when she learned this she was devastated. Her questions were: 'Where can I go? What can I do?' I was asked to work with her. She had had several dreams which we began to work. Attending to the dreams seemed to please her unconscious, and more dreams came. They were dreams to guide her.

Dream 1
She was swimming in the sea, along the waves. She was ready to get out – swam towards a jetty. When she went to climb up the pylons, they were covered in crawly, slimy animals. She swam towards shore – walked up the sand to the top of the sand dune and the world ended. She had to go back down to the jetty and sit and wait.

When we worked this dream she was delighted to find a part of herself directing her. This part was saying, 'You have to wait here.' Sitting on the jetty felt like waiting at the children's home.

Dream 2
She and a friend were hitchhiking. The first car came by and it was so full they couldn't fit the two girls in. The next car had suspicious-looking people in it and her friend said, 'Wait for the right ride.'

The message of this dream was repeating the earlier message. There were many other dreams all of which helped her to wait until she was able to move forward, guided from within.

Comments

This child was agitated, unsettled, her psyche was 'on the move'. When Patricia heard the first dream she felt dreamwork was the process to choose. The child's unconscious had already given a clear starting point.

Even though the child had to discover the meaning for herself, it seemed to be a simple, clear message. Every symbol in a dream is a part of the dreamer. So in Dream 1 some of the symbols Gestalted were:

- the ocean
- the sand dune
- the creepy, crawly animals
- the jetty
- the child

As this young woman became each symbol she was reclaiming a part of herself:

- the ocean: a strong, fluid, refreshing part of her
- the sand dune: a strong, warm, stable part of her
- the animals: the churning, 'don't know where we are going' part
- the jetty: solid, a place to see from, a place to wait on

Patricia needed to wait until the young woman had felt and heard all this and then ask: 'What do you think your inner world is telling you?' The answer was clear, she was excited: 'To wait.' She was able to connect with and hear her own inner guidance.

CHAPTER SEVEN

Moving forward on the inner journey

We have not even to risk the adventure alone,
for the heroes of all time have gone before us,
the labyrinth is thoroughly known.
We have only to follow the thread of the hero path.
Where we had thought to find an abomination, we shall find a god;
where we had thought to slay another, we shall slay ourselves;
where we had thought to travel outward, we shall come to the
centre of our own existence;
where we had thought to be alone, we shall be with all the world.

Joseph Campbell, *The Power of Myth*, ABC Radio Tape.

Exploring the unconscious

It is quite appropriate and healthy for children to be very outward-oriented. The task for all of us in our first 25 years or so is to establish ourselves in the world. Children move with varying ease into outer involvements with school, friends, hobbies, sport and leisure activities.

Children also easily enter into their inner world and, indeed, find comfort, solace and support there. Many children need support in today's world. Outer support is essential. They need to find their own inner support, which not only heals but also gives them the gift of experiencing themselves. To have a connection with 'Who I am' is a gift beyond price. This connection sets a child on a path in life that enables confident and free exploration.

It is with these two considerations in mind that we include this chapter on the inner journey. The work presented in this chapter comes from an understanding of the need for:

- Balance between inner and outer living. Outer living that is disconnected from the inner becomes empty and eventually burdensome.
- An awareness that each child has an unconscious world that is operative. Making friends with this large energy source within decreases fear and allows them to be in charge of life.
- A language that gives a child a way of talking about what is happening in the feeling world, dream world, imagery world, fantasy world.
- A conceptual framework within which a child can understand the dynamic interaction that occurs between the inner and outer living.
- An attitude of interest in the inner world so that the treasures, gifts, potential, fullness of a child can come to fruition.

Exploration exercise

Exploring the conscious and the unconscious

Suitable for children aged 6 to 12 years.

Have ready copies of the 'My Own Consciousness' diagram (see page 150); crayons, pencil or pen; soft music; lively dance music.

1. Give children a copy of the consciousness diagram and tell them it represents the outer boundary of themselves – their skins.

2. Ask them to close their eyes, take a big breath in and then let it out.

3. Invite them to remember five things they know about themselves (do this one at a time). This may need to be directed for younger children; for example:
   - *Name something you know about your age.*
   - *Name something you like to eat.*
   - *Name something you like to do, or don't like to do.*
   - *Name something you are good at.*

Moving forward on the inner journey

4 *Write the facts near the small section at the top of the diagram.*

5 Tell the children:
You are conscious of these facts about yourself. These words, 'are conscious of', mean 'know'.
Expand on this with them. Get them to say the word 'conscious'. They may like to tell you lots more that they are *conscious* of.

6 Now ask them to close their eyes again and take a big breath in and let it out. (Put on some soft music.) Ask them to watch inside their 'mind's eye' for a picture of a special animal or bird to come. Ask them to be sure to wait for it to come. (Turn music down and off.)

7 When the picture has shown itself they can tell you what it is. Notice the energy of surprise, excitement. (If a picture does not come, it is important to emphasise how wise the unconscious is and how true to themselves the children are. When they need to access this symbol from the unconscious or they are less afraid, it will happen for them.)

8 The children could be asked now to draw this picture in the lower portion of the diagram.

9 Help the children to discover which aspect of themselves their unconscious wants to show them. This could be done via a Gestalt process (see page 140) or simply by asking 'What is the most special thing about this animal?' This may need to be followed by other questions until they arrive at such statements as:
- It is strong.
- It can dive deep to hide, explore etc.
- It can fly high and be free and see.

10 Take children back to their diagram. Ask them to draw the animal or bird in the lower portion of the diagram. Now help them to acknowledge 'I have a part within me that is strong like this . . .' (tiger or lion or . . .)

11 Draw a line from the picture up to the conscious (upper) section of the diagram and write this statement in the top part.

12 At this point tell the children about the *unconscious* part of themselves – the part that they do not know, or are just beginning to know. Tell them that it is also called 'the shadow'. Help them to see how big it is compared with the *conscious* and that the more they get to know about themselves the more balanced a person they become.

13 Get them to make the top part of their diagram bigger and the bottom part smaller.

14 Recapitulate the concepts, the language and help them celebrate this learning about themselves.

15 Complete this exercise by putting on some stronger, livelier music, and invite the children to dance the energy of their animal – to feel the 'strong' or the 'free' or the 'fearless' etc. in their bodies. This truly helps this awareness of themselves to stay in consciousness.

To consolidate the child's learning and experience, the above process could be repeated many times using different visual imagery.

Emotional release for children

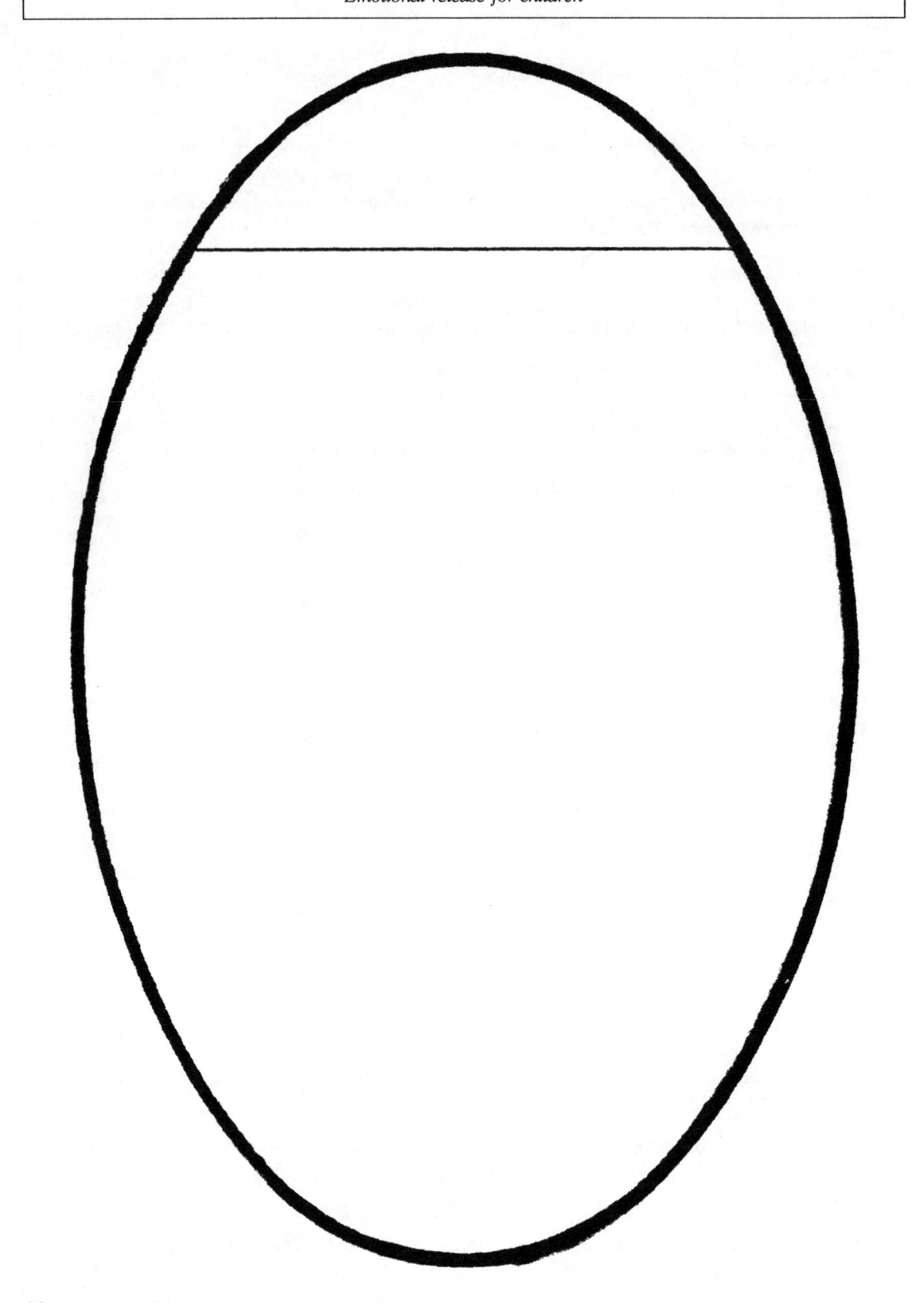

My own consciousness
This diagram can be enlarged and used by children over and over, as they discover more about their unconscious. It can then be used as a record of the accumulation of reclaimed parts of themselves.

Moving forward on the inner journey

Coming to wholeness exercise

Receiving a gift from the unconscious

Suitable for children aged 6 to 12 years.

Have ready the diagram 'My Own Consciousness' (see page 150) with the conscious and unconscious marked; crayons, pen or pencil; some alive, yet soft music.

1. Having done the preceding exercise, ask the children to change the line on this new diagram to indicate they are beginning this next exercise from a more balanced place in themselves.

2. Ask the children to:
   - draw an arrow out from 'My Conscious Mind'
   - write near the arrow some things they know about themselves – that they are *conscious* of

3. Tell the children you are going to help them find one treasure, a beautiful part of themselves, that is hidden in the *unconscious* – the *shadow* part.

4. Ask them to:
   - close their eyes
   - take big breaths, in and out, to help them relax
   - begin, now, to look inside themselves
   - see themselves in a beautiful jewellery shop
   - see themselves being attracted to a magnificent jewel or object – out of all the wondrous things in the shop that they could have, this is the only one they want
   - take time to see it very clearly
   - find a place inside their body where this beautiful object lives – yes, it is alive and inside
   - let it speak and tell about itself – it might say things like:
     - I am your ... (ruby, lapis, gold, silver)
     - I am ... (keep letting it describe itself until the words feel really true inside). The words might be like these:
       solid
       strong
       precious
       sparkling
   - colour in a small area in the unconscious part of the diagram, making it the same colour as the jewel/object chosen and adding a line up to 'My Conscious Mind' to indicate that this gift is now recognised and felt and owned

Before concluding this exercise it is important to recapitulate, using the terms 'conscious' and 'unconscious' in reference to the diagram and to the inner world of the children. It is also important to help the children to integrate their new knowledge of themselves. Each one could tell about their jewel – where it lives in them, what quality it has.

Visualisation work

Visualisation work is active use of the imagination or unconscious. It can be directed, given boundaries, or free form. No matter which method is used it can reveal the true inner state of the psyche. Most visualisations lead children on a journey that brings them to a threshold, a place of familiar markings – a natural place that is the doorway into the realm of their own unconscious. The journey part of visualisations prepares a clear space in their psyche for the unconscious (or imagination) to reveal its contents. We have the children explore beyond the threshold in their own imagination.

Threshold journeys are ideal for use with groups. They help the child awaken to inner wonders, allow them to speak the discoveries as they find them, to a partner who simply listens. This helps them stay in touch with the journey. Sometimes they could draw during the journey, but usually lying down with eyes closed assists them to enter it more deeply. Quiet music can set the mood.

Visualisation often uses images from children's sandplay, dreams, favourite fairy tales and universal symbols, including the energy of popular heroes from movies and TV. Visualisations explore themes of conquest, discovery of inner treasure, inner stillness, resolution of conflicts, defeat, family dynamics, etc.

Study of drawings done after visualisation trips will reveal much of what is happening in the children's inner worlds.

If there is a difficult conflict in the unconscious, a supported, but free-form visualisation will present symbols that express the conflict. Working with the symbols is a manageable way of approaching the core conflict.

For very active or disturbed children, exercises that alternate tensing and relaxing the body, such as bioenergetics, will be a necessary preliminary to being able to be still enough to close the eyes and allow inner focus.

Visualisation exercise

The gift from a wise part of me

Ideal for completion of a period of group work with children 10 years and over.

Have ready gentle, rhythmic music, sandplay symbols, drawing books and crayons.

1. After some dancing or movement, children sit or lie down and close their eyes.

Part one: The special place

2. *You are going on an adventure. Imagine it, see it in your mind. You are walking along a path to a very special, sacred place. What is it like on this path? How is it, not knowing about the place you are going to?*

Moving forward on the inner journey

You are coming towards the end of the path now. You can begin to see the special place. You are moving closer to it. See it more clearly now.

It could be familiar to you or a place you have never seen before. See what is there, see the surroundings. Is it near the beach? in the forest? in the outback? in the desert? in a rainforest? on a mountain? Let your mind make up the place.

It is a very safe place, a place that makes you happy to be there. Find a spot to sit in this place. This will be your own special spot.

Now, in this place lives a very wise person. In your mind, look up and see this wise person nearby. This wise person will be your friend.

Look carefully. What does this wise person look like? What is this person wearing? How does it feel to be with them? Is he/she near to you now? or far off? sitting? standing? moving?

Now, you didn't know this when you set out on this journey, but there is a gift here for you, in this special place. The wise person knows what it is. It is not a gift like a toy or a camera. It is a gift you feel inside you, like happiness, excitement: something you like to have. It might be a new feeling you have never had before.

Now listen to the wise person. You will be told about the gift and be helped to receive it. This special place can let the gift just slip right inside you very easily. You are surprised to learn that part of the gift is that you will become the wise person of the special place now! Feel yourself changing into the wise person.

Part two: The celebration

3 Now let yourself slowly stand up. See if you can keep your eyes closed a bit longer.

4 Let yourself dance a bit as this wise person and feel the gift inside you.

5 Play some gentle rhythmic music in the background.

6 Now let the gift of the good feeling spread out inside you as you dance.

Part three: A symbol in the stillness

7 Now be very still for a moment. Take some full breaths.

8 Stay connected with the gift inside. Imagine what this feeling would look like if you could photograph it, or go to the sandplay shelf and find a symbol that is like your gift.

9 Show the symbol or draw it, then share the meaning of the symbol. In what way is it like the inner gift, like the wise person? What is the symbol reminding you about?

10 Make a group picture of the symbols, or a group sandplay.

Visualisation exercise

Feeling my roots

Suitable as an individual or group exercise for children aged 8 years and over.

Have ready drawing books and crayons.

This exercise is especially useful for a child who is feeling overwhelmed or vulnerable to outside forces, to allow the child to connect to inner strength, the sacred energy, the essential self.

1 *Stand with your eyes closed.*

2 *Feel your feet firmly on the floor. Your energy passes through the floor down into the earth. Imagine feeling the soil on your feet, really feeling the touch of the soil, the cool, brown earth against the soles of your feet.*

3 *Now there are tiny little roots growing out of the bottom of your feet . . . reaching down towards the earth . . . going deeper into the earth . . . becoming thicker now . . . much thicker . . . very big thick roots . . . getting stronger now . . . very strong, deep roots . . . big thick strong roots . . . going right down deeply into the earth.*

 These roots are your roots . . . growing out of you . . . so strong and deep . . . growing so deeply into the earth . . . holding you to the earth.

 Feel the strong wind blowing into your branches, bending your limbs, making you sway a bit this way and that, feel how your strong roots hold you steady even though the wind tries to blow you over.

 Now there's a flood coming down the valley. Feel the torrents of water rushing into your trunk; it's trying to uproot you. Feel how your big, strong roots hold you firmly to the earth.

 Now a bushfire is coming, burning your lower branches, burning and singeing your bark. It feels like it's going to burn you right up, but it doesn't. Rain falls and puts the fire out and there you are still standing, deeply rooted.

 You are firmly in your place. Breathe into that strength, your solidness, your connectedness to the earth.

4 *Draw a picture of yourself as the strong tree. For example, draw yourself with the strong roots going down right through your feet.*

5 *Talk about how that feels for you. What happens in your life that you need these strong roots for? When you go home, how could you help yourself when you feel crumply?*

Visualisation exercise

The mysterious island

Suitable as an individual or group exercise for children aged 10 years and over.

Have ready drawing books and crayons.

1. *You are dancing around the fire with your tribe. You dance on into the night. It is a full moon. The moon is shining a silver path out across the ocean. The water is calm. The night is warm. Something is calling you to take your canoe and venture across the water.*

    You paddle out, following the moon's path. You paddle and paddle, but you don't get tired.

    The daylight glows orange and yellow on the horizon. You see an island. You know that is your destination. You paddle ashore to the island.

    On the shore you walk up the beach. You head into the middle of the island through the trees or jungle. There is a track there to guide you. You come to the threshold, a clearing in the middle of the island.

2. Leave them to go into the centre and discover what is there. Tell them it will be a surprise, something wonderful and unexpected. Ask them to discover what is happening there, to watch and see every detail.

3. Then guide them back, stage by stage, from the clearing to their own land and tribe. They report to the chief, drawing what they saw.

4. Gestalt the surprise, work in pairs, get the message of what was going on at the centre of the island (them). See page 140 for the Gestalt questions.

5. Share the messages.

Emotional release for children

Visualisation exercise

Earth people

Suitable as an individual or group exercise for children aged 8 to 16 years.

Have ready drawing books and crayons.

The aim of this exercise is to support children in feeling their individual specialness, and open them to inner purpose.

1 *Sit in a circle.*
2 *Take some deep breaths, all the way down to your tummy.*
3 *Close your eyes and imagine you are part of a special people on the earth. The first tribe. There is something special you have come here for. See yourself as part of this earth tribe. You can be big or small, you can be any colour you want to be.*
4 *Your home is deep down in a cave. See the cave. Feel what it is like in this cave, your home.*
5 *You have come to this place where you are now to experience something special. There is something special in the air. Imagine what this specialness looks like. Breathe it into you.*
6 *With this specialness inside you, part of you, you can know what the special thing is you have come here for. It might come into your mind as a picture, or a memory, or an idea. Wait for it.*
7 *When you have a feeling of what you have come here for, draw a picture.*
8 *When all have drawn, have children hold up their pictures, show the group and speak one sentence about their specialness.*

Visualisation exercise

Swimming a lap in a very big pool

Suitable for children aged 8 to 14 years.

The aim of this exercise is to prepare children to work through or complete a task and to feel a sense of relief and peace.

1 Tell children to imagine that they are diving into a pool.
2 Encourage them to make any sounds or movements they wish.
3 If necessary, remind them to keep breathing deeply.
4 Tell them to keep swimming until the lap is finished – even though it is tiring. When they reach the end they can climb out of the pool and lie down.
5 When children are lying down, remind them just to enjoy the feeling of having completed the lap.

Moving forward on the inner journey

Visualisation exercise

Discovering my special differences

Suitable as an individual or group exercise for children aged 6 to 12 years.

The aim of this exercise is to support children to begin to accept and appreciate differences and to unfold into all of the real self.

1   *Close your eyes and take a big breath, and I'm going to tell you a very special story.*

   Once upon a time there lived a large family of Shushes. They were slow moving. They only ate worms. They were about as big as a matchbox. They had brown and black colours. They lived in sheltered places that were cool and dark.

   There were lots of mums and dads and each of them had lots of children and all of them lived together. One mum and dad and their one hundred other children were living with lots of other Shushes in a hollow, dark, cool log.

   There came a special day when Mum gave birth to a new batch of little Shushes. To her surprise one was very different. He very soon could move and he moved quickly. They all moved very slowly but this one skipped very quickly. He skipped right out of the log into the bright sun and began eating small juicy pieces of soft grass.

   His mother panicked (slowly, of course) because she felt that a bird might eat him. She waddled and slithered so slowly after him. At first she couldn't see in the bright light and then she was just dazzled and then there he was – on the grass a little way off. He was the brightest blue Shush with purple and yellow stripes and he had pink eyes and beautiful golden feelers. A bird hovered over him. This bird was also dazzled by his beauty and of course didn't eat him.

   He was so happy and so different that his mother became proud instead of worried and brought all the Shushes out of their hiding places to see him and said to them:

   'He's different and he's beautiful and he's one of us.' The little Shush of course was being himself. A long time later he could see he was different but he had had such fun being himself up until then that he didn't worry at all and the other Shushes also began to grow differently. Soon there were quick ones and little ones and big ones and skinny ones, and ones that ate dirt and some even that ate ants. Some had pink spots and some had red stripes and some hissed and some grunted and no matter what they looked like or how they moved or what they ate or how they lived, they were all beautiful and they were Shushes and they were themselves.

2   Ask children the following questions:
   - *What is the 'something' that is beautiful that makes you special?*
   - *What is the most different thing about you? Think about this for a moment, then tell me/the group.*
   - *Make up a little story about you. Pretend you are a Shush. If you were that special, brave Shush what would happen in your story?*

Gestalt exercise for reclaiming self-esteem

Owning the richness within

Suitable as an individual or group exercise for children aged 8 to 19 years.

Have ready sheets of A4 paper and crayons.

This is a visualisation and Gestalt exercise to find images that represent the good things of the inner being, inner resources in symbolic form. These images can represent the light that helps them face the darkness of emotional pain. It can also be used at the end of some powerful work to integrate and focus on inner treasure.

1. Children fold a piece of paper in half or quarters, depending on the number of gifts to be explored.

2. *Lie down and relax. Get comfortable and close your eyes.*

3. *You are very wealthy. Very, very rich. So rich that you could buy absolutely anything you desire. Today you are going to buy gifts for yourself.*
   You like only the very best, the most luxurious, the finest quality. Sometimes you go shopping with your pockets stuffed with hundred dollar notes; sometimes you just use a special Golden American Express Card, which has no limit.

4. *You jet around the world seeking out all the very best shops. You have your own jet, of course. See yourself in the jet, sipping some lemonade, issuing orders to the pilot to land in some special country where you wish to go shopping.*

5. *Now you are walking down the street. See the shops, make them up in your mind. You go inside one. What sort of shop is it?*

6. *You are going to buy yourself a very special gift. Check that you feel good buying something wonderful for yourself. Select – in your imagination – the biggest, the best, the thing that attracts you the most. Wait, see what that will be.*

7. *Now draw it.*
   Pause.

8. *Now lie down again. Your chauffeur is taking you back to your jet. Off you go to another country. Watch for voices that tell you one thing is enough. Go to another shop, buy another gift for yourself.*
   Depending on the age of children and the attention span, get them to buy up to four gifts.

9. *Now draw again.*
   Pause.

10. *Now sit up. You are going to become each special gift. Each gift represents wonderful qualities in you – get ready to hear about them!*

11. *Find all the words to describe yourself as you become each gift: what you look like, your colour, shape, size, texture, what you are made of. Say what you are for. Listen to your voice, listen to your words, say what kind of energy you have.* (Refer to Gestalt questions on page 140.)
    Pause. Continue after the Gestalt work.

> 12 Share what you have learned about yourself. Remember that each gift is a symbol for some real quality in you that caused you to think it up. The gifts are symbols, the qualities are real!
>
> **Variation for older children**
> Buy a present, then an exotic pet, then the best meal you could have – and, in the evening, go to the best concert in the world, the one you would love most.

Relaxation and meditation

Choosing methods for relaxation will depend on:
- *attention span of the children*. It is vital to invite stillness and never to force if the child is to continue into relaxation. If stillness is impossible the restless energy may have to be expressed strongly in order to leave a clearer space inside.
- *time available*. This will determine the depth of the relaxation possible.
- *time of day*. Mornings are times for aliveness; afternoons tend to be times of low energy; dusk is a time for quietness, as nature around us begins to settle for the night.
- *current need*. Is the relaxation work a spontaneous need? a parental need? the child's need? a crisis? part of regular work?
- *state of the facilitator*. The work will go well if the method corresponds to the facilitator's experience and understanding. What has helped you most to relax?
- *state of the children*. This determines the type of work – strong/gentle, fast/slow, etc.
- *location*. Is there lots of space? Are there outer distractions? Can full expression be allowed, i.e. lots of noise? catharsis? Will there be amusing or distracting noises from the environment when the child (or children) are quiet?
- *space available*. Will children be sitting? standing? Is there room to lie down? Is it comfortable to lie down?
- *whether it is group or individual work*. In group work it is more difficult to find the right length of time, as there will be a range of attention spans. With individuals it is clear how long the person can sustain relaxation and be still; for example, how long before they start twitching, wriggling, scratching or opening eyes and peeking around?

Emotional release for children

Meditation/relaxation exercise

Watching the candle flame

Suitable for children aged 3 to 12 years.

Have ready a birthday candle, holder and matches.

1. Children gather in a circle, about 2 or 3 metres from the candle.
2. Set the candle in a holder, slightly raised, so that the children's eye line is slightly downward.
3. Light the candle.
4. Tell the children:
   In a little while I am going to light this small candle. All the time it is burning, I want you to watch the candle and breathe deeply. While you are watching the candle, you can make any sounds you want and any movements you want. Just keep breathing deeply all the time the candle is burning. You can blink as much as you need to.
5. When the candle has burnt out completely, tell the children they can sit or lie down for a few moments with eyes open or closed and just enjoy whatever the feeling is and rest.

Relaxation exercise

Visualising relaxation

Suitable for children aged 12 to 19 years.

Have ready some cushions or books (to use as a headrest).

This is a sequence based on the Alexander Technique, which uses both physical relaxation and visualisation to assist the body to let go and assume its natural posture, and come to a quiet state.

Children lie on their backs, on a carpeted floor with a cushion or books under their heads. (These should be as high as the child's middle finger.) This keeps the neck lengthened and the head supported. Knees are up with feet flat on the carpet, in a balanced position, holding themselves up. The arms are by their sides, with the hands resting on their sides.

- *Imagine your neck is going floppy – and growing longer.*
- *Let your trunk be free to lengthen and widen; picture this happening. Imagine or think this rather than doing it.*
- *Feel your chest and belly. Give them permission to let go now, to melt down like an ice block on a hot day.*
- *Visualise your shoulders going apart from each other. Allow your body to follow this image.*
- *Tune into your belly. Is anything tight? Let go in the belly now.*
- *Imagine your legs letting go from the hips, as if the joints were getting softer. Then imagine this with your hips.*

Moving forward on the inner journey

- *It is quite likely that you will find your body taking some full breaths, so encourage this.*
- *Imagine the legs moving up towards the ceiling, in the direction the knees are pointing. A tiny magic force is at work! Feel what it is doing inside you.*
- *Check through from head to toes. Could any parts do with some more melting?*
- *Stay like this for a little while.*

Relaxation exercise

Walking meditation

Suitable as a group exercise for children aged 12 to 19 years.

This exercise is aimed at supporting stillness and body awareness.

1. The group begins to walk around the room, all in the same direction, and in silence.
   - *Begin to feel the floor under your feet.*
   - *Relax your whole body:*
     - *Drop tension in neck.*
     - *Allow shoulders to drop.*
     - *Let yourself take full breaths.*
     - *Allow your belly to be soft.*
   - *Be aware of knees. How are they? tight? relaxed?*
   - *Now slow down the walking.*
   - *Take three large breaths and let them relax out.*
   - *Become aware of your feet, feel how your toes, soles and heels touch the floor.*
   - *Try to walk and relax your ankles at the same time.*
   - *Practise walking and feeling your feet from the inside for a while.*

2. *Now follow a leader, and go outside.*
   Decide whether the conditions allow for bare feet. If bare feet, choose a path which provides different textures for the feet to experience.

3. Draw children's attention to differences in:
   - texture
   - temperature
   - hardness/softness

4. Remind children to bring their attention back inside themselves to feel their feet.

5. Come to a quiet place, and have the group stop, close eyes for a moment and feel the earth under their feet.

6. Discuss:
   - what it felt like to walk this way
   - how attention is drawn to the outside so easily
   - how they feel after this exercise

Relaxation exercise

What is here now?

Suitable for children aged 8 to 19 years.

Have ready drawing books and crayons.

1. Children lie down on a carpeted floor with a cushion under their head and closed eyes.
2. *Remember yourself at home early this morning; visualise all the things you were doing. Visualise each step up until now.*
3. *Follow each step, each feeling of your day until now, as if mentally watching a home video.*
4. *Feel your body and its energy now.*
5. *Focus on your energy. What does it feel like? Is it mostly in your head? in thoughts? in a part of your body?*
6. *Is there a feeling of being at home in your chest? belly? hands? legs?*
7. *Spend a few minutes dropping all your thinking.*
8. *Allow your body to relax more, to go floppy, to melt.*
9. *Watch. Become a watcher who looks inside. One who simply observes what is in there.*
10. *Let your awareness come to the breathing; let it relax.*
11. *Let your awareness keep dropping down with each breath into your body, let it drop into the middle of yourself, like your mind was sliding into a tunnel that is through the middle of you.*
12. *Every time you think about something else, come back down inside this tunnel in you.*
13. After about five or ten minutes (three minutes for children aged 8 to 10 years) bring the children's attention back to the surroundings and invite their breath to deepen.
14. Invite children to quietly sit up and stretch.
15. Ask them to draw the tunnel, the colours, the shapes, what it was like inside.

Relaxation exercise

Tension and surrender

Suitable as an individual or group exercise for children aged 10 to 19 years.

This is a simple relaxation exercise to release deep tensions and is good to do before quiet relaxation work. It uses over-stressing to assist a deeper let go. It is ideal for children who cannot keep still enough to do relaxation work.

1. Each child lies on a carpeted floor, stretches out limbs, contracts and expands their whole body a few times.

2. They picture themselves as a five-pointed star, with each limb and the head as a point. They picture themselves floating, twinkling in a clear night sky.

3. They begin tensing parts of their body in this order:
   - right hand, right arm, hold for a moment, let go
   - right foot, right leg, hold for a moment, let go
   - left foot, left leg, hold for a moment, let go
   - left hand, left arm, hold for a moment, let go
   - face, trunk, hold for a moment, let go

4. Get a rhythm going: Tense! Tense! Hold! Relax!
   (In group work you can use a drum beat to help establish the rhythm.)

5. Go round the limbs about three to six times.

6. Children then lie still and feel themselves twinkling, pulsating as this star, with lots of quiet energy.

Relaxation exercise

Moving in slow motion

Suitable for children aged 10 to 19 years.

Have ready some quiet, flowing music.

This simple exercise follows on from the previous tension and surrender exercise very well. It helps the body self-awareness. Keeping the movements at a very, very slow speed forces the awareness to come into the limbs. This has a quietening effect on thoughts and feelings.

1. Children lie on the floor on their backs, limbs spread out a bit.
2. Read out the following directions to them slowly, pausing between each step. Play music in background.
3. *Leaving the arms resting on the carpet, begin turning the wrists very, very slowly – so slowly that the movement is between the point of stillness and movement.*
4. *There is nothing now but this movement, the little changes in the muscles as the movement continues.*
5. *Leave the wrists after a while, and work with the ankles – they can turn the same way, or opposite, it does not matter, don't think about it, just feel the movement.*
6. *Work like this with the head.*
7. *Work with an ankle and a wrist – opposite sides of the body. Change.*
8. *Add the head.*
9. *Don't think about it! Lose yourself in the slow motion.*
10. *Kneel up. Let the upper torso turn through space – keep it slow! Add the wrists and head, either all together or one at a time.*
11. *Stand. Try all, then add turning the whole body through space, encourage letting go of all control now, surrender to the flowing.*
12. Give time to feel the stillness when the body finally stops. Encourage the children to take a moment to *be* inside themselves.

Relaxation and stillness exercise

The sunset

Suitable for children aged 10 to 16 years.

Have ready drawing books, crayons, music for shaking the body, drum beat music.

This exercise is helpful for children who are agitated or restless. It allows the restlessness to move, in order to make space for stillness.

1. *Take the body stance of, or play act, the following attitudes. Feel what happens in your body with them.*
   - *'I don't want to do this!'*
   - *'I'm ready, I'm open.'*

   This may have to be repeated a few times.

2. *Shake loose. Shake out the things that are locked up. Take some deep breaths.*
   (Play music for shaking.)

3. *Your breath is magic. It helps you change into lots of different things:*
   You are a firecracker. Gunpowder is packed inside. See what happens when you are lit.
   - *What colours are coming out?*
   - *What movements do the sparks make?*
   - *What sounds does this firecracker make?*

4. *Become the energies, sounds, movements of these:*
   - *an ant*
   - *a snail*
   - *a bee*
   - *a robot* (Change music to a drum beat.)
   - *all school children on Earth on Friday afternoon at home time*

5. *Now you are a young tree, a sapling in the bush. There is space around you, a breeze is blowing from all directions, it changes directions. You are flexible. Feel your roots in the earth. Feel your branches reaching up.*

6. *You are now the sunset – the most beautiful sunset ever. Around you birds are becoming quiet, the humans settle down, the world becomes still. You are the colours, you are the horizon, the distance, stretching so wide.*

7. *Be this for a while. Feel: what is your main quality now? peacefulness? colourfulness? What is it?*

8. *Draw the colours and shapes of the sunset you were.*

9. *Tell the group about your main quality. Show your drawing if you wish.*

Emotional release for children

Guided meditation

At home in my hands

Suitable as an individual or group exercise for children aged 10 to 19 years.

Have ready a tennis ball or apple or orange for each child; quiet music in the background, with an even rhythm; journals and biros; drawing books and crayons.

1 Children sit comfortably, in a way that allows the breath to be full, and the energy to flow up and down the spine. The left hand rests on the knee. The right is turned up holding the ball (or fruit). The inner eye, the inner focus, is on the right hand, feeling the weight of the ball.

2 Children are encouraged to allow breath to be full, and to feel the sensations of the hand, to feel it supporting the ball, to feel what is inside the hand, to feel the air on the skin, to feel the texture of the ball.

3 Tell them that thoughts, ideas, distractions will come, but the inner work is to keep coming back to the focus on the hand, to let the thoughts float away.

4 After a few minutes, change the focus and the ball to the left hand. If the attention span is short, keep changing the hand for focus.

5 After about a total of five minutes with each hand (for children over 13 years make it a bit longer) have them place the ball on the floor in front of them and then continue as if they were still holding it.

6 After a few minutes the focus comes into the middle of the body.

7 End with a simple question such as:
What is it like to be at home, inside yourself?

8 Children could respond to the question in words, writing or with drawing.

9 Repeat this exercise on a regular basis.

CHAPTER EIGHT

Caring for the carers

If [an educator's] own inward life is in disorder
and he talks about order...
the student will realise this is double-talk
and so will not pay the least attention to what is being said.

J Krishnamurti, *Letters to the Schools*, Volume 2, Mirananda/Wassenaar, 1985.

The hurt inner child in carers

In work with children our reactions and responses to children are very much coloured by the unfulfilled parts of our childhood. For example, if you give a lot of time and attention to your own children or children that you are working with professionally, deep inside there is a part that feels: 'Hey! I never got this!' Here you are now as an adult, able to give and pay deep attention to children. If you listen inside yourself, you hear a voice that is calling for this too. And it doesn't want it from you – it still wants it from your mother and father!

A lot of the problems in relating to children in intense emotional support work come from this reaction. Although it's usually just below the conscious level, occasionally it's very clear – out in the open – and then we can work with it, express it appropriately and clear it. But when it goes on, crying out inside, bringing its resentment to the current good work, we find ourselves exhausted, running out of patience, beginning to give to children and ending up demanding of them. We get burnt out. This constant crying out from our past has been awakened by all the giving and feeling of children's deep pain.

While we remain unaware of this longing we unconsciously try to remedy the situation in later years. We sometimes even reproduce a situation similar to the child's in order to try to correct it, to get it right this time. This is done with job situations and particularly when seeking partners and friends. ERC sessions can reveal how we have actually chosen our partners because of a characteristic of one of our parents that has fallen short in offering real mature love. We find that we have exaggerated and provoked this characteristic in them so that the child in us can try again to make the changes it wants. This never works!

When our inner work of releasing the past from mind, heart and body returns us to a natural state, unencumbered by a lifetime of disappointments and repressed hurt, our impulses of love, tenderness and compassion re-emerge. We no longer expect to struggle as the child did. These feelings can now guide us towards a new and deeply rewarding lifestyle determined more by the aims of giving and sharing than by old needs to get and keep.

One of the glories of emotional release work is that it breaks the chain of negative conditioning. For example, your father was shaped in his ability to relate to you, by his father. Your ability to relate to your son has been extended or stunted by the modelling of your father. Of course, both parents are models – we get learned characteristics from both.

Generation after generation, the repressed feelings of hurt and inner and outer disconnection they engender are passed on. A son looks to his father for love and support. He doesn't see that while his father seems to be moving ahead in life, emotionally his father has his back turned. He is longingly looking back – consciously or unconsciously – towards his own father.

These childhood hurts are the main material that emerge for adults in ERC sessions. Adult clients discover why they have struggled for so many years to attain something which has in fact always eluded them. They learn why they have stuck with a project, job or a relationship that did not bring satisfaction and struggled for years, trying as they then realise, to get what the 'child' wanted. Whole negative belief systems are exposed. Learnings of the child have become beliefs for the adult, and many of these have actually made it seem 'right' to the adult that they have not gained fulfilment or satisfaction in life.

Personal development work that includes the child/adult concept also reveals the 'child's' posture in our body. It is usually one of contraction and slumping. Moving through the pain of childhood allows the freed body to find a new adult posture, one of strength and expansion (similar to the posture of an untrammelled toddler).

Outcomes of healing the hurt inner child

In separating from this child part we begin to recognise the adult steps life is calling us towards. We promise the hurt part that it will be given more time to feel and release the repressed material. This is an ongoing process and may take some time. We find that each new freedom and insight is swiftly tested. We also begin to find that the rewards of healing the child's pain and moving towards adult fulfilment do not seem to have a limit. Gradually we notice decreased reactions to those we have always been reactive to. We notice fewer fears in life. We notice, maybe without ever directly setting out to achieve it, that life has become fuller, richer and our human side is experiencing more and more fulfilment. This sense of well-being becomes the foundation for further spiritual work. Our professional work with children becomes less taxing and we discover new ways to support them in opening to their deepest potential.

Facilitator's journal exercise

What calls me to this work?

Since we all have a tendency to want to give what we didn't get it is good to clarify what we deeply wish to offer children, and to examine if it is really what they are needing.

1 Give yourself a quiet moment, relax and breathe fully.

2 Make a list of what originally motivated you to want to help children – it might be to children in general or to a specific child.

3 Note if you feel successful in this task.

4 What are your current motivations?

5 Examine this list and ask yourself:
- Which reasons are from my inner child?
- Which reasons are from the adult part of me?
- Have I in any way re-created my childhood struggle in my present work with children?

The child/adult concept in carers' personal development

Which moments in our relationship to the children we work with belong to us, and in which ones are we propelled by the past imprints?

As our own personal development work progresses it clearly exposes the fact that we have an 'inner child' which is made up of the strong needs and wants of our childhood. This child part frequently runs our lives. Those who look within honestly can see, with horror, where they have been driven by these needs. This entity within denies us our autonomy, and keeps us automatic. When we come to know it and catch it at its tricks – of using us to struggle for what it wanted – we find a lot of freedom. After feeling any hurt from the past we eliminate the unconscious pressures that drive us to set up new hurts in the present.

All the positive, joyous, fulfilled aspects of ourselves as children have been incorporated into our adult personality and character. Every now and then we allow ourselves to feel childlike and enjoy life for a moment – with a sense of wonder – like a healthy child. It is probably this part of us that is responsible for the great pleasure we felt in starting to work with children. Our capacity for spontaneity has not been lost.

The parts of us that were not met, that were not satisfied and have not been integrated, remain almost as a person inside us who is perhaps three, four or five years old.

As children we had extremely high expectations of parents, teachers, and carers. The parts of us that were not met hang on, wait and struggle to get what was missing. This unfulfilled aspect can take control of us and can actually set up extremely negative patterns for our adult relationships. There will be struggle where there need not be any – struggle for what was not forthcoming back then – and rejection now of the very things we as adults want. Agreeing to feel the depths of not having needs met back there will begin to free us of their stranglehold on our present fulfilment.

These same needs that may have been asleep under the surface, or well managed in our lives, can be powerfully triggered as we are confronted with the same needs in our own children or those we work with. Having supervision time and support to clear the needs releases the energy and freedom to be creative and fulfilled now!

Those in the helping professions will often find these inner needs triggered by all their giving. When they are able to clear themselves or step aside from what is unfulfilled, their giving can be truly enriching both to the child and to themselves – rather than depleting them.

What is burn-out?

People who work with children suffer an alarming (and extremely expensive) rate of exhaustion. Quite often the most gifted and caring in this field feel they have to leave, never to return, choosing alternative careers or a simple, steady, non-emotional job elsewhere. They have not had the help needed to cope with the emotions stirred up by their caring work, and so have little option but to withdraw from it.

Burn-out is really caused by:
- the endless effort to satisfy the child's wounded inner child
- the compulsive energy of your own inner child's struggle to save the child (to win)
- the tension of holding down your own pain – the pain which is repeatedly triggered through the support of children – and needs expression, release

Connected with the effort that can lead to exhaustion is the struggle to be perfect. Are you unconsciously trying to live up to an idealised self-image of the perfect parent, the eternally patient counsellor, the most caring and understanding teacher? A dynamic part of the professional's own release work is to allow the self to feel and express (in private with a facilitator) the total opposite of this angelic, ever-patient, perfect, giving person! If this image is used as a measuring stick, everything positive you do will feel inadequate and little satisfaction can be drawn from your real achievements.

It can be quite illuminating to weigh your image of perfection against your feeling of the way you actually are – with all your faults. Usually when these are compared, you find that both are exaggerated in your mind and there is a middle path that is closer to the real way you operate.

Facilitator's journal exercise

Are you heading towards burn-out?

Many people who open themselves to offer healing work, rather than just behavioural management, find a growing level of stress building up. These questions can help you identify the source of the stress.

Ponder and write down your answers to these questions:
- Is your own wounded, dissatisfied inner child trying to fix, heal, make something right by attracting you to this work?
- Is there a feeling reaction, you often have, in this work that makes you feel like a hurt child?
- What situations bring on this feeling? Are these situations in any way like situations from your childhood?
- Note any ways that you sabotage your energy for this caring work.

- In what ways do you suffer the gap between your indealised self-image in this work and your actual human responses?
- How do you feel about the quantity and quality of your rest and recreation? Is there something new needed?
- In what ways does your body celebrate and/or suffer from work in this profession?
- Have you identified the thing you most want to change in most children? Have you admitted that it needs changing in yourself? Can you change it in yourself?
- How often do you remember to honour your own inner life? What are the best ways you have found to listen to it? Where does your emotional support come from?

Facilitator's Gestalt and journal exercise

Discovering my reactions

To extend insights about a particular child who has become quite a challenge and to learn more about your own reactions to the child, use this simple Gestalt method. It can bring some freedom from continually being emotionally triggered and it can help release any held energy so that there can be a truer relationship with the child, a relationship with no projections.

1. Let your body become like the child's – take the child's typical posture, facial expression and gestures. Exaggerate these a little.

2. Take the child's emotional stance.

3. Say the child's standard phrases.

4. Let yourself move like the child.

5. Do any actions, say any words, which might be typical of the child, and which particularly irritate you.

6. Take some breaths and feel deeply what it might be like to be this child.

7. Write down the answers to these questions:
   - What do you recognise in yourself?
   - What are the main similarities and the main differences between you and the child?
   - What have you projected on to the child?

Self-help methods for carers to use at home

Drawing

If you haven't shouted out enough in the car on the way home, do your own emotional release drawings when you get home. Draw your responses to the children. Try this before loading your partner or friends with it all.

When things have gone marvellously well, do a mandala of your new energy and realisations. Put these up on the wall somewhere to remind you of this high time.

Journalling

Write down your intentions, your aims for yourself and for your work. Review these aims from time to time.

Record your insights about yourself, your growth, your challenges.

Record any events that trigger big reactions in you. What can these teach you about your own inner child and the strength of your adult part?

Dance

When did you last dance? Try some strong dance to release the holding and armouring in your body. At work you may have had to brace yourself against the onslaught, but when you are home let it be shaken out so you feel relaxed again. Try to make a habit of this. Even five minutes will greatly help you let go of the day. Strong dance can release energy, use any excess energy, dissipate nervous energy, release excitement, release anger.

Gentle, quiet dance is also useful (especially after the strong dance). Gentle dance helps reconnect us to our inner self, the quiet place where our energy flows. When we are relaxed, gentle dance or slow motion movement (similar to tai chi) can become a meditation that stills us within and opens us to the world around us.

Dreams

The Gestalt method of working with symbols (see page 140) is ideal for integrating the energy and messages of our dreams. At times of great challenge we may find our unconscious offering more help via our dreams.

Time to relax

Of course, all of us do plan to stop and relax, but how many days have gone by since you took more than five minutes quietly for yourself? Hot baths, beautiful music, massage, being at home alone (with the phone unplugged) – all these are vital aids to relaxation. Without some definite time for ourselves, for letting go, we can burn out – we can find that suddenly we feel we have very little to give and very little left over for ourselves.

The effect of my inner work on my children

From Mary Peacock

Having my three children with me has been a great gift. It has been tough going at times as they certainly don't give much space – but they do keep my feet on the ground! Even though the children may appear to be 'out of control' by most other people's 'dead' standards, I'm thrilled to see them saying what they feel. Getting this new expression into the appropriate time and place is the trick.

I've explored various methods that teach parents how to 'manage' children, but I have come to realise that the key is with me. Often I find myself relating to my children from my own inner child or from the father or mother in me. The challenge for me is getting to know how my inner child functions. I see that as I can deal with her, I'm much clearer in how to relate with my own children.

I feel that the greatest gift I can give to my children is my unswerving commitment to my own inner work. People often ask how the children react to me taking time for my own inner work. This isn't an issue really. They, like many children, react to me not spending every waking moment catering to their every whim!

I do perceive them differently now as a result of my inner work – since I perceive myself differently now. I have realised that unconsciously I was expecting an equal relationship. Now I know that I am the adult and they are the children! I understand the impact of their birth imprints now. I allow temper tantrums and expressions of anger. I see this as expression rather than 'bad' behaviour, or a personal attack on me.

The main change I have tried to implement is freedom of expression. We share feelings, both theirs and mine. I try to teach them the difference between expressing feelings and 'dumping'.

I often notice people's disapproval – some express this and some don't. The children's free behaviour obviously triggers the disapproving adults' unresolved issues. For example, they actually say: 'We were never allowed to behave like that.'

I do have doubts at times. I wonder sometimes if I'm allowing the development of bullies and tyrants! There is no one yet to look to who has actually survived these ideas and experienced the results.

I would advise others who might want to begin bringing up their children in more freedom to have lots of inner work, lots of ERC sessions, themselves. Also to remember that children don't have to like everything the parent wants them to do.

One thing I've become very aware of recently is that it is vital to bring to awareness the very large hidden negative reaction to being a mother. All I was previously aware of was the positive reaction, and put all my effort into living this out. The negative was in the background and it sabotaged my clarity.

CHAPTER NINE

Stories from the counselling room

I believe there is no way you can make a mistake
if you have good will
and refrain from interpretation and judgements.

Violet Oaklander, *Windows to Our Children*, Center for Gestalt Development, 1988.

We hope these stories, and the stories throughout the book, add colour and cohesion to the theory and methods we have described. These stories show the subtle way the threads of a child's healing process can lead to new life. They show the way in which the exercises can be woven together to form a counselling session.

They are a tribute to the patience, creativity and versatility that flow out of the care for the children. The counsellors' sensitivity to the full spectrum of the child's psyche is a direct result of not only the study and practice of ERC methods, but also of their commitment to their own experiencing of the inner world.

We have made comments after some stories to highlight the unseen aspects and the progression of the processes.

From Elysha Neylan

Alexandra, 8 years old, second sandplay

Alexandra started to play in the sandtray. At first she smoothed out the sand and then, using the sandplay objects, created a home which consisted of a kitchen, bedroom, loungeroom and back garden. The back garden was full of animals and the animals and the home belonged to a little pixie. I asked her, 'Are you any of these objects?' She said, 'Yes, I'm the pixie.'

She told a story about the little pixie's day. It started with getting out of bed, eating breakfast, feeding her animal friends and then playing with her animals. That was the end of the story.

I asked her, 'Does the pixie have people friends as well as animal friends?' She replied, 'Lots', and pointed to many people objects on the sandplay shelves who befriended the pixie.

I then asked her, 'Are there any objects that are not friends of the pixie?' She pointed to several objects that she regarded as mean and ugly. I invited her to find a place for these mean and ugly ones. She chose to place them in another sandtray. The mean and ugly ones consisted of a skull, devil, witch, mask, tall dark figure and skeleton.

I asked her, 'What do these ugly ones say that makes them mean?' She said, 'I can't tell you.' I assured her that I didn't mind hearing 'mean' things. She was very surprised by this and then felt safe to share, 'They say things like, you're an idiot and I'll kill you.' I asked, 'Who do they say that to?' She replied, 'the little pixie . . . it makes her feel sad.'

I then asked, 'What do they do that's mean?' She replied, 'They take treasure away from the pixie . . . The treasure belongs to the pixie, and that's the end of the story.'

I just mirrored back how the story ended by saying, 'So the pixie's treasure stays with the mean and ugly ones.'

Not satisfied with this ending, she got one of the pixie's friends from the shelves and played out how the friend retrieved the pixie's treasure and placed it back where it belonged, with the pixie, in his home. The story continued to unfold. The skeleton chased the pixie's friend and tried to steal the treasure again, but was unsuccessful. The skeleton went back to the mean and ugly ones and was 'told off' by the tall dark figure for not stealing the treasure. The skeleton no longer wanted to be with the mean ones so he went over to the pixie's home and promised not to steal the treasure and asked if he could live with the pixie. The pixie then welcomed the skeleton as one of the 'good' guys now. The tall dark figure got a sword and came after the skeleton and chopped him several times for not stealing the treasure . . . and that was the end of the story.

Again I mirrored back how the story ended by saying, 'The story ends with the skeleton lying on the ground after being chopped.'

Dissatisfied with the ending, she continued the story. The skeleton got his own sword and hesitated. I assured her that it was safe here and the skeleton could do what he wanted. I wanted to support whatever needed to be expressed and released.

The skeleton then went after the mean ugly ones and chopped up the tall dark figure, the devil, the skull, the mask, the witch and the tall dark one's sword. She said, 'The skeleton is doing to them what they did to him.' The skeleton and his sword were then placed in the home of the pixie. And that's the end of the story!

Again I mirrored back the ending by saying, 'The mean and ugly ones are chopped up. The skeleton, pixie, friends and treasure are all back home.' Alexandra didn't need to change or add to the story. The story was then complete. Something was complete within herself.

We both then drew. Without thinking much, we just let colour, lines and shape emerge on paper as an expression of how we were feeling. We took some time just looking at our own drawings. I asked her, 'See if there is a feeling or any words that describe your picture.' She replied, 'I love you.' I asked, 'Who do you love?' She said, 'I love me, myself.' (The treasure was back at home with the pixie!)

Alexandra's mother has told me there has been a change within the girl after just two sandplays: she has been less upset and generally calmer.

Adam, 13 years old, first counselling session

Adam's mother brought him a long way to see me because he refused to go to school and generally exhibited many serious behavioural problems.

We started the session with Adam talking about his week. He told me about an accident he had. He continued to talk and told me about many accidents he had had throughout his life.

I asked him, 'What is one accident that really stands out for you?' He told me about a time when he was ten and a friend deliberately threw a rock at the back of his head. He didn't know why his friend threw the rock. I asked him, 'How did it feel?' He replied, 'My head bled and it really felt sore.' I mirrored back, by saying, 'It physically really hurt. How did you feel inside?' He replied, 'I don't know.'

I invited him to to make his friend in the sandtray by using the sand. He built a mound of sand and said this was his friend's face. I asked him, 'What would you really like to do to this face?' He pounded the mound of sand down with his fists and said, 'I'm beating him . . . smashing his face in.' He then said, 'I'd like to walk all over him with my feet.' I wanted to support his body in expressing his rage, so I invited him to take off his shoes and let his feet walk on the face in the sandtray. He refused and said, 'I'll just imagine my hands to be my feet.' For some time he let his hands squash the sand. He finished and said, 'He's gone.'

For three years – since he was ten – he held in his rage and within the safety of the sandplay, he was able to express and release this rage. But this accident was one of many.

I asked him, 'Has anybody else hurt you like your friend did?' He replied, 'No.' I just mirrored back by saying, 'Nobody else has hurt you.'

I asked the same question again – but within a more specific context; that is, 'At home?' The reply was 'No'. At school? He said, 'Yes.'

He spoke about a boy at school who called him a name and picked a fight. Adam walked away. He said, 'There won't be any fight because I won't go to school.'

I invited him to make this boy in the sand. He built a mound of sand, greater in size than the previous one. Again he described the mound as the boy's face.

Again I invited him to do whatever he wanted and needed to do to this face. He smashed the mound of sand with his fists saying, 'I'm beating him.' He picked up the sand with his hands and squeezed it, saying, 'I'm wringing his neck.' His hands then became quite claw-like. I said, 'Let your hands do what they want.' His hands kneaded the sand, and he said, 'I'm ripping his head apart.' He picked up the sand and threw it into the corners of the sandtray, saying, 'I'm feeding his brains to dogs and they are eating his brains . . . He's gone.'

He no longer wanted to work with the sand. I invited him to draw, letting any colours, lines, shapes emerge to express how he was feeling. He drew several drawings and shared the feeling, which was anger.

After the drawings, he said, 'I feel tingly in my back, neck, head . . . it feels like I have the shivers.' I asked him, 'Is that a pleasant or uncomfortable feeling?' He replied, 'It's all right.' I explained that his tingly sensation was his lifeforce. He said, 'I feel happy.'

Once his rage was allowed to totally express and release, he was able to connect with his lifeforce.

Adam has had four other sessions similar to this one. In each session he has needed a safe place to express his rage. As a consequence of his inner work, he is less fearful of the 'bullies' at school and has gone back to school. At home, his mother has noticed changes in how he relates to his friends. He is less aggressive and more cooperative. She also notices changes in his general behaviour – both not as negative and more positive.

Comments

When Adam presented for his first ERC session his symptoms were refusal to go to school, and 'many serious behavioural problems' (We are not privy to the details).

Elysha, his counsellor, knows these symptoms from his mother, but in her talking with him is looking for an energy opening, a 'way in' to his inner world. Her question in paragraph three, 'How did it feel?', is the beginning of a possibility. Although having prepared many options, Elysha may not have made the final decision to use sandplay at this stage. Reaching a block at the end of paragraph three, she decides to move to the sandplay. Her hope would be that Adam would open to feeling some hurt that makes him avoid school, rather than discuss any rational reasons why he should go to school; to use the problem to access the hurt and encourage the release of emotions. This eventually happens as Elysha follows a thread and watches carefully for a way to help Adam address his real issue around school. Her question 'At home?', with the word 'home' hanging in the air and then 'At school?' helped this to happen.

So gradually, without pushing and ever so gently, the reason for refusing to go to school comes out. Elysha would have read energy in his voice, noticed body gestures and stance, and felt another 'boy in the sand' would assist the release of hurt. The release is strong – verbal as well as physical. Elysha knows that on the other side of his rage is something precious, something close to his essential self. She also knows that it is this energy of 'tingling in my back' that operates for him after the session.

It is the new energy and not the remembrance of the expressing of rage, that gives him the courage to go back to school.

Linda, 8 years old

I had been working with Linda for a couple of months. Her main problem was lack of confidence and low self-esteem.

We started the session by doing a simple exercise where you focus on what is inside of you, which animals live inside your zoo (see page 83).

The animal she liked the most was a giraffe who lived inside her feet. I asked her to imagine being this giraffe and tell me what was special about being the giraffe. She went with her imagination, letting her body take the shape of the giraffe and then said, 'I'm a baby giraffe and I love being a baby because I get lots of attention from Mum and Dad.' I then asked the giraffe,

'Does Linda get lots of attention from Mum and Dad?' She answered, 'No.' I asked, 'How does that make Linda feel?' and she replied, 'Really sad.'

The animal she didn't like was a snake. This animal lived in her mouth. She imagined she was the snake and described herself as long, black, brown, having large fangs, hissing a lot and biting people. I asked, 'Why does the snake bite?' She replied, 'People try and kill me and put me in a bag.' I asked her to imagine being in this bag and then I invited the snake to do what it needed or wanted to. The snake fought itself out of the bag and bit all the people who tried to kill her. She said, 'I feel free and much better.'

I asked her, 'Why do you think people try and kill the snake?' She replied, 'People don't like the snake – they think it is ugly.' I asked her, 'Do you ever feel like the snake?' She said, 'Yes, kids at school call me names and say they don't like me.' I asked her to take some deep breaths and tell me how that feels. She said, 'Really sad.' I wanted to support the expression and release of any anger towards these children, so I invited her to imagine the children on the cushion and let the snake in her do or say whatever it wanted. She let the snake energy squash, bite, scare and swallow the children.

I then asked her, 'Have you ever felt not liked by anybody else?' She replied, 'No.' I asked her, 'Do you ever feel Mum or Dad hasn't liked you at times?' She closed her eyes and sat quietly for a while and then gently nodded her head and said, 'Yes, when I'm in trouble.'

I invited her to close her eyes and see if she could remember a time when she got in trouble. For some time she was quiet and then told me about a time when she was three. Her voice wasn't an 8-year-old's voice – it had become like a 3-year-old's. The 3-year-old in her was telling me about a time when she was drawing and ran out of paper and she drew on the wall. She didn't know she couldn't draw on the wall. Dad yelled at her and said, 'I don't like you.' She started to cry. I gently placed my hand on her back to let her know I was there. I assured her that it was good to cry. I mirrored back her pain by saying, 'You feel really hurt.' When there were no more tears, her face had quite a frown on it. I expected there could be anger towards her father, that needed to be released. I invited her to imagine Dad on the cushion and she could say and do what she wanted. She said, 'I hate you . . . you're mean and ugly . . .' She used the cushion to kick him.

When she finished there seemed to be a calmness within her and her voice was back to an 8-year-old's.

She had held in the anger/grief around not being liked by her father since she was three and within the safety of the session, was able to let the 3-year-old in her express and release those emotions.

She finished the session by doing a sandplay. In the centre of her picture was an object of a hand. She imagined herself to be this hand. The qualities of the hand part of herself were friendly and likeable.

Comments

Once again we see that Linda has a particular energy – the presenting problem seems to indicate low energy, a contracted personality.

Elysha has therefore chosen a body-oriented exercise to begin with, hoping that it might allow Linda to let this contracted energy 'speak'. In the expression would be the de-contracting.

In the third paragraph the first clue from her unconscious comes: 'I get lots of attention from Mum and Dad.' Elysha would see the incongruence between that statement and the initial energy stance. She could safely suspect that Linda felt she didn't get Mum's and Dad's attention. Her question does not, however, impose this knowledge. She simply asks, 'Does Linda get lots of attention . . .?' Out of this she can at least nominate a feeling of sadness, though there is no release yet. In many cases this recognition is a relief in itself for the child.

The snake energy is alive and has a shadow quality. It has the potential for activating the emotions that are being held about not being noticed. It is often helpful for children to feel their emotions indirectly at first. Elysha encourages her to let the snake energy in her do or say whatever it wanted. Having released this anger she is able to address more directly her feeling around Mum and Dad. There is now a space in her psyche for receiving memories. A memory comes and with it the layer of emotion under the anger of the 'snake'.

The voice energy often regresses when emotions from the past are being felt, and in this case this was a good indicator for Elysha that the fruits of this process would be lasting.

Again there is need for some further work that is gentle and quiet to allow Linda the chance to experience the new feeling: what was contracted energy and low self-esteem is now transformed. Linda's words indicate this; she has found a friendly, likeable part of herself.

From Irene Pecheniuk

I work with children in care in foster homes, using many of the processes developed by Mark and Patricia. I also work with foster parents, looking at how they can facilitate the natural expression of children's emotions and feelings, while at the same time looking at their own blocks around expression.

The children with whom I have worked have had varying degrees of resistance around opening to the pain in their life. With most of these children, this pain in all its aspects has been extreme. The fact that they do not live with their natural families increases that pain, their rage and their awareness of rejection and abandonment to a high degree.

I have found that sandplay and work with hand puppets allows the children to express their deepest hurts as they would never have done in the usual face-to-face encounter. Sandplay in particular seems to take the children to their core hurts within minutes and they can then connect with their rage by demolishing their creations in the sandtray or by symbolically killing the people who have hurt them, or through war scenes where magically only the nasty adults are killed and the children and the adults that they love are kept safe.

Michael, 6 years old

Michael was only 4 years old when the child welfare services received its first notification of physical abuse against him by his stepfather. There were five more notifications over a two-year period. All attempts to engage the family in counselling, parent education and child behaviour management programs failed.

Michael finally came into foster care through the court system. He was torn by the abrupt change in his life. He was very pleased to be out of an intolerable situation, but at the same time he was very bonded with his mother and his sisters and the sudden separation was very traumatic. The mother had never departed from her view that their family was normal and happy, even though she was herself a victim of domestic violence through two marriages. During the year that followed there were two attempts by the parents to regain custody of Michael by agreeing to the Department's condition that they successfully undertake family therapy.

However, in each of these attempts things were fine until the therapist began to touch on sensitive issues and the therapy was terminated by them at that point.

It was my view at the time that the depth and breadth of the family secrets and family pathology was so huge that to open up even a small part of it would open the floodgates with the force of a tidal wave.

At first, Michael was very fearful of his foster family and of adults generally. He was extremely reluctant to talk about his family and managed to skilfully change the subject when asked about any aspect of his home life.

I began work with Michael in his foster home, a very informal, non-threatening environment, by introducing him to body awareness work and the concept of having different sorts of feelings in the body. I tried to familiarise him with the idea that it was normal to have feelings. I was greatly assisted in this process by his foster mother, who is very much in touch with her own feelings. She therefore has no fears about the expression of emotion. It was not too long before Michael was saying, as he gave his foster mother a huge hug, 'I just love you so much, my body tells me that I just have to love you.'

As we worked we played hand puppet games where Michael became various animals and told stories to my hand puppets. In turn, my puppets told him stories about little animals who have to be separated from their families and how this made them feel. I would ask his puppets to expand on how they would feel in the same situation. I learned a great deal about Michael's fears and hurts through this type of fantasy.

When he settled and started to feel safe enough to be fully himself, I started to bring him into the more structured setting of the sandplay room. On many occasions he set up elaborate structures of cattle sale yards, where his stepfather, who reared cattle for sale, sometimes took him when he needed help with the work. Invariably, the sale yards in his sandtray would be attacked by robots (transformers) and all the fences were destroyed, the adults were killed and all the children and animals would run away and be free.

At other times he would set up scenes in his mother's kitchen with his sisters and his mother sitting around the table. He would then surround the kitchen area with transformers and monsters who protected them from the bad men.

The intensity of his rage at these times was remarkable. He was a hopeful fighter and would not be defeated.

There was one memorable sandplay experience following the threat from his parents that they would move away and leave him behind unless he said that his abuse was all lies. He took the biggest truck he could find, which would not even fit into the sandtray, and loaded it up with the sandplay furniture. On top of the furniture he placed his mother and his sisters. This was a symbolic 'goodbye' to his loved ones. He then broke down and sobbed deeply, connecting with the deepest sorrow he felt for what he came to see as the inevitable, given that his mother had chosen his stepfather over him.

Usually after these sandplay sessions Michael became very angry for a time at home and even began to act out his anger in various inappropriate ways. We bought him some worry dolls, some feeling dolls, a large kicking doll and his own special punching pillow, all of which were well used for almost a year.

The worry dolls and the feeling dolls were used at bedtime in a sort of ritual. They held his worries and his feelings for him so that he could sleep. The feeling dolls were used mostly to mind his sadness, his anger and his fear for a little while, and then he could take them back in the morning if he felt that he needed them. He actually found that he needed them progressively less as he learned to recognise and release his feelings.

Whenever Michael was getting irritable, his stepmother learned to take him to the room where the kicking doll and the punching pillow were kept and just be with him while he kicked the doll, pretending that it was whoever or whatever was making him feel 'yuk'. After about six months this kicking doll became his stepfather and stepgrandparents, and all his anger was consciously directed towards them.

The family did eventually leave the area and move away, but by that time he had anticipated the event, and had already undertaken a lot of emotional release work. He was able to openly express his feelings about the event. He was clear that although he loved and missed his mother and sisters, he did not want to live with the family again while his stepfather was with them.

Michael no longer seems to have guilt about loving his foster family. Over time he has developed the courage to remember and share more and more about his life with his natural family.

Michael's drawings and stories depict various members of his family being hurt by the stepfather and trying to run away from him. His play and his drawings generally revealed themes of threat, escape and capture. That had been his reality. It took time and hard work for him to cease expecting to be hit at any moment and to feel safe to play, to laugh and to be dumb and silly at times.

We believe that he is beginning to fully experience his childhood and develop a sense of his own worth. He is developing a sense of the higher spirit. Occasionally a figure creeps into his sandtray which feels significantly like a symbol of the divine.

From Maurine Boon

Tommy, 11 years old

I met Tommy during the first weeks of the school year. He was a consistent patient at sick bay, presenting with classic symptoms of stress and anxiety. His mother asked me to work with him, as she had known her son to be prone to stress and phobic fears before.

Tommy, a tall, freckle-faced kid, intelligent and very articulate, was eager to talk about his fear at our first session.

The first day he had arrived at secondary college he had been attacked by a bully in Year Ten. This older, larger boy had tripped Tommy over in the schoolyard, much to the amusement of his friends. Tommy had been badly frightened by the incident and was convinced that the boy was 'out to get him'. He had built this fear into such an overwhelming phobia that he was unable to function. His schoolwork suffered because of this fear and the major stress symptoms that followed the schoolyard incident. He could not stay at school and, at times, was even unable to get out of bed to attend school at all. So strong had this fear become that Tommy would walk long distances around the school to avoid a meeting with this bully. This resulted in Tommy arriving late, if at all, for class, causing him more stress and anxiety.

At our second session Tommy did his first body outline exercise. It was also at that session that he identified his Power Animal. His feelings were mainly fear and tension. His animal was an eagle that was held in his chest, near his heart. He was excited by this exercise and understood the meaning of a power animal very clearly.

Many sessions followed. Tommy loved to draw, so during these sessions he made many drawings of the 'monster', who he decided was his symbol for the bully in Year Ten. His eagle was also depicted in many of these pictures, fighting the monster. Tommy was drawn sitting on his eagle's back, looking strong and positive as they went into battle together against the monster.

During this time I worked with his anxiety and stress symptoms using relaxation and visualisation techniques. The eagle was the focus for the symbol of strength and self-esteem.

I clearly remember a session I had with Tommy after a long weekend. He came into my office looking elated and eager to tell me his story. He and his father and his friend Tony had gone fishing during the weekend. He liked his friend Tony, even though Tony could run faster and throw things better than he could. Soon after they had arrived at the fishing spot Tommy found a beautiful eagle's feather lying in the grass. He was so overjoyed by his find that he picked up a stone and threw it, hitting a tree several metres away. His friend Tony was so impressed. He said, 'How did you do that?' Tommy told him about his eagle and the feather.

Tommy said, 'I gave Tony the body outline to do when we got back home. Tony has a dog as his Power Animal.'

The feather now has pride of place on Tommy's bedroom wall along with a large poster of an eagle, a gift from his father.

Tommy's progress after that was quite dramatic. He drew several pictures of the eagle destroying the monster. During each battle Tommy was proudly sitting on the eagle's back. He no longer needed to take long, roundabout ways to get to class. On one occasion he met the bully face to face in the corridor without feeling scared. His psychosomatic symptoms left him. The breakthrough came when one day the Year Ten boy was sent to spend time in Tommy's class for misbehaving. Tommy related this to me with a big grin on his face. 'And I wasn't even a bit scared of him,' he said.

Tommy is now 'one of the mob'. He moves freely about the school, and hasn't been near sick bay this term. His mother says he is sleeping well, eating like a horse, and loves school.

During the last week of the school year Tommy called by my office, bright and cheerful. 'Can I do one more drawing?' he asked. This last drawing depicted a very tranquil scene of a beach, palm trees, sun shining and a large eagle flying towards the sun. When I asked him, 'Where are you?' he replied, 'I am the eagle!'

From Bernadette Wallis

Jules, 7 years old, sandplay session

Jules came with his mother. He had had two or three sessions with me. To begin with we did some bioenergetics with music, then moved into the sandplay. He was excited about using the sandtray.

To tune into himself I asked what he was feeling: his response was 'thirsty'. I suggested he move over to the sandtray and feel how thirsty he was. He put his hands into the sand and started to form a lake. He asked for a drink of water, so his mother brought in a glass from which he sipped and poured the rest in the lake. He then chose a limited number of symbols – a bull, pig and sheep and built a fence around them. That was the farm on the hill and the animals came down to the lake to drink the water. The pig lay down in the mud in the yard. This symbol seemed to be the one that had the initial energy. After some time playing with the animals and forming and re-forming the lake and hillside and farmland, I suggested he become the pig. He rolled around and snorted, really enjoying himself.

Then he became the bull and allowed his anger to emerge as he pawed the ground and growled. He was holding the pillow in his bite but could let it out and a different tone formed as his anger became strong.

There was a lull and he then became the sheep. 'Sad' was his feeling because the sheep was 'hurt from the shearing'. With the change of energy I asked him who was hurting him. And he exclaimed the names of his older brothers who had been bashing him on the legs and he was bruised and hurt. At this point he took the cushions and with cathartic expression exclaimed, 'I hate you S . . . and A . . .' He then cried, softened and drew his sandplay story to take home. His state was peaceful after the session.

Jules was interested and alert throughout the session, moving quickly through what was happening for him. The 'thirst' seemed to be worked through, forming a lake from which to drink; the anger held in his throat was released when he became aware of biting back what sound was inside. The identification with the sadness of the sheep enabled him to go deeper and feel his helplessness in the bullying of his brothers, and deep rage emerged. The final shift was to a softness and peacefulness. The symbols used: land formation in sand, lake, water, pig, bull, sheep, fence around them.

I concluded with the drawing as an integrative process and talked about this place being a safe place to say what he really felt and the fact that his brothers were really big, and sometimes it's not safe with them when they hurt him, etc.

I saw Jules at a holiday camp about ten days later. He claimed me as 'his' when talking with the other kids. That says to me he is comfortable with working in this way with me – a trust relationship is there.

Comments

It would seem from this report that there was no specific problem presenting, so the sandplay would be chosen as a way for Jules to keep attending to his inner journey.

Bernadette notes towards the end of paragraph two: 'This symbol seemed to be the one that had the initial energy.' She means, of course, that the symbol touched, or opened Jules to his issues. ERC depends on the facilitator helping the child to follow the expression of this energy, the expression of the emotions that are alive at the time, even though they may be hidden. It is the movement, release and aliveness of the combination of body energy and emotional energy that revitalises the whole system.

This initial energy flows out as 'enjoying himself'. Other emotions expressed via different symbols are anger and sadness. Bernadette is watching for the emotions, almost as a barometer herself, that seem most connected, most urgent, to Jules. It is not until the 'sad' of the 'hurting sheep' does she ask who is hurting him.

Because Jules has already been active in expressing the names with energy, the emotions come easily, they flow. Bernadette sees that the energy is transformed and all that remains is for him to integrate gently. She chooses drawing. The final evidence that the session was fruitful was Jules' trusting relationship with Bernadette, exhibited days later at the holiday camp.

Maria, 8 years old

Maria arrived, excited about coming. We began by doing a body outline drawing with the exercise The Little Person with the Radar Inside (see page 66). I was interested in doing this exercise to explore further her pain in her stomach (discussed on her first visit), and to allow her to begin to identify what was happening in her body. I could see this as a benefit to her mother also, who was present for the session.

Maria was quick to lie down on the soft carpet and close her eyes to tune in with some big breaths. The brief visualisation exercise two days earlier prepared her for tuning in. She identified coldness, warmth, pain, sadness, anger, happiness, the strong and the weak parts, the part she did like and the part she didn't like in her body. Of particular interest were her tummy and chest, which had sad and angry in them. They were drawn in colours and lines that indicated that for her.

I then suggested that with her angry and sad part she might like to pretend she was little and have a tantrum. With the support of both her mother and myself, the soft cushions surrounding her and some strong music, Maria began to kick and thump, thoroughly enjoying herself with this permission. She then began to use words: 'I hate school, I hate my cousins, I hate my brothers, I hate trees, I hate birds, I hate Daddy, I hate Mummy, I hate everything...' The list went on for some time until she finally went limp and felt she had said everything.

I suggested she stand on her feet and move around. She began to dance with the music in an alive, rhythmical and spontaneous motion. I enjoyed the dance with her and noticed the obvious energy shift.

Maria then moved to the sandtray, which she was looking forward to. After moving the sand with both her hands and with firm energy she described her desert with lots of bumps on it. She was then ready to pick from the shelves two symbols she did not like and two she really liked. They were four shells. She placed them in the sandtray.

Her story began around a treasure in one of the shells and someone was looking for it. She then chose more figures from the shelves: a camel, a horse and a girl for herself. They were all looking for the treasure. This came out in her Gestalting the horse, which seemed to hold the most attraction. The horse belonged to the girl and the girl was running away from home to look for more food – and they found the treasure so they could get more food. Her story seemed to be complete. She then drew her story with crayons.

From Lynn Bishop

Sue, 10 years old, hyperactive

During her last session Sue was very active. We did a visualisation and I got her to wiggle her toes whenever she wanted to move – which was most of the time! Surprisingly, she could still concentrate on what I was saying. Not surprisingly, one of the animals she saw was an ant.

We Gestalted it and she 'anted' – crawled – around the room for ten minutes. She took the cushions, one at a time, and built a hut. We talked about ants and how much energy they had and what they did with it (built things and helped each other).

Her mother rang up today and said Sue had asked if she could do the vacuuming from now on. She's been doing it twice a day, before and after school, for the last three days.

She has also started putting folded-up clothes away one thing at a time! Her mother is thrilled; nothing has ever worked before. After talking for a while I found out that before she had been drugged to calm her down or told what she had to do, never allowed to work it out for herself.

From Patricia Nolan

A 12-year-old boy

The boy had been displaying violence towards his foster mother's friend, who minded the children at times. His own mother had tried to drown him when he was an infant.

He had agreed to explore these violent outbursts in our counselling sessions, yet when the moment came he said he had not had any violent outbursts.

It was suggested that he lie down and let something inside him suggest what he might like to work on. He very quickly came up with: 'It's when people tell me to do things – I feel I don't want to!'

We began to let his inner voices talk with all their energy. The dialogue went like this: (he wrote this down as it happened)
VOICE 1: I don't want to.

VOICE 2: See if I care.
VOICE 1: You don't care anyway.
VOICE 2: I do so.
VOICE 1: You're a liar.
VOICE 2: Sooooooo. (admission and freedom)

He stopped and drew a box at the bottom of the page and wrote: 'I'm getting a relationship going here.'

His energy was soft, he was 'home', he had experienced his inner battle and, hopefully, needn't project the battle out. His foster mother was helped to see that his casual carer's directive orders were triggering an inner battle probably related to having no choice, being forced to 'die'. She was helped to find another way to ask.

Comments

Sometimes the counselling session recreates circumstances that help the child touch into the original trauma. The child had been asked to come for personal work, had agreed outwardly, yet was not really choosing, saying 'yes' inside himself. This is a common occurrence.

Patricia's approach of not buying into an argument, but knowing intuitively that some part of him did know what to work on, is the key to beginning the session. The suggestion to lie down and let his inner world tell him what to work on came from a firm trust that the unconscious will yield the right material, given the right support. Having had the pressure taken off him, he was able to express the problem exactly.

When an inner voice speaks with strong reactive energy there is always an equally strong opposite energy. There is also a middle ground in the child that is not run by either of the opposites. It is a free place, a place of balance, an 'in charge of myself' place. It was this balance that the child reached when he could say: 'I'm getting a relationship going here.' He was at that moment separate from the extremes of 'I don't want to' – resistance – and 'See if I care' – resignation. He was the director of himself and could choose.

Cloe, 14 years old

Cloe's mother has been using the emotional release methods for a number of years. She and Cloe and Cloe's older sister lived together, separate from Cloe's father. The girls spent most alternate weekends with their father. The father had remarried and he and his wife had a new baby not long before Cloe asked to do some personal growth work.

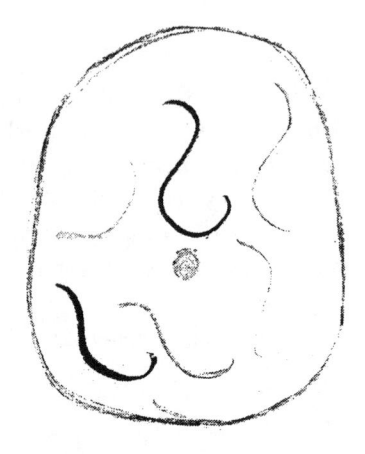

Stories from the counselling room

Session one
Cloe was feeling unwanted, unnoticed at Dad's place because they had the new baby, Harry. She drew her feelings when she, Mum, Dad and sister all lived together. She remembered her contentment.

Then with large breaths and eyes closed she opened to her present feelings. To her surprise, she began to cry. 'I'm lonely,' she said, and then she drew this.

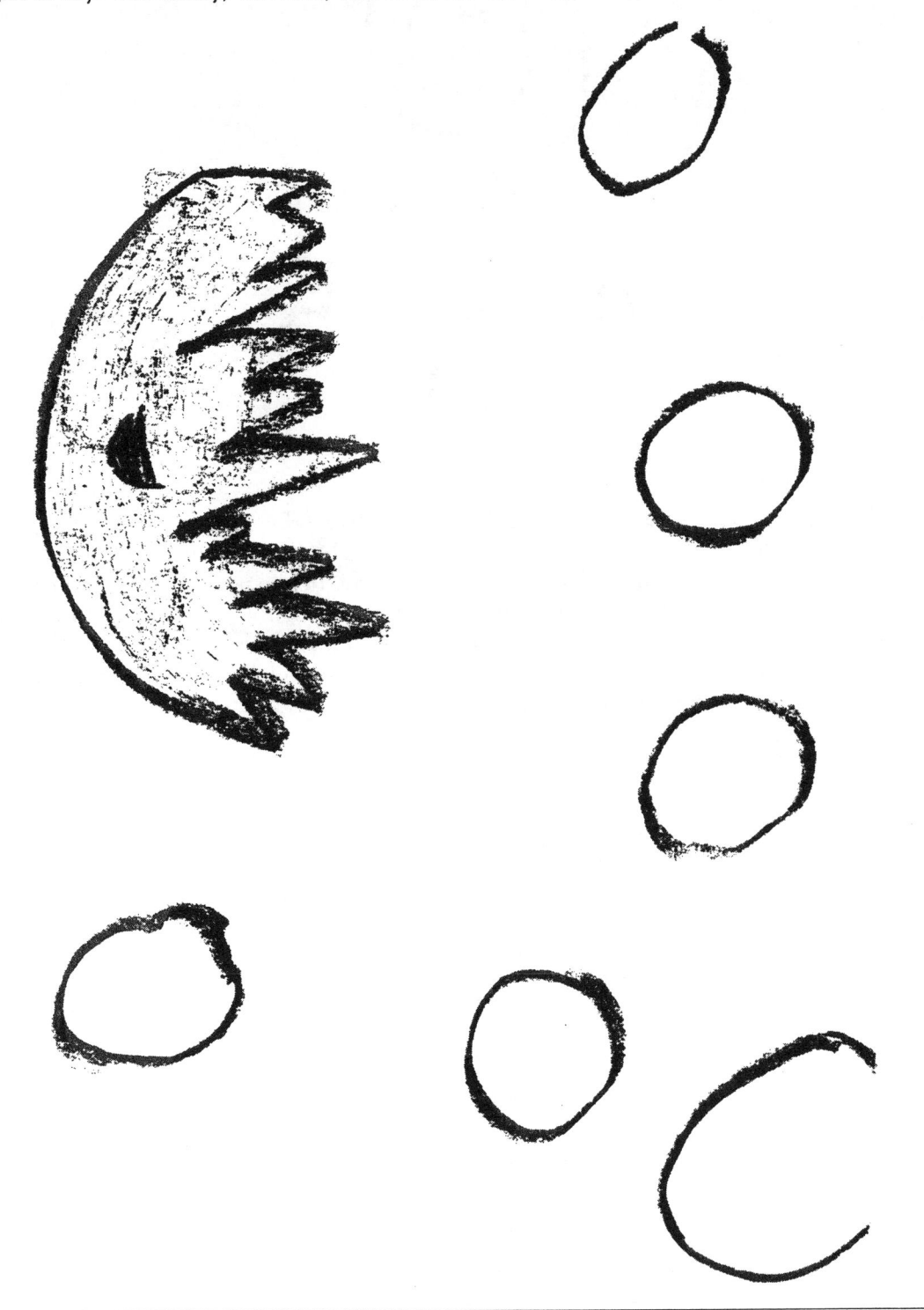

I asked if she ever felt contented now in her life. She closed her eyes, felt inside and took some big breaths: 'When Mum and my sister and I are all together and we are getting on.' She drew this feeling and named it 'contented'.

At this point I could see that Cloe's happiness depended on others and so we did a Now/Then process (see page 58). We called her left hand the *then* hand (of the past, three years old) and her right hand the *now* hand. On the left hand she placed the first experience of contentment – Mum, Dad and sister, and she re-felt the feeling. On the right hand she placed the *now* experience of contentment – Mum, her sister and herself all together. The feelings were the same. To my joy, she was able to recognise and say, 'They both feel like a baby.' So we placed all those baby feelings on the left hand and the right hand remained empty.

I asked her to close her eyes and let herself contact her feelings again from a time when she was really contented within herself, nothing to do with others. A joyous, spontaneous exclamation came: 'Oh! When I'm dancing!' She then drew again, and recognised that any contentment that is dependent on others is her hurt inner child feeling a little bit consoled, and when her contentment comes from within herself it has a very different feeling – it makes her at home with herself.

Session two
Cloe had to have glasses for reading and was worried about wearing them in class. 'I'm worried about what they will say.'

I asked Cloe to breathe more fully, close her eyes and let herself feel what was happening inside and then draw it.

The feeling was 'compressed'. She closed her eyes again, searched inside for memories of a time earlier in her life when she had a feeling like this. She knew very quickly: 'When Mum went to live with a new partner.' She was nine then.

I asked Cloe to let out what she really wanted to say about this. She said to the partner, 'You're creepy', and I got her to repeat it many times until the energy was resolved.

'How do you feel now?' I asked.

'Relieved,' she said, and drew again.

We then did the Now/Then process again so that Cloe could experience how similar were the experiences of feeling 'compressed' about her peers and her glasses, and the feeling she had as a 9-year-old around her Mum's partner. She put the compressed feeling of now on to her left hand with the 9-year-old and on to the right hand came the transformed energy which allowed her to say, 'I don't have to hide because I know my glasses will help me. It's none of their business.'

Session four
Cloe had been to a Yothu Yindi concert and bounced in for her session full of chatter. I decided that she could use this high, joyous energy to find some inner treasure. So I presented the exercise Owning the Richness Within (see page 158).

To my amazement, and hers, there was quite a different agenda going on just below the conscious level. Out of this, of course, came a wonderful treasure.

Cloe's shopping trip from the exercise: 'expensive two-piece swimmers, a new green dress for Mum, a hair salon for my sister in Fiji, a trip around the world for Mum in a private plane.'

My sense of Cloe's energy was that she was regressing from the buoyant young woman who had begun this process. As we Gestalted each purchase, Cloe began to cry and then told me, 'I'm to blame for Mum's unhappiness. If she didn't have to stay with us she'd be having fun. I'm always trying to make up for it.'

I asked her to let herself imagine herself with Mum, 'making up for it'. She went into a contracted small body stance and was wriggling closer to me. She said she felt very close to Mum inside herself. I asked her to let herself move away now and feel herself as a separate person. This didn't feel good to her. Her impulse was to get close to Mum and make her happy. We repeated this many times until she began to feel herself as separate. Her energy began to change and she began to smile. She did a twirl and said, 'I'm free! And Mum's free!'

Session five
Cloe and her mother had had an exchange of words around washing the dishes. Cloe had felt 'not good' afterwards.

We went back to the incident and of course Cloe hadn't done or said what her hurt inner child wanted to. She had suppressed her words and feelings and then felt 'not good'.

I asked Cloe to see herself standing near the sink again. I asked her to take a big breath and then say what she really had wanted to say.

'Get out of my way!' she said, quite strongly, and began waving her hands. I quickly provided a cushion for her to push away. We repeated this several times until she announced, 'I feel so free!'

Later she drew in strong colours: 'Get out of my way!' and 'I feel free!'

Stories from the counselling room

'Get out of my way!'

'I feel free!'

Conclusion

There have been side benefits from this work with Cloe. Because she is feeling better about herself she is able to address successfully some compulsive eating habits. These along with exercise are helping her reduce her weight without recourse to any other more drastic measures. She has more energy for her studies, especially homework. Her mother says that Cloe is sharing much more of herself.

Cloe volunteered her work for this book so that others may see that it's a 'cool' thing to do!

EPILOGUE

New hope for children

He had waded into his fear and was growing strong
with the certainties he was discovering.
He was exchanging his anger and fear and anxiety
for hope and confidence and gladness.
His sadness and sense of defeat were thawing out.

Virginia Axline, *Dibs: In Search of Self*, Penguin, 1971.

Children are constantly bombarded by impressions that evoke a sense of hopelessness. These impressions create a climate of resignation in children and in the community at large.

Saddled with this sense of hopelessness, and even brought to the fore by it, are the unrecognised shadow energies. These are the feelings, the impulses, the energies that have been locked away inside. Because they are unrecognised, yet constantly surfacing to be dealt with, we are drawn to the negative, the violent, even fascinated with the perverted. However outwardly moral or virtuous we may appear, we have an interest in the opposite. The daily newspapers are the proof of this.

The influences around us result in an increase in negative and limited beliefs about new possibilities. They contribute to an increase in general stress levels. They can overpower and obscure the few real models of personal growth, and the ability to creatively resolve real inner and outer problems. It is as if many of our children are living with an inherited hopelessness that brings a contraction in body, energy and spirit.

Children cannot grow without real hope. Hope is the message of most fairy tales. Where does it come from, this hope in something better?

Real hope that is deeply felt and gives strength comes from inner experiences of transformation of our negative shadow material into something positive. It comes from seeing this change and growth in others. It comes from learning that there are not deep dark fears and secrets that need to be locked away, that it is safe (even if painful) to venture within.

Acquiring new skills to deal with our feelings, our inner world, also gives confidence and hope. The great gifts of ERC work are freedom from fear of emotions, and the skills to deal with them.

Inner work may sometimes seem, and actually be, a time of deep self-centredness. But out of it new hope, courage, ability and the intent to support others emerge.

Through dialogue with the unconscious we gain new direction in life. This direction can become like a magnet attracting more and more good. Taking up our real role in life, in our community, and feeling ourselves in the right place at the right time doing what we are called to do: all this gives a deep inner peace and contentment which spreads a sense of hope.

Appendixes

Appendix 1: Milestones pro forma

Age	Family changes	Outer events	Moods, behaviours, symptoms

Milestones

Appendix 2: The people in my life pro forma

The people in my life

Person	1 Their colour	2 Their shape	3 Animal like them	4 Their big problem	5 What I would like to say to them	6 How I feel about them
Dad						
Mum						
Sister						
Brother						
Sister						
Brother						
Stepfather						
Stepmother						
Stepsister(s)						
Stepbrother(s)						
Grandmother						
Grandfather						
Teacher						
Best friend						
Worst enemy						
…………						
…………						

Appendix 3: Sandplay report pro forma

Sandplay report

Date: _____ Facilitator: _____

Child's name: _____ Age: _____

Presenting problem: _____
_____
_____
_____

Process initiated by: _____

Pre-assessment: _____
   body reading: _____
   reported body sensations: _____
   emotional state: _____

Opening directions to child: _____
_____
_____
_____
_____

Choice of objects: _____
_____

While choosing: body energy, posture, attitude, etc. _____
_____

During sandplay: expressions – facial, posture, emotional: _____
_____
_____
_____
_____

Main themes noted: _____
_____

Significant spatial relationships in sandtray: _____
_____
_____

Child's insights: _____
_____

Appendixes

Facilitator's insights and observations: _____
_____

   story: _____
_____
_____
_____
_____

   unconscious meanings: _____
   body movements and sounds: _____
   emotional expressions: _____

Integration processes used:
- ☐ Gestalting   ☐ drawings   ☐ body stencils
- ☐ dance, movement, sounding   ☐ eye-to-eye-processing
- ☐ dialoguing with parts of self   ☐ dreamwork

the process: _____
_____
_____
_____
_____
_____
_____
_____
_____

Outcome: _____
_____
_____
_____

Follow-up recommendations: _____
   stories: _____
   visualisations: _____
   games and dance: _____
   massage: _____
   dreams: _____

Special care recommended: _____
_____
_____

Child's comments at completions: _____

Facilitator's evaluation: _____
_____
   body posture: _____
   energy state: _____
   emotional state: _____

Appendix 4: Choosing music

Here are a few suggestions for music that we have found very supportive for particular feelings and energies. Much of it is film music, as film composers are usually required to focus on one emotion or one mood.

All are available on compact disk. The tracks listed are in order of our recommendation for the particular mood.

Tenderness
Geoffrey Burgon: from the television series *Brideshead Revisited*, especially tracks 1, 2, 3, 4, 5 and 6.

John Barry: from the film *Somewhere in Time*, especially tracks 1, 6, 2, 8, 4, 7; and the suite from the film *Indecent Proposal*, track 7.

Mark Knopfler: from the film *Princess Bride*.

James Newton Howard: from the film *The Prince of Tides*, especially tracks 2, 3, 7, 13, 22.

Grief, sadness, loss
John Barry: from the films *Out of Africa*, all tracks, and *Dances with Wolves*, tracks 2, 3, 8, 9, 12, 13; as well as the compilation CD *Moviola*, especially tracks 13, 12, 6, 8, 5.

Anger
Trevor Jones: from the film *The Last of the Mohicans*, tracks 1, 2, 5, 8, 9.

John Barry: from the film *The Black Hole*, most tracks (tape or record only).

Jerry Goldsmith: from the film *Total Recall*, tracks 1, 9, 3, 5.

Powerfully alive energy
Vangelis: from the films *Antarctica* and *1492*, especially tracks 2, 6, 5; and the compilation *Themes*.

John Barry: from the film *Dances with Wolves*, tracks 7, 15, 1, 10, 16.

Stillness, relaxation, letting go
Ennio Morricone: from the film *City of Joy*, tracks 7, 2, 9, 15, 19, 10, 3.

Terry Oldfield: *Cascade* and *Illuminations* (From New World Productions).

Brian Eno and Harold Budd: *Plateaux of Mirrors*, all tracks.

Patrick Bernhardt: *Atlantis Angelis*, all tracks.

Tony O'Connor: *Bushland Dreaming* and *Serenity*, all tracks.

Alan Stivell: *The Renaissance of the Celtic Harp*, most tracks.

Tim Wheater: *Green Dream*, *Before the Rains*, tracks 3, 4, 5, 2, 6, 1.

Strong movement and celebration
Sirocco: *Port of Call*, tracks 8, 2, 3, 9; *Breath of Time* (ABC Music), tracks 5, 6, 8, 11; and *Wetland Suite* (ABC Music), tracks 1, 3, 11, 12, 17.

From the film *Zorba the Greek*, especially tracks 6, 1, 2, 7, 4.

Heroic
Maurice Jarre: from the film *Lawrence of Arabia*, especially main theme.
Vangelis: from the film *1492*, especially tracks 2, 6, 5.
James Horner: from the film *Willow*, especially tracks 3, 8, 1, 6.
Ryuchi Sakamoto: theme from the film *The Last Emperor*.

Tribal rhythms
Gabrielle Roth: *Totem, Ritual, Bones, Trance* (Spiral Booksellers).
Prem Das: *Dreaming Drums*, all tracks.
Scott Fitzgerald: *Thunderdrums*, all tracks.

Science fiction/outer space
James Horner: from the films *Krull*, tracks 1, 2, 3, and *Cocoon*, tracks 11, 12, 6, 10.
John Williams: from the three *Star Wars* films.

Suppliers

Film music
Ava and Susan Records
Shop 20 Town Hall Arcade
Sydney
Phone: (02) 264 3179 for mail order service.

Hard-to-find film music
Barry Stahl
PO Box 74
Springwood NSW 2777

New Age and relaxation music
New World Productions
PO Box 244
Red Hill Qld 4059

Gabrielle Roth suppliers
Spiral Booksellers
269 Smith St
Fitzroy Vic. 3065

Appendix 5:
Contacts for workshops and training

Contacts for information on workshops, training courses or individual sessions in Emotional Release Counselling around Australia:

NSW Patricia and Steve Nolan
     The Inner Journey Centre
     86 Tom's Creek Rd
     Ellenborough NSW 2446
     Phone: (065) 87 4356

     Mark Pearson
     15 Railway Pde
     Woodford NSW 2778
     Phone: (047) 58 8032

     The NSW Emotional Release Counsellors Association
     Sydney Blue Mountains Branch
     PO Box 465
     Springwood NSW 2777
     Phone: (047) 51 1634

     The NSW Emotional Release Counsellors Association
     North Coast Branch
     9 Sherwood Rd
     Kempsey NSW 2440
     Phone: (065) 62 8249

Qld The Queensland Emotional Release Counsellors Association
     189 Herries St
     Toowoomba Qld 4350
     Phone: (076) 33 1383

Vic. The Victorian Emotional Release Counsellors
     PO Box 91
     South Caulfield Vic. 3162
     Phone: (03) 528 3014 or (052) 33 1230

NT   Bev Quinn
     Phone: (089) 27 5986

Glossary

armouring:
: Permanent contraction of muscles into a fixed body stance; for example, retracted pelvis. De-armouring: releasing muscular tension and allowing the flow of energy into those parts of the body that have been armoured.

bioenergetics:
: Specific exercises devised by Alexander Lowen that awaken and help the flow of emotions and energy within the body.

breathwork:
: See *rebirthing*.

centred:
: A state of focused attention on the sensations in the body. Such a state enables us to become calm and more attentive.

clear:
: When the psyche or body is relieved of a trauma that has been long held there is a state of clear or free-flowing energy.

completion drawing:
: Similar to a mandala, but not necessarily drawn in a circle. May be more intentionally drawn, planned, than a mandala.

conditioning:
: A modification of behaviour learned through receiving positive and negative responses from people and society. Usually the conditioning replaces natural responses.

connection:
: Consciousness again includes the emotional state, the contents of the mind, or the fullness of spiritual life, from which it was previously distracted.

defended:
: Rejecting feedback on one's state; not wanting to know about inner life, and maintaining muscular tension in order to avoid feelings.

ego strength:
: A mature ability of the personality to organise life in a productive way and relate to external life in a realistic way.

emotional release drawing:
: A drawing done as part of the process of releasing emotions. Usually abstract, drawn with the energy of the emotions; for example, strong, thick angular strokes of black and red are often drawn as the child contacts anger.

energy field:
: Relating to the fact that human bioenergy spreads beyond the skin and can permeate and deplete or stimulate another's energy. Also relates to the fact that strong attention from a facilitator may stimulate a client.

essence:
: The part of our make-up that we are born with, not affected by conditioning or education. A part that cannot be wounded, but which can be covered over by the moulding in childhood, and disconnected from.

inner child:
: That part of the psyche that remains unhealed from childhood hurts – sometimes described as a sub-personality.

lifeforce:
: Strong, alive, healthy bioenergy that is rarely fully utilised, yet holds the potential for full and vital life in the body, feelings and intellectual functions.

Glossary

mandala:	A drawing which results from an emotional release experience or a time of contacting the unconscious and is expressed in a circle.
mirroring:	Feeding back to another the perceived emotional state in order to assist connection with it.
neurosis:	A disorder of mental and emotional functioning whereby people become abnormally reactive and are driven by unconscious impulses into unusual behaviour.
opening, to open:	On a physical level muscular expansion accompanied by an attitude of willingness to perceive something new.
personality:	A learned part of us. The part that is presented to the world – sometimes like a mask. It usually covers the essence.
primal pain:	A term coined by Arthur Janov to describe the first recorded memories in infancy of emotional and physical suffering that could not be integrated into the nervous system.
processing:	A way of expressing the hurts in a current problem in order to discover and experience this same hurt – or reactionary energy – which really belongs to a childhood event or trauma.
project:	To ascribe to another a feeling that originates within oneself, but which is not conscious.
psyche:	The mind, both conscious and unconscious, and its interaction with feelings, body sensation and spiritual potential.
rebirthing:	A breath process that allows us to experience the repressed memories of the birth and childhood traumas. In so doing there is a return to the original whole self. Same as *breathwork*.
release:	The letting go of enough control so that a held feeling is able to be felt again, and transform. The muscular contraction associated with it relaxes.
repression:	The shutting away of undesirable information from consciousness. Repression happens unconsciously.
shadow:	A term used by Jung for describing those parts of the human psyche that are suppressed and/or undeveloped. They reside in the unconscious.
sounding, sounding out:	Allowing uncontrolled release of noises, which may include words and phrases, spoken or shouted, and which have been held in the body for a long time.
suppression:	Pushing away from consciousness unpleasant facts or feelings.
transference:	The act of transferring emotions for one person on to another. (Counter-transference occurs when the one transferred on to is triggered into transferring also.)
trauma:	Serious physical, emotional or spiritual wounding.
trigger:	Someone or something outside a person that stimulates a reaction within. They are then said to be in a state of reaction, and have been 'triggered'.

Recommended reading

There are many, many good books on work with children. This is a short list of the books we have found to be most useful for the ERC processes.

Books on work with children

My Daddy Died – Supporting Young Children in Grief, Heather Teakle, Collins Dove, Aust., 1993.

I Thought I Was the Only One – Coping with Grief and Loss in Schools – A Resource for Teachers, Hazel Edwards, Collins Dove, Aust., 1992.

On Children and Death, Elisabeth Kubler-Ross, Macmillan, 1983.

Dibs: In Search of Self. Personality Development in Play Therapy, Virginia Axline, Penguin, 1971.

Windows to Our Children: A Gestalt Therapy Approach to Children and Adolescents, Violet Oaklander, Center for Gestalt Development, NY, 1988.

Grief and Dreams, Mary Symes, Rene Gordon, Vic., Aust., 1987.

The Secret World of Drawing: Healing through Art, Gregg Furth, Sigo Press, USA 1989.

Loving Hands: The Traditional Indian Art of Baby Massage, Frederick Leboyer, Alfred A Knopf, NY, 1976.

Relaxation for Children, Rae Crook, Second Back Row Press, NSW, 1988.

Children of the Future: On the Prevention of Sexual Pathology, Wilhelm Reich, Farrar Straus Giroux, NY, 1984.

Emotional First-Aid for Children: Emotional Release Exercises and Inner-life Skills, Mark Pearson & Patricia Nolan, Butterfly Books, NSW, 1991.

The Spiritual Hunger of the Modern Child: A Series of Ten Lectures – from 1961, J G Bennett et al., Claymont Communications, USA, 1984.

Banished Knowledge: Facing Childhood Injuries, Alice Miller, Virago Press, London, 1990.

Books on sandplay

Sandplay: A Psychotherapeutic Approach to the Psyche, Dora Kalff, Sigo Press, USA, 1980.

Images of the Self: The Sandplay Therapy Process, Estelle Weinrib, Sigo Press, USA, 1983.

Healing and Transformation in Sandplay: Creative Processes Made Visible, Ruth Ammann, Open Court, USA, 1991.

Books related to adult personal development

Birth without Violence, Frederick Leboyer, Alfred A. Knopf, New York, 1984.

The New Primal Scream: Primal Therapy 20 Years On, Arthur Janov, Abacus, Britain, 1990.

Imprints, Arthur Janov, Abacus, Britain, 1977.

The Adventure of Self Discovery, Stanislav Grof, State University of New York, 1988.

A Dictionary of Symbols and Imagery, A de Vries (ed.), North Holland, Amsterdam & London, 1974.

Fear No Evil, Eva Pierrakos, Pathwork Foundation, USA, 1992.

Gestalt Therapy Verbatim, Fritz Perls, Real People Press, USA, 1969. (on Dreamwork)

The Courage to Heal: A Guide for Women Survivors of Child Sexual Abuse, Ellen Bass & Laura Davis, Harper & Row, New York, 1988.

From Healing to Awakening: Introducing Transpersonal Breathwork, Mark Pearson, Inner Work Partnership, Aust., 1991.

Index to Exercises

Adolescents
Getting to Know Each Other   104
Symbols of My Life   105
Focusing with Deep Breath   105
Exploring Unconscious Feelings towards Parents   107
Body Focus   109
Finding the Positive in Trapped Body Energy   110
No Stone Unturned   111
Dealing with Anger   112

Anger work
Body Focus   109
Dealing with Anger   112
Reclaiming the Energy of Anger   113
The Giant and the Little People   115
Waking and Releasing Anger and Strength   116
Finding an Animal Language   117
What Does Your Heart Long For?   119
Riding the Magic Carpet   120
What Would You Really Like to Do?   121

Bioenergetics
My Fireworks Display   97
My War Dance   98
Bioenergetic Games   99
Reclaiming the Energy of Anger   113
Waking and Releasing Anger and Strength   116

Birthing games
Leaving Mother   33
Baby Learns   34

Body awareness
The Little Person with the Radar Inside   66
My Belly Circle   68
My Face Mask   69
Stories in My Body   70

Index

Painting the Body   71
What Is in My Chest?   93

Breathing games
What Is in My Chest?   93

Classroom/schools
See pages 44 to 48

Clay work
My Mask Face   84
Talking about Families   85
Modelling the Shadow Parts   86

Counselling
Talking about What Is inside Me   54
Breaking the Ice   55
Developmental Milestones   55
My Family, My Life   60
My Family at Dinner   81
A Visit to the Aliens' Home   82
The People in My Life   100

Creative writing and storytelling
My Inner Parts Go on a Journey   76
My Life as a Myth   77
Going ahead of Mother Duck   78

Drawings
Are There Messages in My Mandalas?   73
Preparing for Mandala Drawing   79
Learning More from My Drawings   80
My Family at Dinner   81
Getting Ready for Emotional Release Drawing   90

Drama
See page 45 for list of exercises

Dreamwork
Methods for Exploring Dreams   142
Questions for My Dream   144

Emotional Release
Getting Ready for Emotional Release Drawing   90

Index

The People in My Life   100
My Real Face   102
Am I a Puppet on Strings?   103
Focusing with Deep Breath   105
Exploring Unconscious Feelings towards Parents   107
Body Focus   109

Energy release
There's a Zoo in me!   83
I Love a Tantrum   94
The Dragonfly   96
Roaring at the Monster   97
My War Dance   98
Using up Potentially Disruptive Engergy   98

For facilitators
Dealing with a Difficult Child   42
What Calls Me to This Work?   169
Are You Heading towards Burn-out?   171
Discovering My Reactions   172

Gestalt work
Messages from the Sandplay   131
I Am ...   140
My Beauty Revealed   140
What Do They Think of Me?   141
Owning the Richness within   158

Grief
What Does Your Heart Long For?   119
Riding the Magic Carpet   120

Inner child
Separating My Hurt Child from Me Now   58

Integration
Bringing New Life into My World Now   34
Are There Messages in My Mandalas?   111

Meditation
See Relaxation and Meditation

Relaxation and meditation
Watching the Candle Flame   160

Index

Visualising Relaxation   160
Walking Meditation   161
What Is Here Now?   162
Tension and Surrender   163
Moving in Slow Motion   164
The Sunset   165
At Home in My Hands   166

Sandplay
Messages from the Sandplay   131
Journey to the New World   136
Inner Treasure   137
Family Portraits   137

Self-esteem
Owning the Richness within   158
See also Visualisation

Sounding Games
Exploring My Sound   94
I Love a Tantrum   94
Roaring at the Monster   97
Am I a Puppet on Strings?   103

Storytelling
See Creative writing and storytelling

Teaching children about the unconscious
Separating My Hurt Child from Me Now   58
Exploring the Conscious and Unconscious   148
Receiving a Gift from the Unconscious   151

Visualisation
A Visit to the Aliens' Home   82
My Real Face   102
No Stone Unturned   111
A Gift from a Wise Part of Me   152
Feeling My Roots   154
The Mysterious Island   155
Earth People   156
Swimming a Lap in a Very Big Pool   156
Discovering My Special Differences   157
Visualising Relaxation   160

General index

abuse 28
academic psychology 2
acting out 21
active imagination 4
active listening 10, 51
affirmation 43
agitation 46, 165
Alexander Technique 160
Almaas, A H 5
anaesthetic 26
anger 11, 112, 113, 116–119, 121
armouring 5, 8, 31–32, 203
artwork 45, 79–83, 173
Axline, Virginia 35, 193

behaviour modification 7, 12–13
belly 68
bioenergetics 5, 16, 36, 97–99, 113–118, 203
birth 23–27
birthing games 23, 32–34
body awareness 61–72, 162, 163
body focus 109, 110
body outline drawings 61–67
bonding 17, 38
breath xi–xii 9, 11, 13, 91
breathing games 92–93
breathwork xi, xii, 203
breech birth 27
Buddhism 5, 6
burn-out 171–172

Caesarean birth 23, 27
Campbell, Joseph 147
carers 167–174
celebration 19
chest 93
child/adult concept 10, 57, 59, 170, 189

childhood trauma 27
Christianity 5, 6
circumcision 31
classroom 44–49
clay 84–86
clinical psychology 2
completion 15
confidentiality 50
consciousness
    levels of 2, 3
    non-ordinary states of 3, 4
    higher 6
counselling sessions 36–37
crayons 14
creative movement 46, 165
creative writing 45, 74–78
cushions 14, 36, 89

dance 17, 46, 173
defence mechanisms 9, 11, 41
drama 45, 103
drawing 14, 79–83, 90, 173, 203
dreams 144
dreamwork 15, 36, 142–145, 173
dumping 21, 112

ego 3, 7, 203
emotional triggers 10, 204
energy release 83, 91
evaluating 40, 47
eyes 14, 91

face 69, 84, 102
family 60, 81, 85, 137
fantasies 4
fear of emotions 4, 7
firstborns 26
focusing 105
Freud, S 4

Gestalt 5, 15, 16, 36, 80, 130, 139–141, 143, 158
goal-setting 43
Grof, Christina 4
Grof, Stan xi, 2, 4, 26
groups 9, 14, 17, 37–41, 104
Gurdjieff, G I 5, 6

hands 166
hero 77, 147
holotropic breathwork 4
homework 37
hope 193
hyperactive children 16, 185

imagination 152
individuation 3
induced labour 26
inner child 10, 43, 52, 57–59, 168–171, 203
integration 17, 18–19, 37, 130

Janov, A xi, 2, 4, 24, 26
journalling 17, 37, 72–73, 100, 112, 173
Jung, C G xi, 2, 3, 4, 5, 8, 122, 142

Kalff, Dora 5
Krishnamurti, J 167

leadership 37
Leboyer, F 4, 22, 25, 31, 32
lifeforce 8, 203
Lowen, A 4, 16, 115

mandalas 14, 18, 73, 79, 204
mask self 8

211

General index

Maslow, A 3
massage 5, 16, 70
meditation 6, 17, 159–166
midwives 32
mirroring 10, 51, 84, 204
music 16, 39, 46, 90, 200–201
myths 75, 77

neurosis 7, 204
nightmares 144

Oaklander, Violet 53, 175

parents xiii–xiv, 29–30, 100, 107
Perls, Fritz xix, 2, 5, 41, 139, 143
persona 8, 9
Pierrakos, Eva 107
Pierrakos, John 5, 16
power animal 182
processing 7, 9, 36, 88–121, 204
Progoff, Ira 5
projection 10, 12, 41–42, 51, 139, 172, 204
psychology, three levels of 2–6
puppets 180

Reich, Wilhelm xi, 1, 2, 5, 31, 115
relaxation 6, 36, 37, 159–166
repression 7
resistance 36, 38, 51

sacred psychology 2, 5, 6
sandplay 5, 15, 18, 37, 123–139, 176, 177, 180, 183, 198–199
schools xii, 44–49
scriptwriting 75, 76
self-awareness 20, 71
self-destructiveness 8, 30
self-esteem 9, 15, 21, 43, 158
  low 29
separated parents 29–30
sexual abuse 28
shadow 8, 11, 88, 204
sounding xii, 11, 13, 16, 93–96
step-parents 31
stillness 165
stress in carers 47
support groups 49–52
surrender 14, 163
symbols 15, 105, 128
  see also sandplay

tantrum 94, 117
teachers 47
Teakle, Heather 87
threshold journeys 152
touch 16
training 202
transference 41–42, 204
transpersonal breathwork xi, 203
transpersonal psychology 2, 3
trauma xii, 7, 10, 204
trust 9
twins 23

unconscious 7, 148

visualisation 15, 19, 36, 78, 102, 113, 152–159

walking meditation 162
Weinrib, Estelle 122
Wilber, Ken 42
womb experience 24

Zen 5